RE-IMAGINING COMPUTERS AND COMPOSITION

RE-IMAGINING COMPUTERS AND COMPOSITION

Teaching and Research in the Virtual Age

Edited by

Gail E. Hawisher & Paul LeBlanc

Boynton/Cook
HEINEMANN
Portsmouth NH

Boynton/Cook Publishers, Inc.
A Subsidiary of Reed Publishing (USA) Inc.
361 Hanover Street
Portsmouth, NH 03801-3912
Offices and agents throughout the world

Reimagining computers and composition : teaching and research in the
    virtual age / edited by Gail Hawisher, Paul LeBlanc.
        p.   cm.
    Includes bibliographical references.
    ISBN 0-86709-307-2
    1. English language—Composition and exercises—Study and
teaching.   2. English language—Computer-assisted instruction.
3. English language—Rhetoric—Study and teaching.   I. Hawisher ,
Gail E.   II. LeBlanc. Paul, 1957–
PE1404.R385   1992
808.04207—dc20

Cover design by Twyla Bogaard
Printed in the United States of America
93 94 95 96   9 8 7 6 5 4 3 2

Contents

Foreword by Edward P. J. Corbett vii

Preface ix

Part I :   Re-imagining the Profession: Teaching and the Virtual Age. . 1

Chapter 1 :   Computers and the Writing Classroom:
A Look to the Future by Charles Moran 7

Chapter 2 :   Preparing English Teachers for the Virtual Age:
The Case for Technology Critics by Cynthia L. Selfe 24

Chapter 3 :   Political Impediments to Virtual Reality
by Elizabeth Sommers 43

Chapter 4 :   Exploring the Implications of Metaphors for Computer
Networks and Hypermedia by Janet Carey Eldred and Ron Fortune. .58

Part II :   Looking Beyond Virtual Horizons:
Teaching Writing on Networks 75

Chapter 5 :   Electronic Meetings of the Minds: Research, Electronic
Conferences, and Composition Studies by Gail E. Hawisher 81

Chapter 6 :   Breaking Down Barriers: High Schools and Computer
Conferencing by William W. Wright, Jr. 102

Chapter 7 :   Teaching Composition in Tomorrow's Multimedia,
Multinetworked Classrooms by Hugh Burns .115

Chapter 8 :   Social Epistemic Rhetoric and Chaotic Discourse
by Paul Taylor 131

Part III :   Navigating Virtual Waters:
Where Do We Go From Here? 149

Chapter 9 :   The Virtual Context: Ethnography in the
Computer-Equipped Writing Classroom
by Marcia Curtis and Elizabeth Klem 155

Chapter 10 : Computers and Composition Studies: Articulating
a Pattern of Discovery by Christine M. Neuwirth
and David S. Kaufer 173

Chapter 11 : Ringing in the Virtual Age: Hypermedia Authoring
Software and the Revival of Faculty-Based Software
Development in Composition by Paul LeBlanc 191

Chapter 12 : What Are They *Talking* About? Computer Terms That
English Teachers May Need to Know by Richard J. Selfe 207

Contributors: 219

Foreword
Edward P.J. Corbett

People who pick up this book are going to ask, "What is Ed Corbett doing writing a Foreword for this collection of essays on the computer?" If I am known in the profession at all, I am known as one of those gnarled old guys whose notions about communications are still rooted in the Greek and Roman traditions of oratory. Sure, I've done my share of teaching and preaching about composition in our colleges and universities. "But what does he know about re-imagining computers and composition in the virtual age? With his fading eyesight, he probably read the word virtual in the title of the book as *visual.*" And indeed I did, and one of the first things I did was to go to Richard Selfe's glossary of computer terms in the last chapter of the book to find out what *virtual* means in this context.

Well, the simplest answer to the question about why I am writing a Foreword to this collection is that Gail Hawisher and Paul LeBlanc, the editors of this collection, asked me if I would write the Foreword. They probably regarded me as being representative of the many English teachers in this country who need to read a book like this if they are to continue teaching composition in the twenty-first century. What may have prompted the putting together of this collection of essays may be reflected in one of the sentences from Gail Hawisher's essay in this collection and in one of the sentences from Paul LeBlanc's essay:

> Gail Hawisher: "Yet if our theoretical perspectives have allowed us—indeed have encouraged us—to accept word processing and electronic conferencing, the new technologies have also influenced the ways we think about writing and writing instruction."

> Paul LeBlanc: "The computer reveals new possibilities for the teaching of writing and makes the traditional writing class seem increasingly constrained."

After reading this collection of essays, I came to realize how profoundly the computer has affected the lives of all of us and in particular how the computer has revolutionized the ways in which we will have to teach the literacy skills of reading and writing. I was so excited by the reading of this gathering of essays that I wished I were just starting my professional career instead of terminating it with my retirement. But even if the image of me is that of a old stick-in-the-mud, maybe I can still do a service for the profession by doing some enthusiastic tub-thumping for the educational revolution that this book heralds.

But I am not really as outmoded as I am reputed to be. Back in the early 1980s, I was one of the first members of the English Department at Ohio State University to buy a PC for my study at home. So by the time the University equipped the offices of all tenure-track faculty members with Zenith PCs, I was a seasoned performer on the word-processor. The word-processor radically transformed my writing habits. At a conference on the computer and composition staged by Esther Rauch at the University of Maine in Orono in the summer of 1990, I met many of the renowned pioneers in computer-based writing instruction, some of whom are represented in this collection. The talk that I gave at that conference and that was later published in the November 1990 issue of the journal *Computers and Composition* under the title "My Write of Passage: From the Quill Pen to the Personal Computer" gave an account of how the personal computer had changed my writing habits. But what most impressed me about that conference was the spirited interaction between the speakers and the audience after each of the talks. We learned as much from that interchange as we did from the talk that sparked that interchange. Almost all of the articles in this collection have something to say about the lively and fruitful interchanges that take place in the synchronous and asynchronous conferencing in the computer-based writing classroom. Among other things, it is the on-line interaction between students or between students and teachers or between the members of the writing class and the outside consultants that radically alters the atmosphere of the composition classroom for the better.

Up to this point, I have been talking mainly about how this collection of essays has edified me. What is more important, however, is what this book can do to educate the next generation of teachers in how to use the new technologies most sensibly in helping their students to compose the kinds of writing they may have to do in the business and professional world that they will be entering. This book will have to be a required text in those English Education courses designed to train future teachers of writing in the schools. It should also be on the must-read list of those university courses designed to prepare graduate teaching assistants for teaching freshman composition courses, especially if those courses are taught—as they certainly will be in the near future—in classrooms equipped with a network of personal computers. But I hope that this book will also become a highly recommended text for those who want to read a stimulating and instructive book about a new technology for acquiring proficiency in the arts of reading and writing.

Preface

One of our most basic assumptions about writing is that it is text on a page, inert print matter that lies dormant on paper until another person picks it up and reads. The printed page stores information and acts as a repository for new information that society produces. This assumption informs both our private and professional lives, largely determining ways in which literate members of our society read, write, and go about their daily activities while engaging in acts of literacy. For those of us involved in literacy education, the printed page has additional implications: it shapes the ways in which we teach, equip a writing classroom, educate writing teachers, and conduct research into writing. It underlies our notions of publishing, of authorship, of genre, of disciplinary knowledge, of what it means to be literate. In short, a print culture exerts its influence on the lives of both ourselves and our students in incalculable ways before, during, and after school hours.

When Text Becomes Virtual

Now imagine what happens to our notions of literacy when text becomes virtual—when it is produced, transmitted, and consumed in electronic form on a computer. Imagine what happens when printed materials are not the primary school media through which we teach and learn. Imagine what happens when electronic writing and electronic media become the currency of school life. As these changes begin to influence and re-form institutional settings, old assumptions regarding writing and the teaching of writing may no longer hold true in the virtual age—in this age of print we may not be preparing students adequately for the future demands of literacy. The central thesis of this book is that as notions of literacy change so too must our approaches to writing and writing instruction. In order to examine this premise further, we must first identify the kinds of changes taking place, recognize that they may require new approaches to writing, research, and teaching, and begin to develop and test our recon-ceptualizations of composition instruction in an electronic-based medium.

Exploring Virtual Spaces

The basis for writing as we now practice and teach it is in the relationship of fixed physical entities that largely resist change. The typical writing classroom is a physical place where students and instructor congregate at specific times. Student text is submitted on 8″ x 11″ sheets of white paper, double-spaced with fixed margins in what used to be called "manuscript" form. Although in the late 20th century, there are variations of the above, it remains standard practice for most high school and first-year college writing classes. Few of the relationships between these entities have changed. When writing teachers receive dot-matrix print-outs from students who have failed to separate the pages at the perforation, teachers don't like it. Essentially, they resent receiving a "scroll" instead of a "paper." Imagine how they might react if students handed in work as stacks of notecards variously connected by lengths of string, the physical analog of hypertext. Our expectation that student papers be written on single sheets of paper and that the text follow a discernible linear sequence is the product of our mature and highly stable print culture.

Indeed, print culture is so ingrained in our thinking that understanding virtuality requires a difficult conceptual leap. Whereas print culture is largely defined in physical space, virtual culture is defined within electronic space through the use of software and computer memory. As such, virtual space transcends many of the time and space boundaries that now govern traditional print culture.

Imagine the following scenario:[1]

> The date is October 5, 2000. Alexis Quezada is a freshman at a prestigious institution of higher learning. Her classes are typical for a freshman of the year 2000: Algorithmic Mathematics, Physical Science, Art History, English Composition. . . . It is a nice day, so Alexis rides her bike over to the park before the lecture [for her class] starts. At 10:00 A.M. sharp *Tablet* [her 8″ x 11″ lightweight computer] informs her that the Physical Science lecture is about to start. She directs her attention toward the screen as the lecture begins. (Young, et al., 10)
>
> In English Comp class at 2:00 P.M., the professor indicates that she has finished grading the previous assignment and returns them. Instantly, the corner of the [screen] display contains a copy of Alexis's graded paper—B +, not too bad. Alexis pages through the paper by touching the screen. She touches the video-mail icon for comments about a particular page. Segments of her text become highlighted in color as they are discussed. Unfortunately, her teacher is pretty boring, and so she turns on her soap opera instead. (Young, et al. 11)

In this description by a group of students from the University of Illinois, Alexis does not go to her classes—instead she takes her classes with her as she bikes to the park with her *Tablet* under her arm. She writes notes with an electronic stylus on the *Tablet's* screen and may never print them out as hardcopy; she may instead transmit them electronically to her teacher and fellow students through a modem, or she may choose to keep them "filed" in her *Tablet*. Communication for Alexis on this typical school day takes place within a virtual framework; that is, it remains in electronic and not physical space.

Consider another example, this time related to hypertexts and hypermedia. Reading this book, you encounter a number of references to other texts, and you pursue these by looking through the list of works cited, going to the library, and doing the requisite footwork necessary to get the texts in hand. Because of the sheer size and cost of the books, we cannot supply you with the actual referenced texts. If, however, you read this book in virtual form, that is, as electronic text stored in computer memory, accessed through software, and read on the screen, we could use hypertext technology to make all those resource materials available to you. As you read, for example, Janet Eldred and Ron Fortune's chapter on metaphor and come to their reference to Vannevar Bush's seminal 1945 *Atlantic Monthly* article outlining the basis for hypertext, you simply click on the reference with your mouse. Immediately the text of the article appears on screen, giving you instant access. You would then continue to access any other references you wanted by following this simple procedure. In electronic form we could overcome the physical constraints imposed by the print medium. The intertextuality we believe to exist in print culture can actually be manifested in virtual culture.

Our willingness to accept electronic texts and communication as conventional depends on the degree to which they allow us to do something at least as well as we can do it with print. For example, we would argue that the widespread use of word processing has relied on the ease of revision and the time savings that it offers us over longhand or typewritten revision. But word processing still most frequently results in a print document. In contrast, the technologies described in the above examples exist electronically or completely on-line, beyond print, and as their use spreads, the movement from print literacy to virtual literacy will accelerate.

For those new to the field, a brief overview of networking and hypermedia may be useful. Richard Selfe's guide to computer terminology at the end of this book might also be helpful.

Networking

While there are many networking systems, they perform the same basic function: linking individual computers for the transfer and sharing of information. While networks are not new, the ability to network microcomputers at a reasonable cost is, thus the recent proliferation of networked computer writing classes in schools across the country. Among the capabilities of networks most interesting to writing teachers are

- the easy sharing of documents for comments, revising, and collaboration;

- electronic mail and bulletin boards for asynchronous communication between members of a writing class or a larger community;

- "real-time" or synchronous conversation programs that allow on-line conversations.

Through computer networks, we can also easily access other resources like a library's CD-ROM databases (ERIC or PsychLit, for example) and, assisted by telecommunications, we can link with other networks, schools, organizations, and professionals worldwide.

Hypermedia

People use the terms hypertext and hypermedia interchangeably, although they seldom mean to restrict their discussion to only text. Therefore, we begin by arguing that hypermedia is the more apt term in almost all discussion since it describes the non-sequential linking of information in various forms including text, graphics, sound, video, and animation. A hypermedia document contains units of information, called nodes, that are linked electronically. A node might be a graphic, a text which can be scrolled through, a segment of video, or a combination of media. Nodes can have multiple links to multiple nodes, so that a reader (if we might use the term) of a hypermedia document can experience it in an idiosyncratic way depending on what links he or she decides to follow. For example, a hypermedia document designed for a survey course in British Literature includes timelines for various periods, including the Medieval Period, as illustrated in Figure 1. The reader can click on any box on the screen and link into another node.

This node is linked to ten other nodes. Clicking on the "Old English" section of the timeline, for example, moves you to a new node (shown in Figure 2) that provides a background text and five works of literature from the period. A reader can select a work and its text, hear a recording of it being read, get background on the work, or access related texts.

As is obvious from the figures, the number of connections and paths through this large collection of information is quite high. Figure 3 illustrates the web of connections for the Medieval Period node, and that is just one layer in a much more extensive and intricately connected program.

The web of possible links builds and the various paths through this database of information increase as the reader proceeds at will through the program.

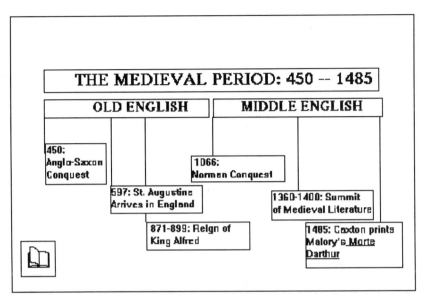

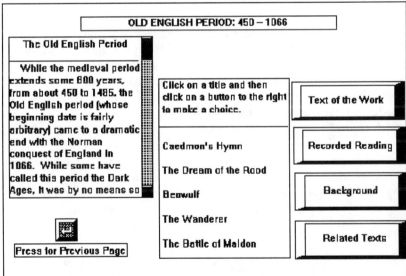

Michael Joyce offers a useful comparison of what he calls "exploratory" and "constructive" hypermedia (11). Exploratory hypermedia, the most common type, allows readers to navigate a body of information in whatever order and structure they wish and to browse through the material at hand. The key to the reader's freedom is that navigation ultimately exists with the author who created the original links. As Joyce suggests,

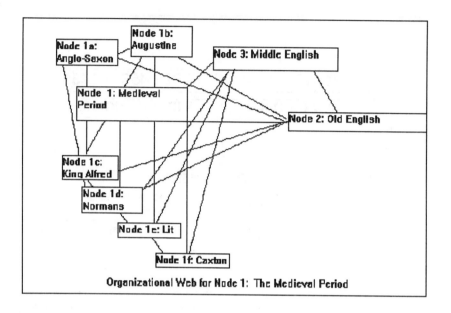

Organizational Web for Node 1: The Medieval Period

"Transformation of knowledge is the litmus test we should use in judging both exploratory and constructive hypertexts" (12). In other words, do readers create new meaning from their encounter with hypermedia? Constructive hypermedia, where the transformation of knowledge can be most dramatic, further dissolves the distinction between author and reader. Unlike exploratory hypermedia, where the author does not relinquish control to the reader, in constructive hypermedia documents the reader acts upon nodes and links, creating new structures instead of various versions of existing structures. In some constructive hypermedia, readers can actually add to the document, building upon it and designing their own links and nodes, as well as altering the ones with which they started. Hence, readers quite literally become authors rewriting the text as they read.

What Do Virtual Technologies Change?

Nancy Kaplan argues that researchers in composition studies look at computer-supported student writing with the same expectations that they bring to printed material—that "although the means of text production changes, the meaning of the term 'writing' remains constant . . . (14)." But as Kaplan goes on to note, the rhetorical conventions of electronic text are not the conventions of printed text and demand new ways to talk about writing. Something as simple as a publisher's suggestion of page length for a manuscript or a writing assignment might make no sense if the document is a hypertext or hypermedia document. Then we might need to talk about the approximate number of nodes required to explore a subject, probably as impossible a task as setting a page length. Or we might need to talk about "scanning" graphics and "importing" video into hypermedia documents to make our writing more visually appealing and effective for the readers of our virtual texts. Thus, along with our understanding of the very act of writing, our terminology regarding discursive practices must change to account for phenomena that are foreign to our notions of paperbound products.

So too must our research into writing change as we examine new writing processes that defy the commonly held assumption that process is independent of medium. Are we prepared, for example, to understand student documents as including animation, sound, or video? What processes or activities do writers engage in as they incorporate new media into their texts? Are our old research methodologies adequate for examining what happens to writers when they write and communicate with other writers across time and space? And, finally, how can we use the capabilities of computer technology to help us with our research? We have barely scratched the surface in exploring ways in which different kinds of research in composition studies can be undertaken with electronic technology.

Our notions of the writing classroom and writing pedagogy must also change as electronic communication becomes increasingly common in our classes and institutions. The very concept of a writing class changes, as illustrated in the earlier example, when classes "meet" over phonelines and through wide-area networks. Even local networks restricted to a given classroom call for new ways of structuring classes. As Thomas Barker and Fred Kemp have argued, a new conceptual framework for working within the networked classroom may be required. Their notion of "network theory" assumes that each piece of student communication—that is, each piece of writing—is a "transaction" between the writer and the other members of the class and must be judged as such. Since the writing belongs to class members, Barker and Kemp argue that the rhetorical skill of each writer becomes increasingly important as student writers seek ways to add their contributions to a common knowledge base. How do notions of the communal classroom and "group knowledge" change our notions of writing instruction? Does student writing over both wide and local area networks improve because of the immediacy of the communication? And, if indeed it improves, what measures are we using to assess this electronic writing? How do we accommodate Kaplan's argument that we're using print conventions to judge electronic text? These are just a few of the questions we must address as electronic environments begin to change our roles as teachers.

Topics prompted by these sorts of questions are among those that the fifteen contributors to this collection discuss as they explore the implications of teaching writing in the virtual age. We have divided the book into three parts. Part 1, "Re-imagining the Profession: Teaching and the Virtual Age" explores the changing nature of the "classroom," the need to educate teachers of writing differently for the virtual age, political issues that arise when technology and composition come together, and the metaphors that shape our research and pedagogy. Part 2, "Looking Beyond Virtual Horizons: Teaching Writing on Networks," offers examples and analyses of electronic conferencing as it breaks down barriers between communities and classrooms, between cultures and countries, between print and other media, and between various genres. This section includes a discussion of chaos theory and social epistemic rhetoric, as well as a review of the research on electronic conferencing. Part 3, "Navigating Virtual Waters: Where Do We Go From Here?" establishes an agenda for our ongoing research. It begins with a description of how ethnographic research can help us understand and re-imagine writing instruction in the virtual age in a more complete way than has been offered so far in computers and composition research in general. This discussion is then followed with a description of a new mode of inquiry, based on cognitive research and software design, for exploring the evolving shape of technology and answering the question, "What should the computers we use look like?" The section proceeds with an exploration of hypermedia authoring programs and their potential for reinvigorating faculty-based software development in composition. And, finally, a glossary is included·to help readers tackle some of the new terminology connected with virtual environments.

Each chapter in the collection presents a different way of viewing the field than teachers and scholars have understood computers and composition studies in the past. The contributors take a broad and bold look, examining the ways our assumptions about writing must evolve in the age of virtual text. They re-imagine our writing, our writing spaces, our teaching, our research, our own preparation, and our most basic notions of literacy, language, and communication.

Notes

1. This passage was taken from a group of Universty of Illinois students' prize-winning proposal for Project 2000, a competition Apple sponsored in January of 1988. Those entering the competition were asked to envision how electronic technology might be used in the year 2000. Luke Young and his fellow students won the competition with their entry of *Tablet,* a computer for the 21st century. The excerpt presented here is taken from the article they wrote for *Academic Computing.*

Works Cited

Barker, Thomas T. and Fred O. Kemp. "Network Theory: A Postmodern Pedagogy for the Writing Classroom." *Computers and Community*. Ed. Carolyn Handa. Portsmouth: Boynton/Cook, 1990. 1–27.

Bush, Vannevar. "As We May Think." *Atlantic Monthly* 176(1): 101–108.

Joyce, Michael. "Siren Shapes: Exploratory and Constructive Hypertexts." *Academic Computing*. (November 1988): 10–42.

Kaplan, Nancy. "Ideology, Technology, and the Future of Writing Instruction." *Evolving Perspectives on Computers and Composition Studies: Questions for the 1990s*. Eds. Gail E. Hawisher and Cynthia L. Selfe. Urbana, IL, and Houghton, MI: NCTE and *Computers and Composition* Press, 1991.

Levinson, Paul. "Intelligent Writing: The Electronic Liberation of Text." Paper presented at the Annual Meeting of the American Association for the Advancement of Science. San Francisco, 1989.

Young, Luke T., et al. "Academic Computing in the Year 2000." *Academic Computing* (May/June): 7–12, 62–65.

Part I

Re-imagining the Profession: Teaching and the Virtual Age

Introduction

> We are living through a cultural revolution that shapes our image of the future in a way that nobody, however titanic, could have foreseen a half-century ago. It is a revolution whose shape we cannot sense, although we already sense its depth.
>
> Jerome Bruner

The cultural revolution that Jerome Bruner alludes to is also a technological revolution. It is, furthermore, one that is happening so fast that we must stop, catch our breaths, and try to imagine what it means for us as educators. In this last decade of the century, we must think hard about the kinds of spaces we and our students inhabit and examine the day-to-day activities that have come to be known collectively as schooling. For those of us who are English teachers, we must also pause and think hard, for the day-to-day classroom practices that constitute writing instruction are changing dramatically as word processing, electronic mail and conferences, hypertexts and hypermedia become integral to our understanding of what it means to teach and write in these revolutionary times.

In recent years, with good reason, it has become fashionable to reflect on our teaching, to examine what it is we do in our writing classes, to look at how our students respond to their assignments, and to modify our practices in such ways—as a result of our reflection—that we can help students learn to write better. Analyzing our teaching carefully and bringing this sort of critical approach into our writing classes suggests sound pedagogy that we all benefit from. But what we don't do or do less of, perhaps, is look forward into the future and speculate about what our teaching might look like in a week, in a month, in a year, in the next century. Although we might say "next week in class the students will meet together in groups to talk about their papers on sexist language," all of which is good, important planning, we don't get much further into the future. Most of us, after all, don't see ourselves as "futurists"; nor do we want to.

But therein lies a problem: the next century is less than a decade away, and most of us can only sense, as Bruner reminds us, the depth of change that propels us forward. We need to speculate about what writing instruction in the future might look like and what it means to us as teachers. For those of us teaching in electronic classrooms, it is especially difficult to imagine our writing classes for the next year, much less the next century. Most of us are using very different computers and software than we started out with in the last decade. As this book goes to press, Apple introduced System 7. and Windows 3.0 was introduced for IBM-DOS environments. Both these developments make it necessary for many writing teachers to learn new ways of using their computers for writing instruction. But we must do more than learn the new software. We must also try to re-imagine what our classes might look like in the very near future and to contemplate our role as teachers in this new age of virtuality.

The first part of this book, "Re-imagining the Profession: Teaching and the Virtual Age," is our attempt to think hard about the future and ask what it might hold for us as writing teachers. Charles Moran in chapter 1 asks us to re-imagine the spaces in which we teach: our classrooms. He maintains that our current physical set-up is "inconvenient" and "uncomfortable," necessitating as it does a specific time and place where teachers and students must gather and sit in contraptions such as "chairdesks" so that writing instruction can take place. In arguing that the classrooms of the future—virtual spaces we experience only on-line—might work every bit as well for us, he presents a provocative yet realistic view of future writing classes. Just as our classrooms themselves change, so must our teaching and our preparation of teachers. Cynthia Selfe, in chapter 2, asks us to re-imagine the profession in relation to how we educate teachers and makes five strong suggestions. Each suggestion aims for English education programs to play stronger leadership roles in preparing teachers to think and act critically about technology as they look to the future. In chapter 3, Elizabeth Sommers steps back for a moment and grounds us in the political present in so far as our work in computers and composition studies in the academy is concerned. She argues that we must reshape English departments within higher education if they are to be comfortable and productive places for those of us who teach writing *and* computers. In imagining a future not terribly different from the political reality of the present, she reminds us that a great deal of work remains to be done within our own English departments. In chapter 4, Janet Eldred and Ron Fortune ask us to consider the ways in which we *think* about the new technologies in relation to our teaching and research.

They argue that the metaphors we construct for computer networks and hypermedia often constrain our thinking and blind us to the possibilities each development offers us as teachers. Eldred and Fortune ask us to extend our thinking into the future and to once again think hard, so that we may capture the full potential each technology affords us both as teachers and researchers.

Thus the chapters in this first part argue that critical speculation about the future is an exceedingly important activity. As a profession, we need to re-imagine our writing classes, our preparation of writing teachers, our academic departments, as well as the metaphors we use to think about the new technologies. In looking to the future, the chapters in Part 1 move us ever more firmly toward imagining virtual spaces for our teaching and learning.

Works Cited

Bruner, Jerome. *Actual Minds, Possible Worlds.* Cambridge,MA: Harvard University Press, 1986. 148.

1

Computers and the Writing Classroom:
A Look to the Future

Charles Moran
University of Massachusetts at Amherst

> The real impact in computers is not the silicon. It's not even the current software. It's the re-thinking.
>
> Robert Frankston

The college writing classroom of the year 2050 will not be what it is today. But what will this writing classroom look like? What shapes and characteristics will it have? How will it be equipped? As Robert Frankston suggests in the epigraph, the future design of the writing classroom will be less the result of the new technology than it will be the result of the deep, merciless re-thinking that this new technology compels us to undertake. So let us begin the re-thinking here by looking at the conventional writing classroom and asking ourselves, "What do these college writing classrooms look like now? Are they now what we want? And what, given the advent of computer technology, are the alternatives?"

The "Real" Writing Classroom

Suddenly the conventional college writing classroom seems an odd place, a "virtual reality" of its own, frozen in time, remarkably similar to the turn-of-the-century urban school classrooms pictured in histories of American education (e.g., Tyack 46, 56). This writing classroom is an expensive, impersonal structure serially inhabited by different classes,

7

none of which leaves any trace in the room. The room serves as a "writing" classroom only when the writers and their teacher appear; at other times, it serves as a classroom for History 102, Economics 312, German 103, Philosophy 201, Management 207. There are no books in the room, except for those that students and teachers bring with them. There is a teacher's desk at the head of the room, a symbol of authority that has in it only the fugitive piece of chalk and perhaps an old blue-book or two. Otherwise, there are no writing materials in this desk, which is a stage device, a prop, and not a workspace. The teacher works at another, "real" desk, at home or in a college office, where there are pencils, pens, staplers, paper, stamps, paper-clips, a typewriter and/or a PC, an address-book; and, somewhere near the desk, there are bookshelves, a bulletin-board with reminders and mementos on it, pictures, a telephone, a file cabinet.

Facing the classroom teacher-desk, there are student desks, not often, these days, bolted to the floor, but still set in rows. These desks, like the teacher's classroom desk, are 'unreal' work-spaces. They are also poor writing places. The writing surface is often irregular, often small, and, for those who are left-handed, awkwardly placed. And if one wants to set up small groups, these pieces of furniture suddenly become awkward and heavy, for they have been built of metal and laminated, wood-grained plastic—to last.

There are other pieces of equipment in this conventional classroom that, given our deconstructive move, now seem as unreal as the unreal desk. Behind the desk is a chalkboard that, in colleges and university classrooms, is usually empty at the beginning of class; a given class meets there so seldom that any messages "saved" on the chalkboard will likely not survive the two-to-four-day interval between classes. On the walls of the classroom there are bulletin boards which, by default, have been taken over by those paid to staple advertising—for vacation travel or magazine subscriptions—on every available open wall-space. These materials have a somewhat hallucinatory connection with the business of the writing class. In an elementary school, where students and teacher spend the full day in one room, the class can post its writing on bulletin boards and thus "publish" on the classroom walls. But here the walls, the furniture, belong to everyone and to no one—as impersonal as a room in a motel.

Reasons for Change

From this perspective, we begin to see that this classroom we inhabit is not an inevitable structure, or even a good one, *for* our purposes. Indeed, to argue *for* the conventional writing classroom is not going to be easy. We would, if we could, re-design these writing rooms, even without the impetus of technological change. We would go to our administrators and schedule writing classes in particular rooms for the entire school day, and we would turn these rooms into writing rooms: equip them with dictionaries, paper, staplers, file cabinets, envelopes, stamps, paper clips, typewriters, copy machines, handbooks, thesauri—anything that a writer might want or need. We might ask for a mix of furniture: some writing desks where a writer could write alone, and some small round tables where writers could read and discuss one another's projects. There might be something like the "author's chair" of some elementary classrooms, a place where, by custom, writers read their work to others, for response and comment.

So we should re-think the writing classroom in any case. But today there are forces that would drive us to re-think the writing classroom in its present form, even if it were now acceptable to us. The first of these forces is the widespread perception that we are not now doing our job very well. We can assign some, and perhaps most, of this public dissatisfaction with higher education to demographic and economic factors, but we are left with an uncomfortable residue—a feeling that we might, somehow, do better. We cannot be long satisfied with the outcome of our teaching if so many others are dissatisfied.

A second force is the cost of the brick-and-mortar classroom. This conventional classroom must be heated and cooled, lighted and swept, secured and re-painted and maintained—and it will be used for two thirteen-week periods during the year—half of the year!—and only for five days/week—130 days!—and at most fourteen hours/day. There may be occasional, or even systematic, use of the facility in the off-season, and colleges on trimester or quarter systems may make better use of their facilities, but even with a summer-school and a conscientious division of continuing education, it would be hard to imagine a classroom that was used for more than 50 percent of the hours in a given year. The cost of constructing, maintaining, securing, lighting, heating, and cooling this largely-unused classroom will, given the inevitable rise in energy cost, force us to consider alternatives.

The third force that will drive change in our classrooms is the precipitous drop in the price of computer technology. Though higher education is not now spending widely, or even wisely, on the acquisition of computer technology (Flynn), it won't be too long before the cost of computer and communications equipment will look like a pleasant alternative to the rising, energy-driven cost of the brick-and-mortar classroom. And we writing teachers are well placed to utilize this technology, because we don't need tremendously expensive systems. One can write now, and perhaps forever, on a simple PC, and one can connect, with this same PC, to other writers on other PC's. Despite the advent of multi-media environments, as writing teachers all we really need to work with is a PC and a wire.

Given these I-think-unarguable facts, I look ahead to the "new" writing classroom not as a techno-groupie but as a moderately rational writing teacher, one who is attempting to see the outlines of a future that is

I don't know sure to arrive. If we were now, as a nation, satisfied with the products of our existing writing classrooms; if our present system of higher education were not rapidly pricing itself out of the American marketplace; and if the cost of computer technology were not dropping exponentially; then the following sections would be, even in my own eyes, self-indulgent. But it seems clear to me and to others (e.g., Tiffin) that the writing classroom of the next millennium will be radically different from the writing classroom of today. In the sections that follow, I will look at two different but related models: the computer-equipped, brick-and-mortar writing classroom, and the "virtual," on-line classroom.

The Computer-Equipped Writing Classroom

It is certain that the new will first inhabit the forms of the old. Indeed, much of the old may persist within the new. We still "drive" automobiles, and we speak of their "horsepower." And the fact that neither of the two books emanating from the recent English Coalition (Lloyd-Jones and Lunsford, Elbow) considers our subject suggests that most of us are not eager to contemplate the changes in school design that lie ahead. We will begin therefore by considering the computer-equipped writing classroom—a brick-and-mortar classroom, with all its attendant energy costs, but one with computers in it—a room that students are scheduled into just as they are into conventional classrooms. This facility will not be more cost-effective than the conventional classroom, but we'll assume that for the near-term we will be reluctant to abandon the ways in which our colleges presently operate in space and time. Students will continue to come to brick-and-mortar classrooms, physical spaces within which teaching and learning occur. Given this assumption, we can ask, "What will these new writing-rooms look like? What will their equipment be? And how will it seem to learn, and to teach, in these rooms?"

I describe here my own college-level, computer-equipped classroom, one that operates on a "MWF" and "TuTh" schedule and serves 16–20 different teachers and classes each semester. The room has a few more workstations than students—to minimize the disruption caused by inevitable hardware failure. The workstations are networked. Each class has its own "area" or section of the subdirectory structure on the file-server's hard disk. Each teacher has, as well, his or her own subdirectory—his or her "desk." Given the ability of LAN-software to "map" and to assign "rights," each class "sees" only its own subdirectory structure, one that can be customized according to its needs but which will remain constant throughout the semester—a "virtual" workplace, where assignments, syllabi, prompts, and peer-responding instructions are kept in read-only form; where work-in-progress is saved in read/write form; and where final products are sent to a "turn-in" subdirectory. In a writing classroom that was not computer-equipped, even one as marvelous as the ideal writing classroom we imagined above, we would not have storage space for all of this paper: we would need twenty file drawers for the writing of all the students in the twenty classes that write in this room; we would need bookshelves for multiple copies of hard-bound dictionaries, handbooks, and thesauri; we would need wall space sufficient for multiple, proprietary blackboards and bulletin boards; and we would need a secure place for teachers to store attendance and grade records. In the computer-equipped classroom, all of this material resides in the system's file-server, which is the size of one instructor's briefcase, or, more accurately, it resides on the file-server's hard disk, which is, at the moment of this writing, the size of a pocket-dictionary.

The materials accessible on the classroom's hard disk become a "virtual space," designed and furnished by the teacher and the students together. We live and work in this virtual classroom through an act of imagining, just as we construct the "virtual" worlds created by novels, plays, poems, and computer-games. Through the screen each class accesses its own bulletin-board, mail-system, virtual filing-and-storage system for student writing, and store of syllabi, schedules, writing prompts, teachers' comments, peer-readers' comments, and attendance records. Teachers may access through the screen their own private files: a "virtual" grade-book, class roster, annotated syllabus, and notes on, let's say, particular students' progress toward particular goals. Given the compression that occurs when you convert print-text into magnetically-charged bits of iron oxide, and given a network with a file server with a 300 MB hard disk—trailing-edge technology, as of this writing—there is room in this system for roughly 150,000 pages of double-spaced student writing, or, assuming that we need 60 MB for software and that in a given semester the system will be used by 20 sections of 20 students, the system has the capacity to store some 300 pages of text per student. Further, students have their own disks, private spaces where they can store hundreds of "pages" of their own material. And all of this electronic text can be made shareable or, to put the matter more accurately, can be copied and re-copied without cost or increase in physical dimension.

In a typical class in this typical computer-equipped writing room, students log in, using their instructor's name and password, and a log-in script invisibly and silently routes them to their class subdirectory structure—their own working environment. What first appears on their screen is a greeting from their instructor, and, let us say, instructions to pick up the day's writing prompt from the Prompt box. Or the instructions may be to read through the final drafts submitted in the Turn-in box, and, opening a second window, to write a response to the author of their, or the teacher's, choice. In one of these "boxes" may also be "magazines" edited by groups of students from work submitted to them in yet another "box." The writers, as they work on their screens, are in their "home room"—a digitized space, a literate environment, filled with writing tools and their own writing.

Where does the teacher fit into this structure? It depends to a considerable degree on the design of the physical and virtual spaces. We could design a computer-equipped classroom that replicated the structure of the conventional classroom—not *my* choice, but a choice nevertheless. To do so, we'd mark a workstation, by position or custom, as the "teacher's place." This workstation could stand at the "head" of the class, facing the students' workstations, in the same layout as that of a conventional classroom, where the teacher's desk faces the students' desks. Or the teacher's workstation could be electronically exalted: through software now available, such as *Real-Time Writer* or *Timbuktu*, the teacher would be given the right to take over student screens, write on them, broadcast to them, or observe them. And the teacher's workstation could have near it an overhead projector, one that permits the teacher's screen to become an electronic chalkboard for purposes of demonstration.

Why would we design a computer-equipped writing classroom in this way? As a small and therefore inefficient lecture hall? Samuel Johnson argued in 1781 that, given the availability of books and the ability to read, lectures were no longer a necessary mode of education (Boswell 1136). Yet in 1987, more than two centuries later, the English Coalition felt the need to argue that the freshman writing course should not be teacher-centered, but should "stress an *active, interactive theory of learning* (rather than a theory of teaching), one that assumes students do not learn by being passive eavesdroppers on an academic conversation or vessels into which knowledge is being poured" (Lloyd-Jones and Lunsford 27. See also Elbow 32). Apparently a change in available media does not significantly change the ways in which teaching and learning are conducted. All I can say, therefore, is that computer technology *presents us with the opportunity* to break with the past and to create interactive writing classrooms.

Let us therefore re-imagine the classroom and the software in such a way that the teacher becomes a member of an interactive community of writers—distinguished from the student writers by degree of writing experience and training, so still clearly the writing teacher, but otherwise inhabiting the same world as the students. With such a goal we would not distinguish a "teacher's workstation" but would set our workstations in sets of six or eight, in "pods" or islands extending from one of the room's walls. The workstations would be identical, but the teacher, given a log-in and password procedure, could be assigned "rights" that students do not have. For instance, the students could be given full read/write rights to several subdirectories, but read-only rights to others.

I am assuming that the teacher and class have the autonomy to build their own "virtual classrooms"—and I need to note here that this is an assumption and a hope, not an inevitable consequence of the character of computer technology. Indeed, network management is difficult, and once you give the users a measure of autonomy, you multiply network management problems exponentially. System managers' need to standardize applications is in sharp conflict with users' need to choose their own applications. At issue here is the teacher's authority within the larger educational system. In America we have been moving to grant teachers more power in their schools. Electronic classrooms will run easier and cheaper from "dumb" terminals which grant access to a single, managed curriculum. Teacher autonomy will be expensive and will make running the system harder—and schools will be tempted to move, as businesses have, toward the "dumb" terminal and the centralized control which this equipment makes easy. What businesses see as an evil—"hanky-panky on the network" (Lewis, sec.3:4)—may be, for teachers and for students, the lifeblood of creative teaching and learning.

This computer-equipped classroom will have in it, in addition to networked workstations, a range of on-line writer's aids: a beginning, simplified word processing program and a more powerful word-processing program for those who feel the need for such features as complex formatting, sorting, searching, indexing, and the inclusion of graphics with text. There will be an on-line thesaurus, an on-line dictionary, and an on-line spell-checker. There can be on-line as well style-checkers and a range of programs that function as heuristics, asking the writer questions that are intended to stimulate invention, the generation of ideas. The limit to the number and range of these writers' aids is the teacher's judgment about the extent to which these programs can be helpful to writers.

To the extent that the teacher wants to have students "discuss" on-line, perhaps as a pre-writing activity, a "chat" program like the Daedalus *Interchange* will permit on-line, real-time, written exchange of views: a quick e-mail exchange, in effect, or a rapid epistolary exchange, with instantaneous electronic copies for all participants. Such a program will permit group interaction but with the written language as the medium through which the self is presented. The teacher will have to decide on the degree of autonomy students will have in these on-line, written discussions. Will the teacher begin the session with a prompt? Will the teacher join in the discussion and control "flaming" or discourse that is potentially hurtful to members of the group? Will the teacher direct the formation of sub-conferences or permit students to set up their own? Will the teacher permit students to adopt pseudonyms and thus change their relationship to their written texts? As I have indicated above, the computer-equipped classroom presents us with choices.

A final choice we will have to make in the design of our computer-equipped classroom is the relative value we give to print-text and on-line text. The computer-equipped writing classroom should have printing facilities in it: ideally quiet, laser- or ink-jet printers. The printers will be available to all workstations, through the network. But what uses should teachers make of these printers? On-line text is essentially "free": once the equipment is available, the cost of "printing" a text on-line is zero. Printers, toner, and paper are expensive. For cost effectiveness, both locally and globally, our classes should operate entirely on-line: students submit their writing on-line, and teachers read this writing on-line.

Yet we now live, and will likely continue to live for some time, in an amphibious condition, one where we function both in the "elements" of print-text and on-line text. College curricula are still print-based: there are bookstores, printed lecture-note services, written and proctored examinations, and libraries with huge investments in printed books. Our students will, outside our writing classes, be writing for teachers who will read their work in print-text form. To the extent to which this is true, we'll not want to force our writing students to work exclusively in an environment of electronic text. We will, instead, want to help our students manage the transition between electronic text and print in ways that take advantage of the special characteristics of the two media.

For this reason, our computer-equipped classrooms will have graphics programs and desk-top publishing programs that will permit student writers to format and to publish their work. In some classrooms, document design will become part of the curriculum. In these classrooms, editing "teams" will work collaboratively, through the network, in assembling documents: flyers, brochures, volumes of essays, all published in printed form through xerography. And, so long as the print-culture of higher education requires students to submit "papers" to their teachers, we will need to have in our classroom at least one workstation with a large-screen, 8 1/2 x 11 black-on-white monitor. With this equipment, we can help our students manage both the rhetorical and formal processes involved in effecting the transition from electronic author to print-text reader.

Beyond Time and Place in the Computer-Equipped Classroom

So far we have been thinking of this computer-equipped classroom as existing in space and time, a function of cinder-blocks, glass, hardware, and wire. We have also, however, considered the extent to which this classroom is a site for the construction of many "virtual" classrooms. The student working in one of these computer-equipped classrooms is physically present but related to a digitized world that is accessed through the class log-in script. In such a networked system that serves many classes, the "reality" that one enters is a function of bricks and mortar, yes, and of the teacher's "live" presence, but this reality is as well a function of one's password, which permits one to enter the virtual world of Prof. Moran's writing class. With another password, you'd enter someone else's class-world, with different software options and a different subdirectory structure, let alone different prompts, messages, journal entries, and files of student writing. In our computer-equipped classrooms at the University of Massachusetts, we see that the computer-equipped classroom begins to break down the physical sense of "the class." When I and my class are scheduled into Bartlett 105, the computer-equipped classroom, I work with my own students, to be sure, but it is likely that there will be in the room also a few students from other sections, logged into their own digitized class environments, and even the occasional teacher, doing class preparation, logged into his or her own subdirectory structure. Our teachers report that on occasion these "visitors" choose to join in, finding the work of the class to their taste. So even in this somewhat retrograde brick-and-mortar computer-equipped classroom, the boundaries of the "class" begin to become permeable, and we begin to see that the "class," defined as a packet of students delivered to a particular place at a particular time, is not a given, unless one accepts the inevitability of the industrial model.

The next step in this deconstruction of the "class" will be to connect our computer-equipped classroom, through bulletin-board or e-mail software, to information sources outside the room. Through telephone lines we can access data bases such as on-line library catalogues. Through these same telephone lines we can connect with resource persons outside the classroom, bringing their expertise and perspective into our rapidly expanding virtual world. At the 1990 Conference on Computers and Writing in Austin, Texas, we heard of a class that had in this way made contact with a District Attorney and had used this contact to gain direct access to both information and professional opinion relative to a topic the group was writing about. The virtues of this system, as explained by the speaker, were those of an e-mail system: the District Attorney could, on his own schedule, read the communications from the students and write his responses. For him, this situation was feasible. A "live" class visit would not have been possible (Hughes). Or we could connect our writing class with another writing class, as has been happening through networks such as BreadNet, which operates out of Middlebury College in Vermont. We could bring together in an on-line conference writing classes that were from different cultures—say a northern urban school with a school in the mountains of Kentucky.

But now I begin to anticipate our next move, a move into the writing classroom that exists entirely and solely on-line. Oh for hypertext!

The On-Line Classroom

The on-line class now exists. Indeed, on page 30 of the November 1990 *Education Life* section of the *New York Times*, there is an advertisement for the "American Open University of NYIT," or New York Institute of Technology. The advertisement reads as follows: "The modern way for adults to pursue an undergraduate degree without having to attend traditional classes. Obtain a baccalaureate degree in such areas as business, behavioral sciences, and general studies through computer teleconferencing anywhere in the world." The phrase *open university* connects the NYIT program with a similar program at the Open University in Great Britain, described in the work of Kaye, Mason, and Rumble. Other academic programs delivered solely through computer conferencing are described by Naidu, Mason, Roberts, and McCreary. And in a recent article Romiszowski writes, "In the state of New York alone, more than 100 educational establishments use some form of teleconferencing to supplement, or supplant, face-to-face education" (234). Research into this area brings us into contact with such established conventions as the abbreviations CC (Computer Conferencing) and CMC (Computer-mediated Communication) and such established journals as *Distance Education* and *The American Journal of Distance Education*.

So in imagining an on-line writing classroom we are not engaging in ungrounded fantasy. There are many on-line courses now being taught. In England, Canada, and the United States, these courses are generally offered, as the NYIT advertisement suggests, to adults who for one reason or another can not be in our conventional classrooms M-W-F 10:05 A.M. and who, because of work and parenting schedules, need to work and learn when they can. In other areas, such as Micronesia and northern Canada, where a physical meeting of a class is not economically feasible, "distance learning" is the only alternative, and, with satellite uplinks, computer conferencing "may well be the fastest growing area of applications of technology to communication and education" (Romiszowski 236).

What would an on-line writing classroom "look" like? It would have three elements, both separable and potentially interactive: 1) a "mail" system; 2) a "filing," or storage-and-retrieval system; and 3) a computer-mediated conferencing system. For the sake of clarity, I will look at these three subsystems separately.

The on-line mail system makes possible a writing course that is much like the learn-to-write-by-mail services that are advertised in such publications as *Writer's Market* or *Writer's Digest*, or the conference-based writing class envisioned by Lester Fisher and Donald Murray. The essential transaction in this model is that between the writer and the editor.

Writers send their writing via a "mail" system; the writing is read, and the editor sends a response by return mail. The editor could be the teacher, or could be students, or both in some mixture and alternation, depending upon the teacher's and students' values and goals.

The virtues of editing on-line are several: the editors can edit at their convenience, picking up the manuscript at any time of day; the editor will comment in writing and, in so doing, practice both writing and editing skills; and the editor can take the time to reflect and even return to and modify the first response with a subsequent re-vision or re-mailing of the second thoughts. Important here is the fast turn-around made possible by CMC; Kaye notes that in a correspondence course the typical turn-around time is three weeks (Mason and Kaye, 12). During this interval, Kaye notes, the student has most often proceeded to a new piece of the course, so the feedback comes too late to be useful. On-line, the turn-around can be rapid and therefore more effective.

The disadvantages of on-line editing are clear: the difficulty of making comments in a "margin" and the difficulty of drawing arrows and lines—the kinds of editing that we have become so used to on paper do not yet have their equivalent on-line. Red-lining programs are mildly useful, but they tend to be unwieldy and they produce a text that, with its embedded deletions and additions, is difficult to read. Yet the speed of response may more than compensate for the difficulties we now have in commenting flexibly and economically on-line on an extended piece of writing. And hypertext holds the promise of an environment where comments-on-text can be more easily made and received.

In addition to the "mail" system, the on-line classroom would include a virtual storage-and-retrieval system. In this electronic filing cabinet would be all texts produced by the group—more-or-less formal pieces of writing, editors' comments, all mail-messages sent during the semester, texts brought in by members of the group as references, examples, authority. Available also would be transcripts of the on-line conferences, retrievable by author or topic. Our class storage area would be connected to on-line, public data bases that students could search as they needed to for their own or their group's writing. We would need to establish protocols that would permit privacy, where appropriate, and access, where appropriate. We can imagine that access to our "classroom's" storage area would be limited to the members of the class itself. It might be important for each member of the class, and here I include the teacher, to have his or her own virtual desk—either housed in memory in the host computer or in the memory of the participant's own workstation—in either case a part of the virtual classroom. The student and teacher would be at their "desks," at school, at home, or wherever, and could log into the "class" at any time.

conference

A third element in our on-line writing course would be the computer-mediated conference (CMC), a process that may, as some predict, "ultimately emerge as a new educational paradigm, taking its place alongside both face-to-face and distance education" (Kaye, "Computer-Mediated" 3). CMC is seen by some (e.g., Feenberg 26) to hold the "promise that writing will once again become a universal form of expression," as "written," on-line conferences and e-mail exchanges begin to be used instead of voice communication by telephone.

The computer-mediated conference is a much more flexible medium than the two-way epistolary correspondence. And, whereas the "mail" and "filing" functions are individual in their orientation, CMC is potentially—some would say inevitably—social and interactive. Through the conference, the teacher and students together can design an on-line classroom that is as full and functional as is the digitized environment stored in the file-server of our computer-equipped writing classroom, described above. That the students are connected to the system by telephone lines, rather than by an Ethernet wire, might seem for most purposes irrelevant. In such a classroom the teacher and students can orchestrate reading-and-writing groups, on-line, written discussions, brain storming bulletin-board sessions, and on-line publication. The response-time in this on-line classroom would on occasion be slower than it is in a classroom where readers and writers are physically present, but it is not clear that a somewhat relaxed and deliberate cycle of writing-and-response is a disadvantage. And quasi-synchronous conferencing sessions, such as those made possible by Interchange in the computer-equipped classroom, are possible to arrange on-line, though for these sessions the class would have to agree to be on-line simultaneously.

Researchers and practitioners have found, too, that CMC is a new and not unproblematic communication medium. Face-to-face communication occurs in a rich context of cues: tone of voice, gesture, facial expression. Andrew Feenberg asserts that "In computer conferencing the only tacit sign we can transmit is our silence, a message that is both brutal and ambiguous" (34). CMC, using as it does just the written word, requires that we pay attention to context-building. This context-building can be the work of the teacher-moderator, whose work, according to Feenberg (35-6), consists of creating an initial context for the discussion, setting norms, setting agenda, recognizing and prompting the participants, "meta-commenting," or dealing with "problems in context, norms, or agenda, clarity, irrelevance, and information overload" (35), and "Weaving," which is "to summarise the state of the discussion and to find unifying threads in participants' comments" (35). Part of the context-building may be one or more face-to-face meetings. All this, Feenberg states, is "an admission of defeat" (37)—the medium is not yet good enough to do what we'd like it to do. Feenberg's teacher-moderator sounds, however, suspiciously like the present classroom teacher who leads and facilitates a classroom discussion. Perhaps Feenberg is right: computer-mediated conferences may require a leader/facilitator. But it is just as likely that we will develop new conventions—such as the "emoti-cons" of e-mail correspondence—once we have learned to live and work in our virtual classrooms.

The structures of the on-line classroom can help the participants imagine not just a "virtual classroom" but a "virtual college," a complete educational environment. Lynn Davie carefully constructs a range of "sites" in her computer-mediated conferences: "I may call the main discussion the seminar room; provide a faculty office for advising; provide a small meeting room for informal interactions or help; provide an in-basket for student assignments; or provide workspaces for small group projects, subjects, etc" (79). Davie goes on to say that these metaphors can "help the student learn to navigate" the conference but notes as well that "we need to examine closely the advantages and disadvantages of different metaphors" (79). The context-setting metaphors can be visual and iconic as well as verbal. Alexander and Lincoln have described a graphical-user interface for their Thought Box project, one that permits students to choose from among boxes in the "Courses Building" which consist of "T101 News," "T101 Activities," " T101 Assignments," and "T101 Forum"; from boxes in the "Student Union" which consist of "Book Exchange," "Forum," "Help and Advice," and "Classified Ads"; and from icons such as "The Library," in- and out-baskets, newspapers, calendars, calculators, and class notes (90–91). With the graphical inter-face used by the Open University, we make a full move from the "virtual classroom" to a "virtual university." The "Electronic Campus Map" of the Open University presents the user with a graphic "map," with paths connecting six "buildings"—the Mail Building, the Staff Building, the Courses Building, the Student Union, the Tutorial Building, and the Resource and Information Center (Mason 117). Each building is faced with panels that represent choices that you'd make by "clicking" on the panel with a mouse: the Mail Building, for example, has panels labelled "in tray," "out tray," "your mail," "tutor A's mail," and so on. To the north of the Mail Building is a park-like space, with strolling people in it, labelled "Conversation area."

The "context" of the on-line classroom can include virtual spaces that stretch or exceed the academic metaphor that seems now to be the norm. Connections to non-academic settings, where students can partici-pate in writing tasks that are being undertaken in worlds outside the col-lege and the university, make possible a virtual "office" space where writ-ers from workplaces join writers from the academy in collaborative writing tasks. In the conventional classroom, the logistics of such an undertaking make it extremely difficult. The working writer does not have time to come to class to explain the context; interaction-at-a-distance is too slow for both sides of this transaction. On-line, we can construct a virtual space where the student writers and writers at worksites meet to discuss the writing task in progress.

What Do We Gain? Lose?

But what is lost in this new classroom? I think of Walt Whitman here, who saw the end of writing in the invention of the typewriter (Traubel 314). Will the on-line classroom be the end of our teaching? Certainly we lose face-to-face contact. But might we not generate another relationship, a different intimacy that might have its own virtues? Might the virtual classroom foster new relationships and new kinds of learning?

Researchers in this field have found that distance learning is often as effective as face-to-face instruction (Chute, George). Barbara Grabowski, et al., have summarized the research in the field, conspicuously citing the work of Linda Harasim, who found that students in an on-line, computer-mediated conference experienced and demonstrated increased initiative and increased responsibility for their own learning, and of Downing, et al., who found that in an on-line engineering course, students "asked more challenging questions, and that students reported high-quality instructor responses to their inquiries" (Grabowski, et al. 278). And Starr Hiltz finds that for some learners, CMC is a better learning environment than the brick-and-mortar classroom. In her study, Hiltz finds also that students reacted more favorably to the on-line environment when the courses were constructed in such a way as to foster collaborative learning. She notes as well that one computer-mediated conference was still going strong a month after the end of the semester, "with over a hundred new entries which continued to discuss the issues raised in the course" (7). Hiltz's findings are supported by Linda Harasim, who argues that "as a medium, it [CMC] is particularly conducive to information-sharing, brainstorming, networking, and group synergy"(61), and by McCreary, who finds that CMC has enriched the entire academic culture at her university, the University of Guelph, Ontario.

Given the research now extant, the proposition that on-line classrooms are somehow cold and impersonal and therefore in some way dangerous is arguable. Is an epistolary relationship less warm, less personal, less intimate than a "live" relationship? Is a class conducted through a computer-mediated conference less warm, less personal, less intimate than a face-to-face classroom experience? Given the powers of the human imagination, are human warmth and a sense of intimacy necessarily dependent upon physical presence? There is some doubt.

The on-line writing classroom has much to offer. It has all the virtues of distance education, in that it opens the class to people who cannot, for one reason or another, travel to a particular place at a particular time. The on-line classroom does not require the heating, cooling, and maintenance of the conventional classroom. And the on-line classroom does not require travel to a physical place, a factor that is now crucial in areas of low population density, but given that the cost of travel increases at double the rate of inflation (Chute 265), it will become increasingly important in all institutions of higher education. But perhaps more important, because the on-line classroom offers such wide access, it creates the possibility that classes could be more diverse than they now are: on-line writing classes could be deliberately composed of writers from different backgrounds, of different ages, and of different cultures. Such classes could become forums for our emerging cultural democracy. Further, the on-line, computer-mediated conference may be a site that will encourage the emancipating discourse envisioned by Boyd, Cooper and Selfe, and Flores—discourse in which status is less than it now is a function of race, gender, and class.

Clearly there are differences between on-line and "live" teaching and learning. These differences may seem to some to be losses. To the extent that students and teachers have experienced agency in "live" teaching situations, both will experience the virtual classroom as change and perhaps discomfort. Shoshana Zuboff has described the dislocation felt by workers at industrial sites as they moved from the foundry floor to the air-conditioned, information-processing booths above the floor. It would be extraordinary to imagine that students and teachers would not feel the sense of loss that attends the change in the nature of their work. To the extent that students and teachers have learned to be "good on their feet" in oral, face-to-face discussion, we'd expect the on-line environment to seem to them restrictive: impersonal, cold, devoid of human contact. And, so long as the on-line environment is created by the written language, students with learning disabilities that affect the production and reception of the written language will be at a disadvantage.

But, despite the fact that for some this will be a difficult transition and despite the fact that questions of access and equity remain to be addressed, for the reasons I have laid out above—our national dissatisfaction with schools as they are, the rising energy-cost of such schools, and the decreasing cost of computer and communications technology— we need to begin now to consider the shape that our writing classrooms may take in the second millennium. The two writing rooms I have described—the computer-equipped, brick-and-mortar classroom and the computer-mediated, on-line classroom—both now exist. From my perspective, writing now in 1991, they will soon, perhaps by the year 2050, seem entirely normal. John Tiffin argues that "the fibre optic telecommunication system will be to the current copper-based telephone system what the railway lines were to a donkey-track." Given the emerging capacity for electronic communication, he argues, "It seems highly unlikely that schools will survive in anything like their present form" (240). I think that Tiffin is right. It is time to begin to build, at least in our imaginations, the writing class of the coming virtual age.

Works Cited

Alexander, Gary and Ches Lincoln. "The Thought Box: A Computer-Based Communication System to Support Distance Learning." Mason and Kaye 86–100.

Boswell, James. *The Life of Samuel Johnson, LL.D.* Ed. R.W. Chapman. London: Oxford University Press, 1960.

Boyd, Gary. "Emancipative Educational Technology." *Canadian Journal of Educational Technology* 16.2 (1987): 167–172.

Chute, Alan. G. "Strategies for Implementing Teletraining Systems." *Educational and Training Technology International* 27.3 (1990): 264–270.

Cooper, Marilyn M. and Cynthia L. Selfe. "Computer Conferences and Learning: Authority, Resistance, and Internally Persuasive Discourse." *College English* 52.8 (1990): 847–869.

Davie, Lynn. "Facilitation Techniques for the On-Line Tutor." Mason and Kaye 74–85.

Elbow, Peter. *What is English?* New York: Modern Language Association, 1990.

Feenberg, Andrew. "The Written World: On the Theory and Practice of Computer Conferencing." Mason and Kaye 22–39.

Fisher, Lester and Murray, Donald. "Perhaps the Professor Should Cut Class." *College English* 35 (1973): 169–173.

Flores, Mary J. "Computer Conferencing: Composing a Feminist Community of Writers." *Computers and Community*. Ed. Carolyn Handa. Portsmouth: Boynton/Cook, 1990. 106–117.

Flynn, Laurie. "Funding PC Purchases is Low Priority on Campus." *InfoWorld* 12.42 (1990): 5.

Frangston, Robert. Interview "Welcome to the *Byte* Summit." *Byte* 15.9 (1990): 271.

George, Judith. "Audioconferencing—Just another Small Group Activity." *Educational and Training Technology International* 27.3 (1990): 244–248.

Grabowski, Barbara, and Suciati and Wende Pusch. "Social and Intellectual Value of Computer- Mediated Communications in a Graduate Community." *Educational and Training Technology International* 27.3 (1990): 276–283.

Harasim, Linda. "On-Line Education: A New Domain." Mason and Kaye 50–73.

Hiltz, Starr R. "Collaborative Learning in a Virtual Classroom: Highlights of Findings." Paper presented at the Computer Supported Cooperative Work Conference, June 1988. Revision for CSCW Proceedings. ED 305–895.

Hughes, Bradley. "The Police Chief, The Judge, The District Attorney, and The Defender: Using Networked Writing to bring Professionals into an Undergraduate Course on Criminal Justice." Paper given at The Sixth Conference on Computers and Writing, Austin, TX, May 17–20 1990.

Kaye, Anthony. "Computer-Mediated Communication and Distance Education." Mason and Kaye 3–21.

———. "Computer Conferencing for Education and Training: Project Description." Project Report CCET/1. Open University, Walton, Bletchley, Bucks (England). Institute of Technology. 1985. ED 273–260.

Lewis, Peter H. "The Executive Computer," *New York Times* 6 June 1990, sec. 3:4.

Lloyd-Jones, Richard and Andrea Lunsford. *The English Coalition Conference: Democracy through Language.* Urbana, Illinois: National Council of Teachers of English. 1989.

Mason, Robin and Anthony Kaye, eds. *Mindweave.* New York: Pergamon Press, 1989.

Mason, Robin. "An Evaluation of CoSy on an Open University Course." Mason and Kaye 115–145.

———. "Computer Conferencing: A Contribution to Self-Directed Learning." *British Journal of Educational Technology* 19.1 (1988): 28–41

McCreary, Elaine. "Computer-Mediated Communication and Organisational Culture." Mason and Kaye 101–112.

Moran, Charles. "The Computer-Writing Room: Authority and Control." *Computers and Composition* 7.2 (1990): 61–70.

Naidu, Som. "Computer Conferencing in Distance Education." 1988. ED 310–374.

Roberts, Lowell. "The Electronic Seminar: Distance Education by Computer Conferencing." Paper presented at the fifth Annual Conference on Non-Traditional and Interdisciplinary Programs (Fairfax, VA, May 1987). ED 291–358

Romiszowski, Alexander. "Shifting Paradigms in Education and Training: What is the Connection with Telecommunications?" *Educational and Training Technology International* 27.3 (1990): 233–236.

Rumble, Greville. "The Use of Microcomputers in Distance Teaching Systems." ZIFF Papiere 70, Fernuniversitat, Hagen (West Germany), 1988.

Selfe, Cynthia L. "Technology in the English Classroom: Computers through the Lens of Feminist Theory. *Computers and Community.* Ed. Carolyn Handa. Portsmouth: Boynton/Cook, 1990. 118–139.

Tiffin, John. "Telecommunications and the Trade in Teaching." *Educational and Training Technology International* 27.3 (1990), 240–244.

Traubel, Horace. *With Walt Whitman in Camden.* New York: Rowman and Littlefield, 1961.

Tyack, David B. *The One Best System.* Cambridge, MA: Harvard University Press, 1974.

Zuboff, Shoshana. *In the Age of the Smart Machine: The Future of Work and Power.* New York: Basic Books, 1988.

2

Preparing English Teachers for the Virtual Age:
The Case for Technology Critics

Cynthia L. Selfe
Michigan Technological University

Today, more than a decade after personal computers first entered the English curriculum in force, few teachers feel prepared to carry out effective instruction in a virtual classroom, and even fewer English education programs can claim they adequately prepare teachers for assuming productive instructional roles in such classrooms (cf. Wresch; Selfe, Rodrigues, and Oates). This state of affairs, while disturbing now, is bound to become increasingly problematic during the next decade as the pace of technological change accelerates. Our profession is not preparing teachers to deal with technology in its current forms, and we are certainly not preparing them to deal with technology as it changes in the future.

Ironically, it is the very teacher education efforts we *do* have underway that contribute most dramatically to this situation, encouraging a nearsighted and limited focus on the technology itself rather than on the instruction that it supports. Indeed many English education programs, in well meaning attempts to prepare teachers for public school classrooms, seem determined to make English teachers into technicians. All too often in these programs, attention is focused on specific hardware configurations; demonstrations of existing software packages, programming languages; or computer-assisted instruction and computer-managed education (cf. Lathrop and Goodson; Lucking and Stallard; and Standiford, Jaycox and Auten). Almost no time, unfortunately, is spent in teaching educators to think critically about *how* and *when* virtual environments can support the educational objectives of teachers in English classrooms.

Nor is our record any better with in-service education. Teachers who graduate and enter our public schools and universities are scheduled into under-supported, under-staffed computer classrooms where they spend too much of their time troubleshooting problems with personal computers, recovering lost files and data on faulty floppy disks, and feeding boxes of perforated paper into the cranky tractors of outdated printers so that their student writers can work. In-service programs, too frequently planned and implemented by computer specialists with no background in English education, bore or discourage teachers with inappropriate introductions to BASIC programming, spreadsheet manipulation, and database management.

Under such conditions, and with such training, it is little wonder that English teachers at all levels too often resort to the simplest computer-assisted instruction for their students, turn to drill-and-practice software packages that require minimal support, or use word-processing capabilities only as a way of making final paper drafts more readable. All too frequently, these teachers must be more concerned with re-writing unreadable user documentation or keeping an antiquated Apple II running than in making informed decisions about how to design and operate virtual learning environments that are both theoretically and pedagogically sound (McDaniel).

If our profession is to succeed in preparing teachers to be effective educators in the virtual environments of the next decade, we will need to help them learn to use technology *and* to function actively as technology critics and reformers in the context of our educational systems. To these ends, we have to teach educators to function as lifetime learners within technological environments *and* to understand technology and technological change in terms of social, political, and educational implications.

The following suggestions are designed to help us think of teacher preparation in these terms. They are far from exhaustive, but they may help to give us a sense of the direction in which our teacher preparation and in-service programs can move during the next decade.

Suggestion #1: Prepare English teachers to be lifelong learners in technological environments.

If, as a profession of English teachers and educators, we have learned anything about computers after experimenting with these machines over the course of the last decade, it is that we have much to learn. In fact, we have just begun to realize that our whole notion of learning must change radically in the face of the challenges posed by the virtual age. Given these challenges, teachers can no longer expect to be content or effective with four or five years of preparatory education in a single content area such as English or language arts; rather, these educators must be prepared for lifelong learning about technology, must see their own experimentation with, and exploration of, technology as part of an on-going process of discovery.

Five years ago, English teachers could experience a rush of satisfaction when they learned to master a word-processing program and could consider themselves well prepared for participation in the computer revolution. Today, these same teachers find they have to learn three or even four such programs as their departments or universities update or standardize their software holdings. Indeed, it is becoming increasingly common to find educators who must learn graphics and layout packages, database programs, bibliography bases, style checkers, outliners and idea generators, and networking and conferencing software to stay current in the fields of composition studies or technical writing. Teachers in English and composition are now faced with new versions of software packages that come out quarterly; missing one of these updates often means struggling with a myriad of new details in later versions. And, as software has changed, so has hardware. In the last five years, teachers have learned to deal with stand alone personal computers, modems, synchronous and asynchronous networks, laptop computers, laser printers and laser disks, CD-ROM, projection devices, full-page and double-page displays. Even this partial catalogue of changes suggests the enormity of the learning curve that confronts teachers of English. But trying to keep pace with these changes in software and hardware may well be the smallest part of a teacher's task in the virtual age.

There are indications, for example, that a larger and more difficult part of that task may involve teachers in learning an entirely new set of what Gumpert and Cathcart term "grammar[s]" (23) those sets of conventions that allow us and our students to operate successfully within communication environments. Indeed, knowledge of the grammars connected with virtual environments (the grammars of computer screens, networks, or hypertexts, for instance), will be a primary marker of a literate communicator in virtual environments—much as a knowledge of other grammars (the grammar of pages, the grammar of books) marks the literate print-based communicator (cf. Selfe, "Redefining Literacy"; Lanham; Slatin).

To understand this point, we must first understand "literacy" as the ability to make meaning through reading and writing texts, interpreting the contents of these texts in light of our own experiences. Given this definition, it makes sense that part of our job in teaching literacy involves the teaching of those conventions that literate communicators share. In a print-based culture, for example, the grammar of a page allows readers to predict certain standard approaches: information on pages generally begins in the upper left-hand corner and proceeds, in a line-by-line fashion, to the bottom right-hand corner. Pages, as they are collected in books, are also generally characterized by running heads, page numbers, static margins, fixed order, and fixed size. This knowledge allows print-based readers to predict, in an economic way, how information will be presented on pages and in books and to use that information—we know what to expect and how to interact with the information on books and pages because we know how it is arranged and what this arrangement signifies.

In important ways, however, the grammars associated with virtual environments—the grammars of computers, of computer screens, operating systems, and networks, among others—represent very different sets of conventions. English teachers, moreover , have just begun to identify and understand these conventions. Text within virtual environments, for example, involves temporal as well as structural conventions and lacks some of the spatial-contextual cues to which page readers have access. Thus, readers of virtual texts, unlike readers of books, cannot gauge the length of an on-line manuscript by hefting it, glancing at its bulk, flipping through its pages. On-line readers, instead, must learn to refer to the memory storage requirements of a text, as expressed in bits or bytes; to move through the text by scrolling, searching for key words, or activating links between hypertext nodes; and to access on-line maps or representations of a text's sections. Different media, in other words, require different strategies for reading and navigating texts.

Such differences exist not only in the conventions used to structure on-line and print texts in formal or physical ways, but also in the conventions readers and writers use to chunk and locate information, move about in texts, comprehend information, and refer to specific ideas. In this way—as Cathcart and Gumpert, Lanham, Selfe ("Redefining Literacy"), Slatin, and others—have pointed out, our notions of literacy tasks and genres, the sense and scope of possibilities we perceive as readers and writers, our very world vision are shaped at essential levels by the media in which we work. It becomes clear, then, that teachers raised in print-based cultures must be prepared to study and acquire entire sets of new grammars—whole systems of different conventions—to operate successfully within virtual communication environments.

At the same time, however, there are some indications that the processes involved in acquiring a working knowledge of new grammars, much like the process of acquiring a second language, may never result in complete fluency, that individuals' "first" literacy so fundamentally shapes their world vision and their ability to function as literate individuals, that complete "fluency" in a second or third literacy may prove impossible. Hence, we can explain the actions of teachers, brought up to be literate in a paper-and-pencil environment, who ask students in computer-supported classrooms to "turn to page three" of an on-line document. To those students, who are operating literately in virtual environments, this simple direction may well be meaningless. There are, for starters, no pages to turn. Students will be used to scrolling through a dynamic text in which particular spatial locations of information change with the margins that individuals have set, the type size they have chosen, or the word-processing system they are using. Or the students will be navigating the links of a hypertext in which information is stored not on fixed pages but in nodes that some writers and readers will see and some will not. In a similar sense, we can understand teachers who teach in computer-supported writing environments but require hard-copy printouts of virtual texts for use in peer-critique groups—even though such an approach does not allow for the use of hypertexts, which can only be represented meaningfully in a virtual environment, or even more traditional on-line documents containing representations of color, emphasis markers like blinking and highlighting, or other on-screen conventions typically available to writers working on line.

These experiences with technology, accumulated over the past decade, have taught us some valuable lessons about how educators must be prepared for the virtual age: we must not only teach individuals how *to learn now* about computers as these machines exist in our classrooms, but also teach them how *to continue learning* as technology shifts in form and concept at an accelerated pace. Moreover, given the fact that most educators are still raised primarily in a print-based culture, we have to prepare teachers to learn, not only from their own first-hand experiences with media, but also from observing their students' experiences systematically.

In this sense, one of the more valuable lessons we can teach educators is how to forget what they *think* they know about how people read and write (information we have gathered from our observations of the print culture) and learn to watch what their students know about reading and writing in virtual environments. From these observations, among other things, we can identify increasingly effective ways of functioning as readers and writers in on-line communities, gain new perspectives on linking information associatively in virtual environments, study techniques of navigating hypertexts and the on-line information bases on which they depend, and formulate new visions of genre boundaries for on-line writing.

This approach to teaching—which involves the recognition that we lack expertise in virtual literacies—may be an uncomfortable one for teachers given our current emphasis on mastery, accountability, and standardized tests. At the same time, it may also be the most valuable perspective teacher-preparation programs can possibly pass along. It represents, in the most fundamental way, the re-definition of both the "teacher" and "student" as central terms in our hierarchical educational system and aligns these terms much more closely with the notion of non-hierarchical learning exchanges. As described by Paulo Freire, such exchanges are based on dialogues in which

> the teacher-of-the-students and the students-of-the-teacher cease to exist and a new term emerges: teacher-students with students-teachers. . . . They become jointly responsible for a process in which all grow. In this process, arguments based on "authority" are no longer valid. . . . (67)

Within such an educational setting, teaching, learning, and the relationships among teachers and students are radically revised, and teachers never stop being learners themselves. Practically, however, there is no quick way to establish this kind of mindset. Teachers who work within virtual environments need to labor constantly to develop and maintain the habit of continuing to learn. They must make themselves attend to and explore student perceptions and behaviors, especially those that seem productively connected to technology and those that are not congruent with patterns typically displayed in traditional learning environments. They must force themselves to adopt the habit of systematically observing students working with technology in ways that seem unusual, of making notes about these observations, and of looking for patterns within these observations. They must seek out those places and times when students' learning with technology seems to resist traditional educational patterns. Teachers in virtual environments, must, in other words, get used to being unsure of what they know and realize that this feeling of dissonance can be productive in leading to new knowledge.

Suggestion #2: Prepare English teachers to see technology critically, as it functions within complex social, economic, and political contexts.

A second lesson we have learned about computers over the last decade is that they cannot be understood *simply* as tools, considered in isolation from the social, political, or economic contexts in which they are developed and in which they continue to be used. Technology, we recognize, is a richly embroidered artifact of a culture. As such, it embodies the values and ideological directions of a society and cannot help but reveal important things about the people who produce it. In this sense, our understanding of computers and their effects within our classrooms has become increasingly complicated. If ten years ago we represented computers as panaceas to educational ills, now we see these machines as multi-valanced forces within our classrooms, one being used by educators to effect both great good and great evil, as Joseph Weizenbaum has noted. Certainly, we recognize that computers are being used as often to support those values we see as reprehensible in our educational system (intellectual isolation, competitiveness, and the continued oppression of women and minorities) as they are to support those values we see as positive (productive collaboration, connectedness, and equal educational opportunity) (cf. Cooper and Selfe, Eldred, Gomez, Jessup).

This newly complicated vision of technology helps us explain why computers so often make very little real difference in our classrooms and why so few teachers have succeeded in using these machines to effect the positive changes that they had hoped for (Hawisher and Selfe, "The Rhetoric of Technology"). When technology, as an artifact of our culture, is employed by teachers who lack a critical understanding of its nature or a conscious plan for its use, and when these teachers must function within an educational system that is itself an artifact of the political, social, economic forces shaping our culture, the natural tendency of instruction is to support the status quo. Technology is, in other words, inherently ideological; and all technological decisions in educational settings are, thus, inherently political. In light of this realization, we can understand why so many school systems set up computer-supported writing classrooms that mirror traditional classrooms, even though virtual learning spaces can differ radically and productively from such spaces; why many teachers insist on lecturing within computer-supported classrooms, even though such an activity is difficult and obviously ineffective in such classrooms; and why most software packages purchased for English classrooms involve traditional drill-and-practice activities in grammar, usage, or mechanics, even when we know such instructional approaches to be ineffective.

To prepare teachers for an age in which learning can take place in productive virtual environments, then, we need to help these educators acquire the habit of thinking critically about technology in complicated social, cultural, and economic contexts. A good part of this habit must come from broad theoretical preparation, cross-disciplinary study in critical theory, cultural criticism, science and technology studies, Marxist and feminist studies, among other perspectives. Each of these fields informs teachers at a general level about the relationships that bind people to one other in cultural groups, the language individuals use to express these relationships of society, and the tools used to give their language form and substance.

Understanding this need for theoretical study may be difficult for preparatory programs that stress application and practice. But practice, especially in connection with technology, provides only one part of a teacher's preparation. Indeed, it has been our profession's nearsighted focus on practice and the lack of theoretical frameworks on which to base this practice that has encouraged the multitudes of what-works-in-my-classroom reports now filling our academic computing journals. These reports—given their reliance on localized constraints and resources, specific student audiences, and particular educational sites—remain isolated instances of "teaching from the hip." More disturbing, perhaps, is the fact that these efforts are often unconnected at any deeper level with a school's educational philosophy, the theoretical foundations of a given writing program, or a teacher's larger vision of language and how it functions. If we recognize that technology and technological decisions are inherently ideological and political, this lack of conscious and systematic links between theory and practice becomes even more problematic within educational settings.

We do not have far to look to find a frightening example of the myopia that can result from an over-reliance on practice and the absence of critical, theory-driven examination. A brief glance at the history of computer access in our educational system can provide us clear direction. During the first decade of experimentation in virtual learning environments, most English teachers went about their instructional business with computers on a what-works-in-my-classroom basis. The reports these instructors did publish focused primarily on practical advice for making hardware and software decisions, pedagogical tips for introducing students to computers, and suggestions for how to use computers to support process-based revision (cf. Jobst, Stephens, Papinchak). In those early days of discovery, in the rush to integrate technology into our curricula, if an activity worked, we used it and passed news of it along to others. There was not often time stop to think about *why* such activities worked so well within the existing systems of our classrooms or what kinds of learning we were promulgating with them.

It was not until educators took a step back from these wholly practical concerns, sometime in the middle of the last decade, that we could begin to consider from a larger and more critical perspective how or if these early efforts were productively affecting students and the learning environments in which they were functioning. When we did pause for this critical examination, we found evidence of disturbing trends, among them differential patterns of access to technology in our schools for whites and non-whites, for those students from well-funded schools, and for those from schools in lower socio-economic areas (cf. Cohen; Cole and Griffin; Miller; Sheingold, Martin and Endreweit). In their survey of schools, for example, Michael Cole and Peg Griffin reported

- more computers are being placed in the hands of middle and upper class children than poor children;
- when computers are placed in the schools of poor children, they are used for rote drill and practice instead of the cognitive enrichment that they provide for middle and upper class students. . . . (43–44)

These patterns, clearly, have been established by neglect, not by design, and are more frightening because of this fact. Despite the best intentions of teachers in individual classrooms, differential patterns of access to technology have grown on the foundations of differential access to political and economic privilege already existing in our schools. These patterns are so deeply rooted in our schools and our educational system that they are invisible to us. As Mary Louise Gomez interprets this case, our computer-based curricula have been operating on an un-examined set of assumptions about

> poor children and nonwhite children and these groups' perceived abilities to learn with and about computers, [that] replicates existing models of teaching and learning with traditional sources. . . . [It] perpetuates stereotypical assumptions regarding the superior abilities and greater interests in technology . . . of . . . whites, and students of higher socioeconomic status. These assumptions guide teachers' expectations of students. In turn, teachers' assumptions about learners' abilities and interests guide the development of activities for students. (5)

Our lesson from this story is clear: schools at all levels must provide rewards for teachers who establish critical and careful links between educational theory and practice. When teachers talk or write only about practices that they have found successful in virtual environments and fail to look critically at these practices or to connect them with existing theoretical frameworks, they cheat not only themselves, but also the profession at large as it seeks to support positive educational reform on a larger scale. One of the primary aims of theoretical examination is to examine a critical or contextual vision of a field—especially within a social, political, or historical framework. As Cary Nelson notes, it is only within a "theorized discipline" that is actively engaged in "self-criticism" that scholars can establish a "site for a general social critique" (48). I would add that only after such a critique is established and accepted that positive changes in our educational system can be effected. This kind of work is, clearly, not easy; it may require long-term, collaborative efforts at articulation among elementary, secondary, and college-level English teachers. It is, nonetheless, necessary.

Until we examine the relationship between computer technology, virtual environments, language, and society from a range of theoretical perspectives—both in our teacher education programs and in our profession—we will continue, myopically and unsystematically, to define our vision of technology by examining isolated bits and pieces of a much larger puzzle, conducting separate studies in isolated classrooms and undertaking isolated research projects that cannot inform work in other settings. We are in danger, through such an approach, of drastically misinterpreting how technology and education relate to one another within our existing educational system. We are in danger of constructing a misleading picture that will fail to give our everyday classroom efforts direction and meaning. "Theory," as Marilyn Cooper (*Theory and Practice*) reminds us, "is prior to, and essential to, good practice" (1).

Perhaps one of the more productive strategies for teachers who want to begin this work is to start reading collections of critical thinking about technology and its uses, and to work on re-framing the themes and concepts from these books within the context of a particular classroom or educational site. Any number of these collections are available and teachers can start with areas of personal interest: feminist theory (Kramarae), cultural criticism (Hardison, Winner, Zuboff), philosophy (Heim), learning theory (Turkle), or composition studies (Hawisher and Selfe, *Critical Perspectives* and *Evolving Perspectives*).

Suggestion #3: Prepare English composition teachers to be classroom researchers who systematically observe technology and its relationship to learning.

If a critical, theory-based understanding of technology is important for teachers in a virtual age, however, it only remains so if continually informed, adjusted, or validated by systematic classroom observations. Theory untested by practice and a systematic research program remains an intellectual exercise that has little to do with the real stuff of instruction. The key word, here, for teachers in virtual environments is "systematic." As Miles Myers notes, "All teachers think about what happens in the classroom, but these thoughts are largely undocumented and unreported, and if they are reported they are usually anecdotal and only for lunchroom discussion" (2). Myers explains further that increasingly systematic teacher research is central to the effort of "making schools better places for teaching and learning" (2).

For teachers operating in virtual environments, the need for systematic observation and research may be even more necessary than it is in traditional environments, informed as they are by a long history of educational trial and error, the many leads our profession has already followed, and the accumulated learning we have amassed. Given the embryonic state of our knowledge about what goes on when instruction is carried out in virtual learning spaces, however, increasing instances of observation and research are essential to directing our efforts during the next decade. Without the information we can gather from such observations, we have little to go on in making decisions about virtual instruction. Our efforts cannot, for instance, be informed by history, for we have put very little time behind us in the virtual age. Nor can we rely solely on our teacher's intuition, given the points made earlier in this chapter, about the limits of our own intellects, trained in a print generation. Indeed, in a virtual age—given the complicating factors of software, hardware, and the lack of training and experience—we might well need *more* observation and research, and different kinds of research, than we have required in other instructional settings in order to reach generalizable conclusions about teaching practices.

Evidence for this last argument is abundant in our early approaches to research on computer-based education in English classrooms. As Gail Hawisher noted in her germinal reviews of research on word-processing, the first forty major empirical studies of word processing, conducted between 1981 and 1988, resulted in research findings that were both "varied and conflicting" ("Research Update," 7). Only "slightly more studies," Hawisher ("Research and Recommendations," 52) reported, for example, indicated that students writing on computers did more revision than they did writing without computers; similarly mixed results were reported for those studies examining changes in writing quality.

It is quite likely that this confusing situation will endure until we learn some important lessons from our early attempts to understand technology and its relationship to virtual classroom environments. As Hawisher points out, to begin to sort out the rather confusing research picture we have thus far constructed, we must first refine our research approaches, designing single investigations so that they build on the findings of previous work; or, better yet, designing series of studies that follow "systematic research agendas" ("Research and Recommendations," 59). Moreover, Hawisher adds, we should encourage longitudinal investigations of proficient student users of technology and complicate our vision of virtual environments by studying computer use within the rich social and educational contexts of classrooms. This advice is supported and augmented by Andrea Herrmann, who points out that we cannot hope to capture the scope of change connected with computer-based writing environments if we continue to rely on single-method investigations. Indeed, as she notes, our "governing gaze" (124) in future studies of virtual environments must envision technology as it is situated in the social, pedagogical, economic, and social fabric of our classrooms and must incorporate a range of inquiry paradigms and research methodology. I would add that teachers working within virtual classrooms may need to think about the different *kinds* of research questions, directions, and methodologies that productive investigations of these spaces may require. If virtual environments do, indeed, involve fundamentally different patterns of learning, literacy conventions, and teaching approaches, then our studies may also need to differ in radical ways if we hope to tease out information about what goes on within these spaces.

It has become clear from these commentaries on our profession's early exploration of virtual environments that such a rich and multi-dimensional vision of technology and change cannot be constructed by teacher/researchers with training only in the use of inferential statistics. Given the complicated interaction of technology, teachers, learners, and cultures in our schools, those educators who set about to observe computer-supported classrooms in a systematic way will need to bring to bear some combination of enthnomethodology, case-study techniques, inferential statistics, formal writing assessment, historical analysis, and naturalistic observation to accurately portray what is happening. Certainly, these researchers will have to look both at what happens within virtual environments themselves (how electronic texts are generated and exchanged, how discourse and discourse communities are formed and how they function in on-line conferences, how individuals construct knowledge representations in hypertexts as they read and author these texts) and what happens within the educational contexts that support these environments (how teachers adapt to the use of computers, how students adapt to virtual environments, how concepts of authorship and ownership are altered by electronic collaboration, how lab/classroom configurations affect virtual writing environments and the uses to which these environments are put). Computers, themselves, may well prove useful research tools in such work by supporting, among other things ethnographic databases and field note compilations, keystroke capture programs, and hypermedia representations of complex research projects.[1]

Finally, given the lack of consensus about technology and its uses in English classrooms, teachers in virtual environments should also be prepared to share their observations with other teachers, either locally or regionally—through workshops, seminars, or district newsletters—or on a wider basis—through professional journals and national conferences. Until we begin to share the results we find, widely and systematically, we cannot begin productive comparisons, replications, or the large-scale collection and analysis of results.

Suggestion #4: Prepare English composition teachers to be architects of computer-supported learning spaces and virtual learning spaces.

One of the more positive side effects of our profession's recent struggle to formulate a rich and multi-dimensional vision of computers has been an accompanying re-vision of our classrooms and curricula as sites in which learning and thinking take place. To make knowledgeable decisions about how technology should be used in our classrooms, English teachers have had to re-think what they, as educators, want to accomplish with instruction and what goals they want students to achieve. Computers, in this productive way, have prompted us to re-examine many of the philosophical and pedagogical assumptions that form the foundation for our teaching, and, in some cases, have encouraged teachers to make changes in the way they approach education in general.

An important illustration of this trend has been the work our profession has done in designing computer-supported writing classrooms or virtual learning environments. Educators involved in such efforts have been prompted by such projects to re-think the connections between the architecture of learning spaces and the activity of learning, to re-consider the traditional hegemonic relationship between teachers and students as it is played out in the architecture of non-computer classrooms. In the course of this re-consideration, there has been a recognition of how the elements of traditional classrooms serve to reflect and sustain a way of regulating power that many teachers consider antithetical within the conceptual framework of a liberatory pedagogy. We have come to recognize, for example, that traditional classrooms privilege the teacher's space as a center of power. The teacher's location clearly designates the "front" of a room and is marked by furnishings appropriate to such a power center (lectern, blackboard, desk). At the same time, traditional classrooms also work to limit the power of students, in many cases, actually bolting desks to the floor to make sure that students must face the teacher at all times and restrict their independent movements and interpersonal conversations.

These realizations about classrooms, of course, are not new, nor do they come as a surprise to most teachers. Michel Foucault ("Space, Knowledge, and Power," 239–256) reminds us that the architecture of learning "spaces" (and other public spaces such as prisons, orphanages, schools) is one of the many sites in which a culture plays out its collective notion of power and its exercise. Architecture, to Foucault, represents a "technology" of power (Dreyfus and Rabinow 188), a way of "coding" ("Space, Knowledge, and Power," 253) our cultural thinking about power.

If we have recognized these connections between architecture, power, and educational spaces, however, we have also recognized that we have been less effective in instituting effective reforms. The overwhelming weight of tradition, of historical precedent, of intellectual habit generally prohibits both teachers and students from experimenting in meaningful ways with the architecture of alternative learning spaces that might more effectively support enlightened education.

Recently, teachers with experience in designing virtual writing environments have begun to suggest that the inertia working against educational reform does not govern so inevitably in computer-supported contexts. For one thing, given the relative lack of historical precedent connected with designing computer-supported facilities for English curricula, administrators are unsure of how these spaces should look or what elements they should contain (Selfe, "English Teachers"). For another, virtual environments are still new enough to our discipline to inspire a sense of experimentation and exploration (c.f. Cooper and Selfe, Levy, Fjermedal). As a result, teachers charged with designing computer-supported classrooms or virtual learning environments often find that they have with an increased amount of freedom to shape learning spaces and, hence, the opportunity to be architects of learning spaces that may more effectively support the student-centered pedagogies or liberatory pedagogies toward which our profession seems to be working. In a single networked environment serving several disciplines within a school, for example, English teachers can—and, in the future, may be required to—customize portions of the virtual learning space to support their specific educational goals or those of the programs (basic writing, gifted programs, ESL) with which they work. This customization may involve articulating a specific educational agenda for this virtual space, creating forums that encourage the kinds of learning and teaching behaviors valued by this agenda, importing commercial software and authoring home-grown software that would support specific educational goals, and identifying assessment procedures for evaluating the new learning space.

From the evidence that we now have, it is entirely likely that this trend toward involving English teachers in the design of computer-supported writers' environments will continue and even grow. Those English teachers being asked to design a computer-based writing classroom this year will be asked to design networked systems next year, and hypermedia environments the next. In fact, this trend is already highly visible at the university level, where some departments of English have moved from halfheartedly supporting small collections of stand-alone microcomputers to being highly dependent on sophisticated hypermedia classroom/laboratories in five short years. If we can train prospective English teachers to be careful, critical architects of these virtual spaces, we can design into these contexts exciting features that will allow students' increased amounts of control over their own learning, increased access to information, and increased participation in communities of writers from around the world.

The challenge, of course, is to educate teachers to think critically about the implications of their architectural design efforts. Virtual spaces, after all, can be designed to be just as teacher-centered and hierarchically organized as traditional classrooms. As Foucault ("Space, Knowledge, and Power") reminds us:

> There may, in fact, always be a certain number of [architectural] projects whose aim is to modify some constraints, to loosen, or even break them, but none of these projects can, simply by its nature, assure

that people will have liberty automatically, that it will be established by
the project itself. The liberty of men [sic] is never assured by the institutions and laws that are intended to guarantee them. This is why almost
all of these laws and institutions are quite capable of being turned
around. Not because they are ambiguous, but simply because "liberty"
is what must be exercised. . . . I think it can never be inherent in the
structure of things to guarantee the exercise of freedom. The guarantee
of freedom is freedom. (245)

Teachers, as virtual architects, then, must be sensitive to the implications
of their design decisions.[2] Among just a few of these decisions will be
concerns such as the following: Who has access privileges to various information sources accorded within a learning community (databases,
national and international networks, on-line conferences)? How are decisions about learning made within a virtual community of scholars and
teachers? How is privacy accorded to writers in virtual environments? To
what extent is it protected? How is group and individual work organized?
Who makes decisions about privacy and the organization of collaborative
group work? How are discourse situations constructed so that they give
voice to various individuals within a virtual classroom?

Suggestion #5: Prepare English composition teachers to be humanists.

As the final suggestion in this chapter, this one seems the most simplistic.
After all, English teachers are *already* educated as humanists. What I
would like to ensure, however, is that our profession sensitize English
teachers—especially those individuals who want to specialize in the use
or design of virtual environments—to the importance of keeping their
priorities squarely in the humanist camp and the necessity of working
actively to make sure that the virtual environments they teach in are
informed by these priorities.

If we let concerns about bits and bytes, computer-assisted instruction
and computer-managed instruction, RAM and ROM eclipse our larger
vision of humanist concerns as we educate teachers to design and implement and teach within virtual environments, we will be making what base-
ball teams would consider "a bad trade." First of all, we will be
surrendering for those teachers the richest and most valuable heritage we
have—one that places people, their feelings, their impressions and interpretations of life, the study of human experience and the written expres-
sions about this experience in the center of our attention. Second, we
would be abrogating the rights of both teachers and students to operate
in virtual learning environments designed according to the value systems
of humanists rather than those designed according to the value systems of
scientists and engineers.

To play this suggestion out at a practical level in any given teacher-preparation or in-service program, I think it is absolutely essential to frame all discussions about technology in terms of their humanistic implications for teachers and students—to refuse to enter into decision-making processes about technology unless these are explicitly set within the articulated contexts of of educational philosophy, learning theory, composition theory, curricular goal setting, cultural studies. If we hold fast a commitment to this approach, it should effectively ensure a productive problematizing of political, social, economic, and educational decisions that English teachers make about virtual environments and, thus, ensure that our profession continues to develop an increasingly critical perspective on and innovative uses of these exciting spaces.

Notes

1. For a more complete exploration of the kinds and range of research questions that teachers in computers and composition studies will be facing in the next decade, see Gail E. Hawisher and Cynthia L. Selfe, *Evolving Perspectives on Computers and Composition Studies: Questions for the 1990s* (Urbana, IL and Houghton, MI: National Council of Teachers of English and Computers and Composition Press, 1991).

2. For additional discussion of how design decisions affect the instructional objectives and operational decisions within computer-supported writing environments, see Cynthia L. Selfe, *Creating a Computer-Supported Writing Facility: A Blueprint for Action* (Houghton, MI: Computers and Composition Press, 1989).

Works Cited

Cathcart, Robert, and Gary Gumpert. "Mediated Interpersonal Communication: Toward a New Typology." *Quarterly Journal of Speech* 69 (1983): 267–277.

Cohen, Michael. "Exemplary Computer Use in Education." *Quarterly Newsletter of the Laboratory of Human Cognition.* 3.5 (1983): 46–51.

Cole, Michael, and Peg Griffin. *Contextual Factors in Education: Improving Science and Mathematics Education for Minorities and Women.* Madison: Wisconsin Center for Education Research: University of Wisconsin-Madison, 1987.

Cooper, Marilyn M. *Theory and Practice: The Case of Technical Communication Programs.* Unpublished Paper. Houghton: Michigan Technological University, 1987.

Cooper, Marilyn M., and Cynthia L. Selfe. "Computer Conferences and Learning: Authority, Resistance, and Internally Persuasive Discourse." *College English* 52.8 (1990): 847–869.

Dreyfus, Hubert L., and Paul Rabinow. *Michel Foucault: Beyond Structuralism and Hermeneutics.* 2nd ed. Chicago, IL: The University of Chicago Press, 1982.

Eldred, Janet. "Computers, Composition, and the Social View." *Critical Perspectives on Computers and Composition Studies*. Eds. Gail E. Hawisher and Cynthia L. Selfe. New York: Teachers College Press, 1989. 201–218.

Fjermedal, Grant. *The Tomorrow Makers: A Brave New World of Living-Brain Machines*. New York: Random House, 1986.

Foucault, Michel. "Space, Knowledge, and Power." *The Foucault Reader*. Ed. Paul Rabinow. New York: Pantheon Books, 1984. 239–256.

Friere, Paulo. *Pedagogy of the Oppressed*. Trans. Myra Bergman Ramos. New York: The Continuum Publishing Company, 1990.

Gomez, Mary Louise. "The Equitable Teaching of Composition." *Evolving Perspectives on Computers and Composition Studies*. Eds. Gail E. Hawisher and Cynthia L. Selfe. Urbana and Houghton: The National Council of Teachers of English and Computers and Composition, 1991. 318–335.

Gumpert, Gary, and Robert Cathcart. "Media Grammars, Generations, and Media Gaps." *Critical Studies in Mass Communication* 2 (1985): 23–35.

Hardison, O. B., Jr. *Disappearing Through the Skylight: Culture and Technology in the Twentieth Century*. New York: Penguin Books, 1989.

Hawisher, Gail E. "Research Update: Writing and Word Processing." *Computers and Composition* 5.1 (1988): 7–28.

———. "Research and Recommendations for Computers and Composition." *Critical Perspectives on Computers and Composition Instruction*. Eds. Gail E. Hawisher and Cynthia L. Selfe. New York: Teachers College Press, 1989. 44–69.

Hawisher, Gail E., and Cynthia L. Selfe, eds. *Critical Perspectives on Computers and Composition Instruction*. New York: Teachers College Press, 1989.

———. *Evolving Perspectives on Computers and Composition Studies: Questions for the 1990s*. Urbana and Houghton: The National Council of Teachers of English and Computers and Composition Press, 1991.

Hawisher, Gail E., and Cynthia L. Selfe. "The Rhetoric of Technology and the Writing Class." *College Composition and Communication* 42.1 (1991): 55–65.

Heim, Michael. *Electric Language: A Philosophical Study of Word Processing*. New Haven, CT: Yale University Press, 1987.

Herrmann, Andrea W. "Computers and Writing Research: Shifting Our 'Governing Gaze'." *Computers and Writing: Theory, Research, Practice*. Eds. Deborah H. Holdstein and Cynthia L. Selfe. New York: Modern Language Association, 1990. 124–134.

Jessup, Emily. "Feminism and Computers in Composition Instruction." *Evolving Perspectives on Computers and Composition Studies: Questions for the 1990s*. Eds. Gail E. Hawisher and Cynthia L. Selfe. Urbana and Houghton: The National Council of Teachers of English and Computers and Composition Press, 1991. 336–355.

Jobst, Jack. "Computer-Assisted Grading of Essays and Reports." *Computers and Composition* 1.2 (1984): 5.

Kramarae, Cheris. *Technology and Women's Voices: Keeping in Touch*. New York, NY: Routledge & Kegan Paul, 1988.

Lathrop, Ann, and Bobby Goodson. *Courseware in the Classroom: Selecting, Organizing, and Using Educational Software.* Menlo Park: Addison-Wesley Publishing Company, 1983.

Lanham, Richard. "The Electronic Word: Literary Study and the Digital Revolution." *New Literary History* 20.2 (1989): 265–290.

Levy, Steven. *Hackers: Heroes of the Computer Revolution.* New York: Dell, 1984.

Lucking, Robert, and Charles Stallard. *How Computers Can Help You Teach English.* Portland: J. Weston Walch, Publisher, 1988.

McDaniel, Ellen. "Assessing the Professional Role of the English Department 'Computer Person'." *Computers and Writing: Theory, Research, Practice.* Eds. Deborah H. Holdstein and Cynthia L. Selfe. New York: Modern Language Association, 1990. 31–39.

Miller, J. J. *Microcomputer Use in San Diego/Imperial County School Districts.* San Diego: University of Southern California-San Diego, 1983.

Myers, Miles. *The Teacher-Researcher: How to Study Writing in the Classroom.* Urbana, IL: ERIC Clearinghouse on reading and Communication Skills and The National Council of Teachers of English, 1985.

Nelson, Cary. "Against English: Theory and the Limits of the Discipline." *Profession 87* (1987): 46–52.

Papinchak, Robert Allen. "Beyond the Classroom with Computers." *Computers and Composition* 2.1 (1984): 8–10.

Selfe, Cynthia L. *Creating a Computer-Supported Writing Facility: A Blueprint for Action. Advances in Computers and Composition Studies.* Houghton: Computers and Composition Press, 1989a.

———. "Redefining Literacy: The Multilayered Grammars of Computers." *Critical Perspectives on Computers and Composition Studies.* Eds. Gail E. Hawisher and Cynthia L. Selfe. New York: Teachers College Press, 1989b. 3–15.

———. "English Teachers and the Humanization of Computers: Networking Communities of Readers and Writers." *On Literacy and Its Teaching: Issues in English Education.* Eds. Gail E. Hawisher and Anna O. Soter. Albany: State University of New York Press, 1990. 190–205.

Selfe, Cynthia L., Dawn Rodrigues, and William R. Oates, eds. *Computers in English and the Language Arts: The Challenge of Teacher Education.* Urbana, IL: National Council of Teachers of English, 1989.

Sheingold, K., L. M. W. Martin, and M. W. Endreweit. "Preparing Urban Teachers for the Technological Future." *Mirrors of the Mind: Patterns of Experience in Educational Computing.* Eds. R. D. Pea and K. Sheingold. Norwood: Ablex, 1987. 67–85.

Slatin, John M. "Reading Hypertext: Order and Coherence in a New Medium." *College English* 52.8 (1990): 870–883.

Standiford, Sally N., Kathleen Jaycox, and Anne Auten. *Computers in the English Classroom: A Primer for Teachers.* Urbana: ERIC Clearinghouse on Reading and Communication Skills and The National Council of Teachers of English, 1983.

Stephens, Gary. "Computer Debating." *Computers and Composition* 1.4 (1984): 7–8.

Turkle, Sherry. *The Second Self: Computers and the Human Spirit.* New York: Simon and Shuster, 1984.

Weizenbaum, Joseph. "Not Without Us: A Challenge to Computer Professionals to Use Their Power to Bring the Present Insanity to a Halt." *Fellowship* October/November (1986): 8–10.

Winner, Langdon. *The Whale and the Reactor: A Search for Limits in an Age of High Technology.* Chicago: The University of Chicago Press, 1986.

Wresch, William, ed. *The English Classroom in the Computer Age: Thirty Lesson Plans.* Urbana: NCTE, 1991.

Zuboff, Shoshana. *In the Age of the Smart Machine: The Future of Work and Power.* New York: Basic Books, Inc., Publishers, 1988.

3

Political Impediments to Virtual Reality

Elizabeth Sommers
San Francisco State University

I walked along the college corridor early one morning, as I had so many times before, carrying my sixty students' printouts, some plastic diskette holders, and a stack of software packages. My colleague passed me, as he had so many times before, *The Norton Anthology of English Literature* nestled neatly under his arm. "How are things in computerland?" he asked me. I suppose he was teasing, but I took him seriously. "Why don't you come to see for yourself?" I asked. "Oh, no, it's all beyond me," he said, and we went our separate ways.

This incident has a meaning that resonates beyond my personal situation. Such occurrences are commonplace in high school and college English Departments, pointing to a critical misreading of computer-based literacy programs. First, our literature-teaching colleagues often have no sense that we are involved in remotely the same enterprise: teaching language to students. Second, they typically have little understanding of what we are trying to do: using our professional energies to create programs for students that acknowledge the growing necessity for a computer-based literacy. Third, our colleagues frequently seem indifferent to or even afraid of our efforts to integrate computers into the curriculum, as though such efforts are outside their realm as English teachers. Finally, our research, software development projects, and publication directions frequently seem meaningless to other English teachers, pointing to a deep-rooted and disturbing clash in values between humanism and technology.

The implications are disturbing: we are in a crucial transformational stage as our culture moves towards virtual reality and we should be

43

leaders in shaping this new textuality, but politics are preventing us from doing so. In this article, I describe the political issues confronting educators interested in computer-based literacy: the underlying problem in its various manifestations, its consequences for our profession and for our students, and some incremental steps leading to possible resolutions.

Professional Foundations

Scholars in computers and composition defy easy classification. We are as varied as the field of Composition Studies itself, rarely dividing neatly into the three emerging ideologies—cognitive, expressive and social— often sharing philosophical and pedagogical characteristics of all three (Berlin 478; Faigley 527–528). But despite the diversity of our ideological roots, most of the pioneers in computers and composition tend to share certain scholarly qualities described by Lunsford in her 1989 address as Chair of the Conference on College Composition and Communication (76). We are, for example, often "interdisciplinary," "collaborative," "exploratory," and "non-hierarchical," and we are fast to embrace innovative technologies to help writers.

While I agree with Lunsford, her address downplays a basic political fact: those of us in composition studies tend to be marginalized in our academic departments, and those of us working with computers tend to be marginalized within composition studies. This marginalization is unmistakable, for example, at national meetings of professional organizations. At the 1990 MLA Conference, just seven sessions involved computers, accounting for less than 1% of the total. At the 1990 NCTE Convention, only 4% of the sessions, special interest groups and workshops concerned computer-based literacy. *What is English?*, the publication resulting from the 1987 English Coalition Conference, includes no mention at all of computer-based literacy in its chapter defining English (Elbow 108–118).

The reasons for this marginalization are complex but also simple. When unraveled, they tend to find their sources in traditional institutional infrastructures (Freire 60; LeBlanc 14; Selfe 118). As Lunsford notes, "As teachers of writing have always been, we are dangerous precisely because we threaten the equilibrium, the status quo" (76). We are also dangerous because we come armed with technology, and humanists are often terrified of the changes our machines portend. In computers and composition, even more so than in composition studies in general, our goals are often radically different from traditional institutional goals. Frequently we intend to reform departments, not only to win assistance for our experiments in computerland, but to also reconcile the cultural clash between the values of humanism and of technology (Nelson, qtd. in LeBlanc, *Development*, forthcoming).

We tend to value the traits Lunsford so appreciates: collaboration and risk-taking, experimentation and dialogue (Barker and Kemp 6; Cyganowski 68; Langston and Batson 145). We challenge current-traditional notions of language learning, calling for an end to teacher-centered classrooms, to the notion of knowledge as a pre-fabricated body of facts to be digested by passive and obedient students (Boiarsky 59; Flores 107). We tend to agree with Freire that "in problem-posing education, men [sic] develop their power to perceive critically *the way they exist* in the world *with which* and *in which* they find themselves; they come to see the world not as a static reality, but as a reality in process, in transformation" (70–71). We also call for an end to sharp divisions among faculty, students and administrators (Shroeder and Boe 35).

In short, we challenge some of the basic tenets of institutional life, and such radical shifts in politics, values, and pedagogy directly challenge traditional power structures. Because so many humanists are leery of changes in institutional structures, afraid of technology, and uninformed about the significance of computer-based literacy, those scholars working with computers and composition tend to confront obstacles at every turn. In the following sections, I describe some typical constraints.

Administrative Issues

Grave problems tend to result from a profound lack of understanding on the part of English departments—of computer-based literacy, its significance and of the irrevocable changes in literacy education that technology requires (Lanham 78). As a result, many scholars contend with administrative resistance (Kaplan, *Ideology 50*), and many also sense a distinct lack of administrative trust (Taylor 126). While it would be too simplistic to claim that administrators are the enemy, Herrmann argues convincingly that high school administrators tend to usurp pedagogical authority (113). In colleges, too, administrators rather than teachers tend to make decisions about computer-supported laboratories (Strickland, *Politics* 317). Frequently jurisdiction over computer laboratories falls outside of English departments, with two predictable results: hardware and software choices are not made by computer and composition scholars (Holdstein, *Politics* 127); and English faculty members often have difficulties scheduling classes in the computer laboratories. Also, English departments tend to devalue the contributions labs make to a campus as well as the professional effort invested in them (Selfe, *Blueprint* 118).

On the other hand, Ray Rodrigues reminds us that administrative motivations can be positive (273). Some administrators are genuinely committed to computer-based literacy, willing to educate themselves, to allocate resources and to ensure a favorable environment for work in computers and composition. But such administrators seem to be in a minority, and even sympathetic administrators are inevitably placed in a position of juggling multiple demands and multiple needs. State-of-the-art computer-supported writing programs pose many problems even when they are not perceived as threatening. They are expensive, and little research shows that they even help writers in any neatly measurable way. Administrators, even those most interested in integrating computers into the curriculum, often need to make decisions based on quantitative evaluation, on proven results we cannot provide about writing (Marcus 120).

As a direct or indirect result, many computer-supported writing laboratories in post-secondary institutions are underfunded (Hughes 69; Wresch 286). But computer-supported writing centers require vast resources of expertise, money, time, energy, and dedication (Selfe, *Blueprint* 123), including knowledgeable faculty administrators and laboratory technicians. When under-funded, computer-supported writing facilities often share a whole slew of other problems. Because hardware and software are both expensive and short-lived, equipment problems tend to be endemic. Selfe estimates the average computer has a lifespan of five years, and computers used by hundreds of students require constant repair (*Blueprint* 125). Software, subject to constant upgrades and changes, is both expensive to purchase and time-consuming to learn and teach.

Teaching and Teacher Training

Erika Lindemann's conception of teaching as a rhetorical act (149) can be broadened to encompass the radical pedagogical shifts required when introducing computers into the curriculum. In Lindemann's model, teacher, writers, and subject exist together in a changing but interdependent relationship to one another. When this relationship becomes unbalanced, difficulties immediately develop in the form of classes which are overly centered on teacher, student, or subject. But computers *inevitably* change the balance in a writing classroom, even a process-oriented and student-centered classroom, creating a whole new set of rhetorical relationships.

If we are to use computers in our curricula, clearly we need to devote considerable time and effort to training teachers and developing curricula, to creating a new rhetorical balance. But such change is problematic. Computer-supported writing programs cannot simply be neatly grafted onto existing writing curricula. Instead, our traditional pedagogies need to be radically revised (Hawisher, *Research Update* 18; Oates xiv). As Hawisher states, "currently, teaching strategies are either not powerful enough to encourage significant change in students and their writing, or individual studies are of too short duration to capture it" (*Research Update* 18). Thus we need to develop more productive, powerful teaching strategies and curricula.

Experienced computers and composition scholars realize, of course, that current-traditional teaching methods won't work in computer-supported writing classrooms any more than they work in other writing classrooms (Handa 160). But resistance to teacher training is a chronic problem in English departments (Holdstein, *Training* 127; Marcus 133). When computer-supported literacy enters the picture, the situation becomes even more complex, often stirring resistance or fear among literature faculty. Again, the cultural clash between humanities and technology is an unmistakable part of the problem. Marcus, for example, claims that teachers have "thinking blocks," leading them to believe computers hinder rather than help literacy (132).

Even when English Department faculty begin to acknowledge a need for training and construct curricula to provide for it, these programs are often sketchy. Wresch reports on a 1985 survey sent to 1800 NCTE members (281–2). While only 176 teacher educators returned the survey, results showed teacher educators spend only an average of 5.7 hours training teachers to work with computers. Such a meager time commitment seems to indicate a lukewarm acceptance at best. Holdstein proposes short workshops with follow-up colloquia (*Training* 133), but such workshops seem inadequate to the substantial task of introducing faculty not only to the teaching of writing but also to the uses of computers in writing instruction.

Of course, some teachers in computers and composition do attempt to reform teacher training programs to take advantage of the potentials of computer-supported instruction. Teacher educators such as LeBlanc and Moran, Peyton, Selfe, Sommers and Collins, for example, have developed curricula attempting to transform outdated models of teacher-student relationships and of teaching and learning writing. But when they do, new problems come into focus, even with the best of intentions and the most motivated of teachers and learners. In Peyton's view, infrastructure changes may be necessary before the classroom microcosm can truly change:

> Our original conception of a revolutionary classroom dynamic was never realized in the way we had imagined. Social distinctions were not necessarily blurred, shifting the teacher out of the role of authority figure and manager of classroom activity and discussion. . . . [I]t may be that our traditional curricula, views of how learning takes place, and ways of measuring learning need to change radically so that writing and thinking in interaction can hold a central place in our planning and assessment, and its full potential can be explored and developed. (30)

Clearly, teacher training for computer-supported literacy education can be not only demanding but virtually impossible, given the present climate in most English Departments. Compounding the problem is the fact that many writing teachers trying to use computers are graduate students, lecturers, and adjunct faculty—those least valued in English Departments. In many cases, the potential power of the microcomputer—to transform the relationship of readers and writers, of teachers and learners, of subject and medium—is never tapped.

Entrenched Resistance to Teaching

While innovative and integrative programs do exist, such programs are presently as rare as they are impressive. This is because even determined college teachers often encounter a related level of problems: entrenched resistance to the teaching of writing at the post-secondary level and intensified resistance to computer-supported literacy. This resistance can be seen in many ways, of course, but two in particular concern me here: the teaching of writing is still seen as lower status work, and work with computers and writing is particularly questionable (Gerrard 39; Holdstein, *On Composition* 69). As Gerrard comments:

> Computer-assisted composition is one of the most exciting and dynamic fields in composition. In some cases, it has utterly transformed the classroom and the experience of learning to write. Yet its universal acceptance as a teaching tool is being retarded partly because of the retrograde status of composition faculty. At many schools, the computer revolution will require far more than a lab down the hall. It will require a revolution in the profession. (39)

Taylor perceives the resistance in slightly different terms, commenting that "composition teachers find themselves in the Mobius catch when, on the one hand, they are suspected of using microcomputers because they can't teach, and, on the other, they're suspected of using microcomputers because they're trying to avoid teaching" (122). In other words, computer-supported writing instruction is often perceived as questionable, even irresponsible pedagogy. In my experience, other faculty members often appear subtly dismissive or frightened of scholarship in computers and composition, denying its authenticity by ignoring its existence or joking about computer-based literacy. Such resistance, grounded in the clash between values of humanism and technology, creates tenacious problems for many computer and composition scholars.

Research and Software Development

In a meta-analysis of early work in computers and composition, Hawisher recommends developing "systematic research agendas" including more longitudinal studies, more studies of experienced users, and more contextualized studies (*Research & Recommendations* 59). The problems in carrying out these excellent suggestions, unfortunately, are substantial. First, English Departments tend to value traditional literary scholarship far more than research and publication in computers and composition (Holdstein, *On Computers* 69; Selfe, *Blueprint* 117). LeBlanc concurs, suggesting that "If composition researchers are still struggling for recognition within departments, computer and composition researchers are more marginal yet" (*Competing* 13).

In reality, few faculty members are unlikely to have the resources to design and carry out long-term, theoretically grounded, sophisticated research studies on various aspects of computers and writing. This is especially true given the special nature of research in computers and writing, which is both time-intensive and complex due to the number of variables: software, hardware, training issues, social environment, and theoretical framework (Bridwell-Bowles 82–83). Such research requires a highly developed knowledge of composition theory, research methods and design issues as well as familiarity with computers and composition pedagogy. Few scholars outside of major research institutions are likely to be in institutional positions to conduct such studies.

Like researchers on computers and writing, software developers within academe often face a thicket of problems. First, their efforts require enormous knowledge, time and effort, yet these efforts are rarely acknowledged and rewarded by administrators and departments (Gerrard 38; Holdstein, *On Computers* 68; Kaplan, *Ideology* 29; LeBlanc, *Competing* 13). Citing a 1988 EDUCOM Academic Software Development Survey, LeBlanc found a lack of incentive for software development in terms of release time, promotion and tenure (*Competing* 14). Not surprisingly, as a result much of the available educational software is weak, and much of the best software has yet to be written. Scholars have the knowledge and the interest, but not the time or institutional support. Since they directly involve teaching, software development projects are often erroneously seen as equivalent to textbook projects, when in fact they usually require much more time, expertise, and development. In addition, software development often requires interdisciplinary efforts, programmers' paid expertise, and state of the art equipment (LeBlanc, *Development* in press). As Strickland observes, for example, we need a new type of software designed specifically to encourage higher order revision goals (*How* 17) . But who will develop it and at what cost?

Consequences of the Problem

The political problems discussed above have grave consequences for computer and composition scholars and for language students. Equally serious, many English faculty and English departments themselves are becoming peripheral, unwilling and unable to cope with the new demands of virtual reality. In this section, I discuss the implications of each of these consequences in turn.

For computer and composition scholars, the repercussions of the many problems tend to overlap. First, the lack of administrative understanding and support has serious consequences for computer-supported language laboratories. Faculty members often inherit the walloping task of laboratory administration, trying to develop and administer facilities without leave time or adequate resources for personnel or equipment. While many writing centers tend to share such problems (North 236), the situation is especially complicated and time-consuming in computer-supported laboratories, where hardware and software expertise is also crucial.

Since many if not most composition teachers also struggle with heavy course loads, the problems of computer laboratory administration can quickly grow overwhelming. Many faculty members grow to understand this and steer clear of such responsibilities despite a keen interest in computer-supported instruction (Gerrard 39). However, not all high school and college educators avoid such professional traps, whether because of pedagogical commitment, scholarly curiosity, or political naivete. My own experience with computer-supported laboratories, for example, is not unusual. When I administered such a facility for a major university, I received no leave time from a four-course load per semester in order to do so. I unpacked computers and configured printers, formatted disks, selected and arranged carrels, scheduled classes and open hours, evaluated software, and taught faculty and students, all the time wondering why my efforts seemed to be viewed with such skepticism by many faculty members and administrators.

Second, the lack of support for pedagogical changes and curriculum development means that in reality few teacher educators have the training, the time, the expertise or the professional incentives to build state-of-the-art programs. Teachers are seldom in a position to remodel classroom and program curricula so they become effective computer-based pedagogies. Selfe and Wahlstrom note:

> The lessons to be learned from teaching computer-supported writing classes are not all pleasant ones. For teachers, the effort of adding a computer-support component to a course generally requires a great deal of time and flexibility—sometimes more than overworked faculty are capable of providing. (268)

As a result, though some teachers sacrifice more traditionally rewarded professional activities to develop sound curricula, more often teachers tend to teach in computer-based situations using ineffective pedagogies. In many institutions, the least experienced instructors teach the computer-supported writing courses, graduate students who may themselves need technical help (Herrmann 115). Without guidance or support, many well-meaning new teachers often imitate their own graduate school teachers, using obsolete teaching strategies that simply do not make sense in any writing classrooms and certainly not in those where computers have irrevocably changed the instructional context.

Those teachers who do take on laboratory administration as well as teaching and teacher training responsibilities do so with predictable consequences: they have less time for scholarly pursuits and, inevitably, fewer professional rewards for scholarly activity. While some teachers do attempt to proceed with research and software development projects, such projects are complex, time-consuming, and poorly rewarded in traditional educational hierarchies. Predictably, few scholars working today have the time or professional incentives to complete sophisticated research projects or to develop software for instructional uses.

The implications of such problems are exceedingly serious for students. The computer laboratories which they use (if they are fortunate enough to have access to such facilities) tend to have far too few computers for the number of students they serve. Their overworked staffs are not necessarily trained to assist with writing instruction, especially when the labs are not part of English Departments. The equipment in such labs tends to be inappropriate for writing instruction, giving students little real assistance. Within English classrooms, the computer-supported literacy programs now available to students are not usually pedagogically effective. Yet these problems will remain unresolved because faculty are not able to conduct in-depth research, develop effective composition software, or construct powerful curricula. As a result, students will remain educational losers, learning little of what they need to know about literacy in the virtual age. They are likely to leave our English Departments having learned outmoded and ineffective writing processes, ill-prepared for virtual reality.

Finally, many English departments as well as their faculties are in serious jeopardy of obsolescence. While computer-supported literacy is often tolerated and sometimes encouraged, it is seldom seen as central to the mission of our schools and colleges. Few English departments recognize the critical transformational stage we have entered in the history of literacy, and the implications of this blindness are not pleasant. English departments are becoming increasingly outdated, unwilling to work to mend the rift between humanism and technology, and so unable to participate in the vast task of building a new vision of literacy. Most English departments abnegate their responsibilities to shape this new literacy, retreating instead into safe, traditional ideas of language instruction. Unless this trend is reversed, English departments will become even less influential than they are today, offering students little of what they need to know as literate adults.

Incremental Steps to Possible Solutions

As scholarship evolves in computers and composition, it becomes clear that we all need much more than personal commitment. Such critical work requires a favorable climate, one most of us working in computers and composition do not now enjoy. Can we demand that our schools and colleges change? I don't think we can afford not to try. And while I can't offer a panacea for our problems, I can propose some incremental steps leading to possible solutions.

First, we can't allow ourselves to be isolated within our own institutions. As we struggle with the problems of administrative support, laboratory facilities, teacher training, research, and software development, we can easily develop tunnel vision. This was my most serious misreading at my last university: isolated, I felt I must be responsible for problems endemic to the system. Had I realized the importance of networking, of explaining the difficulties I faced, of sharing my attempts to build a lab, I might have found both support and guidance. Eventually I realized this and changed institutions; others may be able to change their own situations without changing institutions. But one thing is certain: without systemic support, the energy and idealism of individual teachers is bound to fade. Such support can come in various forms. Within our colleges and universities, we may find interested and supportive colleagues within various disciplines. We may be able to use academic committees as forums; among others, Holdstein suggests making political issues explicit, believing faculty dialogue about political ramifications can result in political power (*Politics* 127) .

In a larger sense, our success—even survival—depends primarily on education. We need to become effective educators of fellow teachers and administrators, explaining both our pedagogical goals and philosophical underpinnings. This education can take place in many forums: in ongoing pre-service and in-service settings, in committee work and in publication efforts, in grant writing and in self-study. It can take the form of classroom visits by peers and administrators. We can initiate deep pedagogical discussions of the sort advocated by Shulman (qtd. in Watkins A:11–12), philosophical explorations of what we mean by teaching and learning. At the heart of this educational process, we urgently need comprehensive training programs designed and taught by scholars with expertise in English Education as well as computer-supported writing instruction. As Oates writes, "English education and training programs should now operate so that others do not have to learn the hard way" (xiii).

We also need to develop collaborative relationships among teachers, teacher educators and administrators (Herrmann 116–117; D. Rodrigues 189; R. Rodrigues 273; Selfe, *Blueprint* 126). Such collaborative relationships have many potential benefits: offering teachers a chance to shape evaluation criteria (R. Rodrigues 272); providing a chance to lobby for the economic and professional incentives we need to continue our work (Herrmann 123); creating educational forums so administrators are aware of our non-traditional curricular goals and their rationales (R. Rodrigues 273); presenting opportunities to educate administrators about the special challenges intrinsic to computer-supported composition instruction; giving new teachers a chance to learn from seasoned practitioners; allowing teachers in schools and colleges to work together.

Nor can we overlook the importance of various professional organizations beyond the boundaries of our own institutions. Electronic networks such as Megabyte University, a computer network initiated by Fred Kemp of Texas Tech University for scholars working with computers and writing, serve a valuable function by providing a forum for pedagogical and philosophical discussions. Consortia such as ENFI share teaching methods, provide support and classroom data for research and software development, and offer inter-university support systems (Batson 7). Computing educators' organizations are now more common, and regional and national professional organizations such as NCTE, CCCC, and MLA might also provide forums for political change. Eventually, too, teachers need to look beyond our own classrooms, our own institutions and our own professional organizations, learning how to funnel economic resources into our programs through local and state political channels (Goodson, Cory, Finkel, and Fletcher 234).

Ultimately, of course, English departments need to recognize the critical nature of work in computers and composition, to perceive this work as central to the scholarship in the discipline. Retention, promotion, and tenure requirements need to be revised to reflect the special nature of work in computers and composition and to fairly evaluate this work (LeBlanc, *Competing* 13–14). Computer-supported writing instruction, as we well know, is labor intensive, often involving laboratory administration, teaching, teacher training, and curriculum design. It may or may not result in publication, given its labor intensive nature, and publications are likely to include software development projects designed for instructional uses. Such projects require a great deal of time, far more than traditional scholarship, and this must be acknowledged. Similarly, research is likely to proceed slowly, especially research which acknowledges the complexities of computer-supported writing environments and attempts longitudinal studies. In short, English departments need to redefine the traditional triad of teaching, research, and service in order to reflect the realities of scholarship in computers and composition.

All of this means a great deal of work, but English Departments have no alternatives. If our students are to be literate into the next century, administrators, faculty, and students have to reshape the academy. The only alternative is unacceptable—to continue to watch individual teachers burn out, to accept an increasing gap between academic language instruction and a society dependent on computer-based literacy, and to resign ourselves to the glaring inequities between the professor with her diskettes and the professor with his *Norton Anthology*.

Works Cited

Barker, Thomas and Fred Kemp. "Network Theory: A Postmodern Pedagogy for the Writing Classroom." *Computers and Community*. Ed. Carolyn Handa. Portsmouth: Boynton/Cook, 1990. 1–27.

Batson, Trent. "The Significance of ENFI." *Proposal Abstracts from the Sixth Computers and Writing Conference*. 17–20 May 1990. Austin: U. of Texas and Texas Tech U., 1990.

Berlin, James. "Rhetoric and Ideology in the Writing Class." *College English* 50 (1988): 477–494.

Boiarsky, Carolyn. "Computers in the Classroom: The Instruction, the Mess, the Noise, the Writing." *Computers and Community*. Ed. Carolyn Handa. Portsmouth: Boynton/Cook, 1990. 47–67.

Bridwell-Bowles, Lillian. "Designing Research on Computer-assisted Writing." *Computers & Composition* 7.1 (1989): 79–91.

Cohen, Michael. "In Search of the Writon." *Writing at Century's End: Essays on Computer-assisted Composition*. Ed. Lisa Gerrard. New York: Random House, 1987. 116–121.

Cyganowski, Carol. "The Computer Classroom and Collaborative Learning: The Impact on Student Writers." *Computers and Community*. Ed. Carolyn Handa. Portsmouth: Boynton/Cook, 1990. 68–88.

Elbow, Peter. *What is English?* New York & Urbana: MLA & NCTE, 1990. 108–118.

Faigley, Lester. "Competing Theories of Process: A Critique and a Proposal." *College English* 48 (1986): 527–542.

Flores, Mary. "Computer Conferencing: Composing a Feminist Community of Writers." *Computers and Community*. Ed. Carolyn Handa. Portsmouth: Boynton/Cook, 1990. 106–117.

Freire, Paulo. *Pedagogy of the Oppressed*. New York: Continuum Publishing Corporation, 1986.

Gerrard, Lisa. "Computers, Writing Faculty, and the Politics of Marginality." *Proposal Abstracts from the Fifth Computers and Writing Conference*. 12–14 May 1989. Minneapolis: University of Minnesota, 1989.

Goodson, Bobby, Sheila Cory, LeRoy Finkel, and Geoffrey Fletcher. "Models of Political Effectiveness at State and Local Levels." *Proceedings of the National Educational Computing Conference.* 20–22 June 1989. Boston: International Council on Computers for Education, 1989.

Handa, Carolyn. "Politics, Ideology, and the Strange, Slow Death of the Isolated Composer, or Why We Need Community in the Writing Classroom." *Computers and Community.* Ed. Carolyn Handa. Portsmouth: Boynton/Cook, 1990. 160–183.

Hawisher, Gail. "Research Update: Writing and Word Processing." *Computers & Composition* 5.2 (1988): 7–27.

———. "Research and Recommendations for Computers and Composition." *Critical Perspectives on Computers and Composition Instruction.* Eds. Gail Hawisher and Cynthia Selfe. New York: Teachers College Press, 1989. 44–64.

———. "Teaching the Future: The Electronic Writing Class and the Traditions of Teaching." *Proposal Abstracts from the Sixth Conference on Computers and Writing.* 17–20 May 1990. Austin: U. of Texas and Texas Tech University, 1990.

Herrmann, Andrea. "Computers in Public Schools: Are We Being Realistic?" *Critical Perspectives on Computers and Composition Instruction.* Eds. Gail Hawisher and Cynthia Selfe. New York: Teachers College Press, 1989. 109–125.

Holdstein, Deborah. *On Composition and Computers.* New York: MLA, 1987.

———. "The Politics of CAI and Word Processing: Some Issues for Faculty and Administrators." *Writing at Century's End: Essays on Computer-assisted Composition.* Ed. Lisa Gerrard. New York: Random House, 1987. 122–130.

———. "Training College Teachers for Computers and Writing." *Critical Perspectives on Computers and Composition Instruction.* Eds. Gail Hawisher and Cynthia Selfe. New York: Teachers College Press, 1989. 126–139.

Hughes, Bradley. "Balancing Enthusiasm with Skepticism." *Computers & Composition* 7.1 (1989): 65–78.

Kaplan, Nancy. "As We May Teach: Some Problems with Computer-Supported Collaboration in the Writing Curriculum." *Proposal Abstracts from the Fifth Computers and Writing Conference.* 12–14 May, 1989. Minneapolis: U. of Minnesota. 1989.

———. "Ideology, Technology, and the Future of Writing Instruction." *Evolving Perspectives on Computers and Composition Studies: Questions for the 1990s.* Eds. Gail E. Hawisher and Cynthia L. Selfe. Urbana: NCTE and Computers & Composition, 1991. 5–38.

Langston, Diane M. and Trent W. Batson. "The Social Shifts Invited by Working Collaboratively on Computer Networks: The ENFI Project." *Computers and Community.* Ed. Carolyn Handa. Portsmouth: Boynton/Cook, 1990. 140–159.

Lanham, Richard. "Convergent Pressures: Social, Technological, Theoretical." *The Future of Doctoral Studies in English.* Eds. Andrea Lunsford, Helene Moglene, and James Slevin. NY: MLA, 1989. 73–78.

LeBlanc, Paul. "Competing Ideologies in Software Design for Computer-aided Composition." *Computers & Composition,* 7.2 (1990): 7–19.

————. *Development of Computer Software for Composition: Overview and Analysis.* Urbana: NCTE and Computers and Composition, forthcoming.

LeBlanc, Paul and Charles Moran. "Adapting to a New Environment: Word Processing and the Training of Writing Teachers at the University of Massachusetts at Amherst." *Computers in English and the Language Arts.* Eds. Cynthia Selfe, Dawn Rodrigues, and William Oates. Urbana: NCTE,1989. 111–129.

Lindemann, Erika. "Teaching as a Rhetorical Art." *Teaching Writing: Theories and Practices.* Ed. Josephine Tarvers. Glenview: Scott, Foresman, 1988. 148–153.

Lunsford, Andrea. "Composing Ourselves: Politics, Commitment, and the Teaching of Writing." *College Composition & Communication* 41 (1990): 71–82.

Marcus, Stephen. "Computers in Thinking, Writing and Literature." *Writing at Century's End: Essays on Computer-assisted Composition.* Ed. Lisa Gerrard. New York: Random House: 1987. 131–140.

National Council of Teachers of English 80th Annual Convention: Educating the Imagination. 16–21 Nov. 1990. Atlanta, GA., 1990.

North, Stephen. "The Idea of a Writing Center." *Rhetoric & Composition.* 3rd ed. Ed. Richard Graves. Portsmouth: Boynton/Cook 232–246.

Oates, William. "Introduction: A History and Overview of this Collection." *Computers in English and the Language Arts.* Eds. Cynthia Selfe, Dawn Rodrigues, and William Oates. Urbana: NCTE, 1989. xiii–xix.

Peyton, Joy. "Technological Innovation Meets Institution: Birth of Creativity or Murder of a Great Idea?" *Computers and Composition* 7. Spec. issue (1990): 15–32.

PMLA: Program of the 1990 Convention. 27–30 Dec. 1990. Chicago, IL., 1990.

Rodrigues, Dawn. "Developing and Implementing Computer-Training Programs for English Teachers: A Game Plan." *Computers in English and the Language Arts.* Eds. Cynthia Selfe, Dawn Rodrigues, and William Oates. Urbana: NCTE, 1989. 179–195.

Rodrigues, Raymond. "Evaluation of Computer-Writing Curriculum Projects." *Computers in English and the Language Arts.* Eds. Cynthia Selfe, Dawn Rodrigues, and William Oates. Urbana: NCTE, 1989. 269–278.

Selfe, Cynthia. "Creating a Computer-supported Writing Lab: Sharing Stories and Creating Vision." *Computers and Composition* 4.2 (1987): 44–65.

————. *Creating a Computer-supported Writing Facility: A Blueprint for Action.* Houghton & West Lafayette: Computers and Composition, 1989.

Selfe, Cynthia and Billie Wahlstrom. "Computer-supported Writing Classes: Lessons for Teachers." *Computers in English and the Language Arts.* Eds. Cynthia Selfe, Dawn Rodrigues, and William Oates. Urbana: NCTE, 1989. 257–268.

Shroeder, Eric and John Boe. "Minimalism, Populism, and Attitude Transformation: Approaches to Teaching Writing in Computer Classrooms." *Computers and Community.* Ed. Carolyn Handa. Portsmouth: Boynton/Cook, 1990. 28–46.

Sommers, Elizabeth and James Collins. "English Teachers and the Potential of Microcomputers as Instructional Resources at the State University of New York at Buffalo." *Computers in English and the Language Arts.* Eds. Cynthia Selfe, Dawn Rodrigues, and William Oates. Urbana: NCTE, 1989. 27–41.

Strickland, James. "How the Student Writer Adapts to Computers: A First-year Student Protocol." *Computers and Composition* 6.2 (1989): 7–22.

————. "The Politics of Writing Programs." *Evolving Perspectives on Computers and Composition Studies: Questions for the 1990s.* Eds. Gail E. Hawisher and Cynthia L. Selfe. Urbana: NCTE and Computers & Composition, 1991. 307–326.

Taylor, Lee. "The Mobius Catch." *Computers and Composition* 4.2 (1987): 121–127.

Watkins, Beverly. "To Enhance Prestige of Teaching, Faculty Members Urged to Make Pedagogy Focus of Scholarly Debate." *Chronicle of Higher Education* 24 Oct. 1990, sec. A: 11–12.

————. "An Education Professor Tries to Put his 'Fantasy School' into Effect." *Chronicle of Higher Education* 7 Nov. 1990, sec. A: 3.

Wresch, William. "Appendix A: Survey of Computer Uses in English Education Programs." *Computers in English and the Language Arts.* Eds. Cynthia Selfe, Dawn Rodrigues, and William Oates. Urbana: NCTE, 1989. 281–286.

4

Exploring the Implications of Metaphors for Computer Networks and Hypermedia

Janet Carey Eldred
University of Kentucky

Ron Fortune
Illinois State University

Simile and metaphor are our handiest tools for defining a technology; they are also our most dangerous. When we encounter new technologies like computer networks and hypermedia, we evaluate and describe with similes: "This is like traditional mail, but faster"; "This is like a phone conversation, only more (im)personal"; "Hypertext works just like a book, but it's more flexible." Sometimes what begins in simile ends in metaphor: we move from "This is like traditional mail" to "Asynchronous computer conferencing allows us to send electronic mail"; from "This is like a phone conversation" to "Synchronous computer conferencing allows us to have electronic conversations"; from "Hypermedia is like having a library at my fingertips" to "With hypermedia, I can take a print or audio-visual resource off the shelf with the push of a button." Metaphor, to borrow from Ricoeur, lives in the domain of both rhetoric and poetry and exists as a powerful means of inscribing the world around us: "First . . . metaphor occurs in an order already constituted in terms of genus and species. . . . Second, metaphor consists in a violation of that order" (Ricoeur 21). By disturbing our methods of describing and classifying, metaphor allows us to understand a phenomenon. Yet as with all features of discourse, we both shape and are shaped by metaphors. As Lakoff and Johnson point out in their ground-breaking book, *Metaphors*

We Live By, it is impossible to understand without metaphors; it is even "impossible to talk about metaphor non-metaphorically" (Ricoeur 18).

Metaphors can be dangerous because of their power and their beauty: they wield their weighty persuasive powers almost magically, invisibly. In *Thinking about Women*, Mary Ellmann describes the effect engendered metaphors, with their implicit sexual analogy, have on our thinking and laments that "not only sexual terms but sexual opinions are imposed." In a study of metaphors for creativity in literary poetics, Terry Castle notices a short period in the eighteenth-century in which authors turned away from organic and physiological metaphors for literary creation and toward a reliance on mechanistic metaphors that deny "the primacy of biological function in all human activity." This brief period in literary history, however, led Castle to question whether it is possible to construct any kind of poetics or any theoretical framework, without relying on physiological metaphors, on some sort of "myth of the body" (202). Ellmann, too, after reflecting on the tyranny of sexual analogy, laments that "perhaps as long as sexual interest is strong" we will understand "all phenomena, however shifting, in terms of our original and simple sexual differences" (43).

Metaphors thus work from a known or familiar frame of reference to explain something whose attraction is based in part on its departure and difference from that frame. The metaphor must limit the phenomena in some way, or the departure the metaphoric frame attempts to embody is no departure at all. The key to preventing a metaphor from undermining its own usefulness lies in our acceptance of and ability to work with its inherent malleability and mutability. In his analysis of art as a metaphorical bridging of formalized public meaning and the immediate and ever-changing world of private experience, Richard Shiff argues that metaphor is central to individual and social advancement because it is the means through which, first, articulating the "new" is possible and, second, transforming the "old" is conceivable. "Acts of genius or dramatic breakthroughs in fields of study can dramatically affect our present world order," he insists, "only if they are joined to it by means of a powerful metaphor" (106). Yet, he is just as adamant about the mutability of metaphors themselves, noting that static metaphors undermine movement toward an ever greater understanding of ourselves and the world around us: "Unless the artistic metaphors themselves change, further knowledge does not lead to . . . truth but becomes a mere . . . accretion [of information] to be added to an already bulging storehouse" (118). The aesthetic of metaphor that Shiff associates with the relationship between art and life is evident in a variety of ways in discussions of computer networking and hypermedia in literacy education, and only when educators take this aesthetic into account are they likely to make the greatest use of this technology in the classroom.

As educators using new technologies, we must realize, as Hawisher and Selfe warn, that "unless we remain aware of our electronic writing classes as sites of paradox and promise, transformed by a new writing technology, and unless we plan carefully for intended outcomes, we may unwittingly use computers to maintain rigid authority structures that contribute neither to good teaching nor to good learning" (64). We need to subject our theory and practice to constant scrutiny. Despite enthusiasm for this new, promising technology (an enthusiasm necessary if we are to successfully integrate it into our classrooms), we must become temporary skeptics and challenge each action and idea. And during these moments of skepticism, we must evaluate the language used to describe this new-found pedagogical tool. We must ensure that our descriptive metaphors are working for us, that we understand not only—in Lakoff and Johnson's terms—what these metaphors "highlight" and allow us to understand, but also what conceptual structures they are hiding. Once we understand what is hidden, we must constantly remind ourselves of its absence—and of what this absence is costing us. This critical perspective is perhaps even more crucial as we begin research in the virtual age, begin to borrow and create a language to describe new technologies and pedagogies. This chapter will explore the use of metaphor in discussing two computer technologies increasingly prominent in literacy education—metaphors of speaking and writing used to define electronic networks, both synchronous and asynchronous, and metaphors for textuality and intertextuality that dominate discussions of hypermedia and its application in the classroom.

Before we begin, we want to define briefly the technical terms we are using. In a synchronous conference, all participants are logged on to a computer system and are communicating at the same time. One can type a message to another user, and the recipient, seeing the message within seconds, responds instantly, thus starting an exchange. These users are most often located in the same classroom, but they need not be. In an asynchronous conference, users log on at their convenience and respond to stored messages. We can, for example, from our offices at home read "mail" from students who might have written their messages from their home or dormitory. Asynchronous conferencing often takes place between users spatially separated, but again, this need not be the case. With both forms of conferencing, participants can be as close as the next terminal or as far away as another country. Hypertext is best defined as a "database that has active cross references and allows the reader to 'jump' to other parts of the database as desired. It is the requirement of active cross-references that makes the computer necessary to implement hypertext" (Schneiderman and Kearsley 3). Hypertext thus deals with linked texts. Hypermedia, on the other hand, might involve text, but can just as easily link "graphics, photographs, sounds, narration (speech), or animated sequences (video)." Hypermedia is thus the preferred term when "documents are multimedia in nature" (Schneiderman and Kearsley 3).

Networked Conferencing

Located between the technology of the typewriter and the telephone, electronic discourse in all its forms shares features of written and spoken discourse, yet resists definition as either "speech" or "writing." Yet even so, it is commonplace in the technological literature to speak of synchronous conferencing as computer conversation (speech) and of asynchronous conferencing as mail or as bulletin boards (writing). There is, then, in the language use a discernible break between speech and writing or between orality and literacy. Given these assumptions, we could sketch a structural model that looks like figure 1 below. Much of the literature about electronic networks reflects this model. (The term "net-talk" is borrowed from Diane Thompson's work "Interactive Networking").

This model appears sound enough; such is the power of metaphor. In fact, when we take a closer look, we see a more complex picture, a picture that depends on our angle of reference; we see the metaphor we are using to examine the phenomena. The model is just that—a framework not a depiction of some scientific, classifiable order. In this particular case, the structure or language chosen—that of speaking and writing—reinforces the politics of the orality/literacy model, one seriously challenged in this decade (Walters). Like any structural system, the speech/writing division does not remain stable as the discussion below will show.

As mentioned above, asynchronous conferencing (e-mail, bulletin boards) is more closely aligned with writing than with speech. Yet, we can locate studies and practices that identify asynchronous conferences— mail and bulletin boards—as speech. For example, Wilkins studies an electronic bulletin board, describing it as a computer "conversation," a "traditionally oral action—interactive discourse—now in graphic form" (57). She uses methods used by sociolinguists to study conversations, the same methods that Thompson ("Conversational Networking") and Murray use to study synchronous computer "conversations." Wilkins thus

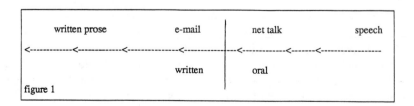

figure 1

operates from the premise that asynchronous conferencing is a form of speech. In literature courses, Eldred has used bulletin boards as an extension of class discussion. Early in the semester, the entries show mainly the characteristics of written discourse, but as the semester progresses, the entries (while still long and edited compositions) show many more features of interactive, spoken discourse.

Figure 1 shows not just a clean division between speech and writing, but also a spectrum, locating writing at one end, speech at the other, and the forms of computer conferencing strategically placed within. Work such as Marx's on peer revision raises questions about the logic of such a spectrum. Marx compares peer revision prepared for an asynchronous network to peer responses written in class. While he notes a spontaneousness characteristic of speech in the mail exchanged, he observes that the network responses have more features of written discourse than the (written) in-class responses: "Conducting exchanges of peer critiquing letters over a distance network requires students to acknowledge the unique demands of written discourse" (26), demands that are not always realized when students compose responses in class. Cohen and Riel's work on an asynchronous network reinforces Marx's observation and makes the argument more complex and interesting because of all the variables their study introduces. Their study looked at student compositions written in Hebrew with pencil and paper, translated by someone else, and transferred onto disk. The students' work was submitted for dissemination on an electronic network, and they were informed that students in another country would read their essays. The control group wrote essays only "for the teacher" for evaluation. When the two groups of papers were compared, Cohen and Riel discovered noticeably higher scores in the papers written for the electronic network. Moreover, they proposed the same intriguing reversal that Marx notes: "Students' writing for the teacher was often similar to an oral account of the events, forming a serial string of sentences, each providing some new information. . . . However, the composition written by the same students for the network usually showed clear chaining of sentences toward the expression of main idea" (153). In studies of asynchronous networks used for peer review or for distribution to peers, the chart then looks more like figure 2. Electronic mail now becomes more "written" than traditional in-class compositions or critiques.

The literature about synchronous conferencing shows a similar problem with any stable structural speech/writing divisions. For example, Diane Thompson describes ENFI (a name given by some to the teaching of "writing" using a synchronous conferencing system (see Batson)), as both "net talk" and as a computer-based technique for "teaching writing by means of writing" (17). In this short essay aptly entitled "Interactive

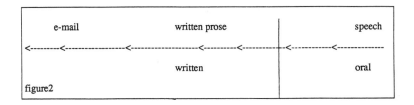

figure2

Networking: Creating Bridges Between Speech, Writing, and Composition," Thompson focuses on the gap between the net-talk (writing?) and "composition." Thompson describes basic writers communicating fluently on the network, "chatting" to one another, and attending to audience and context; students on the network are thus chatting in writing. Still, when asked to compose apart from the network, students froze: non-network assignments constituted "serious" writing. For Thompson, network communication slides from writing to talking and back to writing, but it never reaches the category she calls "composition." Thompson wants to see synchronous conferencing as a means of teaching writing by actually writing, but she is continually thrown back into the language or metaphor of speech.

In another study of synchronous conferencing, Ferrara, Brunner, and Whittemore use the label "Interactive Written Discourse" or "IWD." They argue that IWD "resembles both speech and writing, yet is neither" (9). The definition and the label bring them much closer to seeing synchronous conferencing activity as writing, without completely losing its sense of dialogue: IWD is "written language occurring in simultaneous terminal-to-terminal typed dialogue" (9). Their comparisons lead them to written rather than spoken analogies: postcards, notetaking, and other forms of writing that "appear to try to save time and minimize effort" (13). These classifications remind us that the more precise and various the metaphors, the more we are prompted to imagine and understand the distinct and different characteristics of a discourse and the more we are led to consider context. The comparative genres they choose, for example, are all relatively short; these models thus exclude the kind of longer entries one finds if the network is used for longer class assignments, such as Eldred describes.

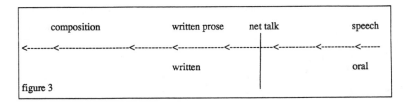

figure 3

Speaking and writing provide us with the vocabulary to discuss what happens when people participate in computer conferences—and they will continue to. This alone is not a difficulty. Yet we must realize that metaphors of speaking and writing now shape theory and pedagogy in networked composition classes. Our classrooms, in other words, are being shaped by the language we have adopted to describe our teaching, our research findings by the language we use to define our methodology. The language now used to describe electronic networks participates heavily in an orality/literacy model. While we implement synchronous networks into our writing courses, presumably as Thompson notes, "to use writing to teach writing," we conceive of this discourse largely as speech, not writing, as a supplement to class discussion. Even though we recognize the "dialogic" nature of printed text, the language of "dialogue" still throws us back into the arena of speech, a problem that has haunted applications of Bakhtin's "dialogic principle" and "speech genres."

Is this distinction much ado about nothing? If we look carefully at classroom policy, we can see the importance of making our presuppositions about speech and writing clearer. The issue of "lurking" brings the speech vs. writing dichotomy to the forefront. ("Lurking" is the phenomenon of people reading the messages in a given synchronous or asynchronous computer conference, but not writing any in response.) Our networked classrooms seem at times reminiscent of Melville's short story, "Bartleby the Scrivener." Melville's story is set in a law office, not a classroom, and the technology at issue here is quill-and-ink copying. But the similarities between this fictional world and the very real world of our classrooms seems instructive. Bartleby's job is to copy documents, a job he eventually "prefers" not to do. Though he wishes to stay at the law office, indeed even lives there, he gradually prefers not to speak to anyone at all. He is, thus, perhaps the quintessential lurker. The lawyer-employer, the representative of the well-intentioned literate man, judges Bartleby's nonparticipation as subversive and ultimately feels compelled to have him jailed. But for a good deal of the story, the lawyer remains perplexed, allowing Bartleby to remain and "prefer not to." Melville thus leaves us with a haunting image of technology and literacy and a frightening image of well-intentioned, benevolent holder of literacy, one who continually tries to encourage Bartleby into the world of speech and legal literacy, but who cannot fathom his employee's silence and resistance. The one word Bartleby uses—"prefer," a word that implies choice—and that even the other copiers eventually assimilate, is one the employer can't begin to unpack. The result is Bartleby's silence and eventual imprisonment. Bartleby moves from lurking, an activity he still controls, to entrapment: a chilling image.

In our classrooms, we, like the lawyer, have no problem requiring students to write. Even considering that we wish to "empower" students, de-center the teacher/authority figure, and encourage collaboration, we still require writing. In the most liberal classrooms, where grades are seen as institutional means of control, the amount of writing becomes even more crucial as the only means of evaluation. Whether through page limits, word counts, or specific assignments, we require students to produce, like Bartleby, enough written prose to receive a grade. (Those challenging the teaching of academic discourses would even argue that our students, like Bartleby, copy a socially-accepted literate form). Conversely, most writing instructors always have been reticent to require ("force" might be the word used) students to participate in class discussion. While we may encourage students—through grading structures or small group exercises—few instructors have mandated speech, unless in a Socratic method, question-answer session, much like one might find in a law school. When we look at how computer networks are integrated into writing classrooms, it becomes clearer that we think of synchronous networks (and even many times of asynchronous networks) as speech: instructors generally do not require students to write a given amount on the network. Instructors, particularly with synchronous networks, allow the "conversation" to shape itself and then evaluate the degree of participation. One of our greatest claims is that synchronous conferencing makes for more egalitarian discussions, but at least one article suggests that the teacher still "gets most of the lines" (Thompson "Conversational Networking"). The situation in asynchronous conferencing is much the same. While some of us stipulate the degree of participation (Marx's students were required to compose peer critiques; Eldred's students were required to write 300-word responses to each novel), just as often, asynchronous conferencing is seen as informal conversation involving lurkers and talkers.

As writing instructors, we find ourselves in the position of Melville's lawyer: we are in the "business" of teaching writing, and yet we watch as students on the electronic networks "prefer not to." And like Melville's lawyer, we have a difficult decision to make, a decision that becomes more crucial when we create policy for a networked classroom. Do we require participation from those who prefer not to? Or do we try to get behind the silence, try to unpack the language (or silence) of resistance? And, perhaps just as importantly, are the two alternatives actually mutually exclusive: Is it possible that allowing nonparticipation simply reinforces silences and ends, not in successful resistance, but in entrapment? The decision we make will be based in part on the language we use to frame the argument. The decision also will be closely related to our purposes in using the network, purposes which are still only vaguely articulated and that lead us back again to orality and literacy arguments. One purpose might be to teach students how to write in the conventional, generic print forms that are now being composed with computers. Another purpose might be to teach writing appropriate for the new technology, whatever that might look like. (If we accept such a proposition, we still have to decide how to finesse (combat?) academic structures such as grades, credit, proficiency, and matriculation.) The rigid perceptions of computer conversations and computer mail, that orality/literacy model, has led us to a new version of the "Great Divide" or "Great Leap" approach to literacy (Walters 174). We envision a tremendous gulf between speech and writing, even when that writing is composed using computer networks; on one shore is conversation (dialogue), on the other written academic discourse. We see the computer as a bridge over that gulf, or we judge that bridge too tenuous to cross and argue that students should stay firmly on one shore or another. Though the literature of computer networking worries about and studies the problems of social inequities and problems with hegemonic discourse, finally, our very language reinforces one of the most hierarchical models of literacy we have. The real gulf is not between orality and literacy but between different social/discursive communities.

What can we do? We might redefine our purpose to teach "communication" in all its forms with no recognized division between speech and writing. We could adopt Bakhtin's "speech genres," perhaps renaming them "discursive genres" to remind ourselves that the categories of "writing" and "speech" become subordinate to genre classification. Instead of all discourse being divided into speech and writing (a division reinforced by the split between communications and English departments), we could divide speech by genres, making "speech" and "writing" mere descriptors like tone or setting or diction. A romance, in this model, could be either a novel, a lyrical ballad, an engaging soap, an intimate tale shared at a kitchen table, a fiction multi-authored on a computer network, or an electronic flirtation conducted online. Yet even given such a unified theoretical model, we still face the speech/writing question in practice: Given our radically different treatment of speech and writing in composition classrooms, what kind of policy should we implement for electronic discourse? The solution seems easy: If we conceive of electronic discourse as speech, we will not enforce participation in computer conferencing. If we think of it as writing, we will require students to participate. However, if we see electronic discourse as a hybrid of the two, if we accept the argument that the orality/literacy distinction is a false and dangerous one, then our original question remains unanswered and problematic: What kind of participation policy should we implement for computer conferencing in writing classes?

Hypermedia

Most of the metaphors that have been used to discuss the application of hypermedia to literacy education have derived from conventional notions of textuality and intertextuality. As with the speech/writing metaphors used in discussions of networking, these metaphors of textuality and intertextuality exhibit a tension between what they reveal and what they hide, between how they work for us and how they undermine our efforts.

Metaphors of textuality common in references to hypermedia predictably focus on the notions of text that have long dominated education. The "electronic book," the metaphor used here to exemplify the complications attendant on our use of metaphors to conceive of the possibilities of hypermedia, is one of the most common metaphors for a hypertext document. The "electronic book" immediately triggers a whole constellation of associations based on features characteristic of conventional books. Indeed, the metaphor has so dominated our understanding of hypertext that it has consistently constrained the classroom applications of this technology. One symptom of this domination is the reductive nature of so many classroom applications of hypertext, which often do little more than transfer the printed page to the computer screen. In a discussion of the uses of hypertext to develop the reading abilities of disabled readers, Ernest Balajthy concludes that "most hypertext applications are summarized textbook chapters transferred to the computer screen with simple graphics" (187). It could be argued that the "electronic book" metaphor does not cause this prevalent reductiveness. However, even if this were the case, it does not explicitly and aggressively challenge the notion of hypertext underlying these applications. At best, then, the metaphor complies with a reductive application of this powerful technology.

The irony to the prominence of the "book" metaphor is that so many discussions of hypertext explain the nature of the technology by differentiating it from conventional books. John Slatin's exploration of hypertext and reading, for example, begins, "The basic point I have to make is embarrassingly simple: Hypertext is very different from more traditional forms of text. The differences are a function of technology and are so various, at once so minute and so vast, as to make hypertext a new medium for thought and expression" (870). The emphasis here and in other discussions on the newness of the medium should begin to suggest how a metaphor strongly rooted in a conventional medium will begin to wear thin. Generally, the "book" metaphor constrains the understanding, and by extension the use, of hypertext in three areas. Hypertext departs from conventional books in the range of materials it brings together, in the nonlinear and nonhierarchical processing that it allows, and in its reliance on the user to determine the paths to be followed in processing the material contained within the hyperdocument. The differences are so basic that trying to elaborate the possibilities of one medium through the metaphorical use of the other quickly diverts new users from seeing the most potent features of the new medium.

From the learner's perspective, the most counterproductive effect of the "book" metaphor is that it implicitly encourages users to approach the hyperdocument with the same processing assumptions and strategies they would use with a conventional text. With reductive applications that could just as readily be presented in the form of a conventional text, encouraging the use of assumptions and strategies appropriate for printed books is not a problem except for the waste of technological resources and the greater difficulty involved in trying to read a book on screen rather than on the printed page. However, with the hyperdocument that takes full advantage of the technology, new users are inevitably disoriented and frustrated because the best use of such a hyperdocument does not accommodate their attempts to work with it as if it were a print-bound book. Aware of this problem, designers of many hypertext applications often provide users with "front ends" geared to compensate for the gap between the processing strategies suited to conventional books and the special challenges and opportunities implicit in the structure of a true hyperdocument. Ironically, however, the "book" metaphor often even dominates the thinking that goes into the design of these front ends. That is, they often amount to no more than tables of contents or lists of topics characteristic of conventional books. George Landow notes just how inadequate this strategy is: "By abandoning the table of contents or list mode that characterizes page-bound, printed text, one liberates hypertext from the restrictions of print and enables it to do what it does best. . . . If hypertext is characterized by connectivity, to realize its potential one must employ directories that focus on that quality. Lists, tables of contents, or indexes do not work in this manner" (141–142). The key to designing truly useful front ends may lie in developing metaphors that more closely get at the essence of hypertext, metaphors that begin with an emphasis on movement and connectivity.

With the tension between the conventional associations implicit in the "book" metaphor and the character and possibilities of hypertext, the immediate agenda seems apparent: We need metaphors that both capture the essence of this technology as we currently understand it and at the same time have the power to continue to extend our grasp of its potential. Two routes for pursuing this agenda emerging in the literature on hypertext include developing alternative metaphors or changing the concept of "book" so that, while the metaphor itself stays the same, it triggers a greatly expanded range of associations capable of embracing possibilities well beyond those connected with page-bound books.

One metaphor that seems to avoid many of the constraints associated with the "book" metaphor in discussions of hypertext focuses on the document as geographical space to be navigated. Discussing interactive fiction, for example, William Costanzo states, "Readers move through the text; they inhabit the text. . . . Hypertext reinforces the notion of a textual topography. It's as if you were following a three-dimensional web of words" (31). Elsewhere, Jay David Bolter connects the topogrpahic metaphor with the non-hierarchical nature of hypertext: "A hypertext has no canonical order. Every path defines an equally convincing and appropriate reading, and in that simple fact the reader's relationship to the text changes radically. A text as network has no univocal sense; it is a multiplicity without the imposition of a principle of domination. In place of hierarchy, we have a writing that is not only 'topical': We might also call it 'topographic'" ("Writing Space" 112). And it is common to hear the user referred to as a traveler through the world of the hyperdocument and to hear the hyperdocument itself called "hyperspace." These metaphors expand the range of associations we connect with hyptertexts and in the process expand the range of assumptions and strategies with which students approach hypertexts. Students are invited to employ, in their interaction with hypertexts, the assumptions and strategies evident in their navigation of the universe around them. The critical shift is from a dependence on a set of conventions that exist outside the students to a protocol determined and driven by the students' own problem-solving navigational choices. However, the point here is not that these metaphors represent some final frame for getting at the "real" essence of hypertext. While topographical metaphors attract us because they free us from the constraints of the book metaphor, we are also aware of the "politics of mapping," of the complications implicit in topographical metaphors. These mapping images suggest that the user traverses the geography as it exists; what in fact is being explored is a particular construction, a very open mapping, but a mapping nonetheless, charted by whoever wrote the application. Still, the topographical metaphor—though not free of its own politics—does move us along in our understanding of how this technology can change in dramatic ways the nature of teaching and learning in the classroom. And perhaps in ways we do not understand now, they anticipate the metaphors that will succeed them.

In *Writing Space: The Computer, Hypertext, and the History of Writing*, Bolter argues that the "electronic book" is a completely appropriate metaphor for hypertext. He does so, however, by enlarging our notion of "book," putting it in the broadest historical context and demonstrating how the common conception today, based on centuries of experience with printed documents, is artificially constrained. Tracing the development of the book from papyrus to the electronic versions we call hypertexts, he argues that what changes is a particular instantiation of the concept "book," not the concept of "book" itself: "While electronic technology does not destroy the idea of the book, it does diminish the sense of closure that the codex and printing have fostered. The imposing presence of the book is gone. . . . The electronic book therefore is not available as an object for decoration in the medieval tradition. Instead the book is abstract—a concept, not a thing to be held" (87). While Bolter approaches the limitations in the metaphor not by changing the metaphor but by transforming our approach to the concept on which the metaphor is based, his efforts point in the same direction as efforts to devise alternative metaphors. He moves from the common notion of book as a printed document to the metaphor of the world as the book of nature and in the process accommodates the same set of assumptions and strategies invited by other metaphors such as the topographical one discussed above. In Shiff's terms, both types of efforts together exhibit the dialectic between metaphor and meaning, a dialectic through which both metaphor and meaning are transformed.

There are as many metaphors for intertextuality as there are for textuality in discussions of hypermedia, and the two concepts are so interdependent that any metaphor for one necessarily includes the other in some way. For the purposes of this discussion, metaphors of highlighting the intertextual aspects of hypermedia are marked by their emphasis of connectivity. They focus on illuminating the ways in which the components in a hypermedia application relate and interact. Perhaps the most common metaphor for the intertextual aspects of hypermedia is the "web." Writing in 1945, Vannevar Bush described the associational processes of the human mind: "With one item in its grasp, it snaps instantly to the next that is suggested by the association of thoughts, in accordance with some intricate web of trails carried by the cells of the brain" (10). As Bush's representation of the mind at work later informed the development of hypertext and hypermedia, his "web" metaphor became central in descriptions of what these technologies had to offer. This metaphor is used to describe the organization of multimedia documents in "Intermedia," perhaps the most elaborate instructional hypermedia project now underway at Brown University.

The web metaphor works well in suggesting the connectivity of hypermedia. However, as the theory surrounding hypermedia has evolved, it has attached increasing importance to the "centerlessness" of a hypermedia application, and the metaphor is less useful in communicating this dimension of the technology. As Landow explains, "Intermedia has no center. . . . Anyone who uses Intermedia makes his or her own interests the de facto organizing principle (or center) for the investigation at the moment. One experiences Intermedia as an infinitely decenterable and recenterable system" (150). But the "web" is an inherently centripetal image, and as long as it is used to communicate to students the nature of hypermedia, it will connote a centripetal structure. In describing students' work with hypermedia in his literature courses, Landow also notes that students tend to be centered in their use of it: "In practice, students employ Intermedia as a text-centered system, since they tend to focus upon individual works with the result that even if they begin sessions by entering the system at an individual author overview file, they tend to spend most time on files devoted to individual works" (151). It may be that their behavior is driven more by their past experience and instruction in literary reading, but even if this is the case, the "web" metaphor seems to accommodate this behavior. As a result they may miss out on the power of hypermedia to allow them to navigate their way to a constantly shifting and evolving perspective on themselves and the world around them. What is needed, then, are metaphors that capture and communicate aggressively what Landow characterizes as the "decenterable and recenterable" learning which hypermedia is uniquely capable of promoting.

While this discussion of metaphors of textuality and intertextuality has concentrated on the "book" and "web" metaphors, other metaphors—e.g., the "card and stack" metaphor for textuality and the "tree of knowledge" metaphor for intertextuality—could have been studied as easily. As metaphors, they are subject to the same dynamic as the "book" and "web" metaphors, and although they might exemplify that dynamic differently, they adhere to the dynamic's essential principles. The challenge for teachers of reading and writing is to understand how metaphors both assist and block students' efforts to learn and then to adapt their metaphors to make them optimally support and extend learning in a classroom that takes advantage of the new technologies.

Conclusion

Metaphors are central to the task of defining a field or phenomenon. As we embark on research in the virtual age, we perform a particularly important function: influencing through the metaphors we choose the direction of research and the shape of classroom practice. A critique of the metaphors we use is thus a crucial project. One way to proceed is by removing ourselves temporarily from the literature on computer technology and writing instruction to study the literature of the metaphors we are using: the literature surrounding orality and literacy (speech/writing divisions), the history of the book and printing press, the politics of mapping. And while critique might seem a frustrating option—one that at times seems to show only the error of our ways—we must remember that the project is never one of finding the "acceptable" metaphor and then making a quick substitute. Lakoff and Johnson note that understanding the tyranny of a particular metaphor does not entail an automatic escape from it. For example, they describe how Americans are shaped by the "life is a puzzle" metaphor, the idea that "problems are PUZZLES for which, typically, there is a correct solution—and once solved, they are solved forever" (145). They tell the story of an Iranian student who visualized "the solution of my problems" differently. This student envisioned "a large volume of liquid, bubbling and smoking, containing all of [the] problems, either dissolved or in the form of precipitates, with catalysts constantly dissolving some problems (for the time being) and precipitating out others" (143). In this chemical metaphor, Lakoff and Johnson note that "problems would be part of the natural order of things rather than disorders to be 'cured'" (144). Yet if we decide to adopt this distinction, a mere decision would not be sufficient to have us "live" it. Lakoff and Johnson stress how difficult it is to supplant ingrained metaphoric structures. And if we could make such an easy substitution, we would soon degenerate into a world of static language, an impossible place for communication. Metaphors are the handiest—and best—tools we have to define and describe and make the virtual age. To use them responsibly and productively requires continual commitment to critique and creativity.

Works Cited

Bakhtin, M.M. "The Problem of Speech Genres." *Speech Genres and Other Late Essays*. Trans. Vern W. McGee. Ed. Caryl Emerson and Michael Holquist. Austin: U of Texas P, 1986. 60-102.

Balajthy, E. "Hypertext, Hypermedia, and Metacognition: Research and Instructional Implications for Disabled Readers." *Reading, Writing, and Learning Disabilities*, 6 (1990): 183-202.

Batson, T. "The ENFI Project: A Networked Classroom Approach to Writing Instruction." *Academic Computing*, 2 (February/March 1988): 32-33, 55-56.

Bolter, J.D. "Topographic Writing: Hypertext and the Electronic Writing Space." *Hypermedia and Literary Studies*. Ed. Paul Delaney and George Landow. Cambridge: MIT Press, 1991. 105-118.

————. *Writing Space: The Computer, Hypertext, and the History of Writing*. Hillsdale, N.J.: Lawrence Erlbaum Associates, 1990.

Bush, Vannevar. "As We May Think." *Atlantic Monthly* 176 (July 1945): 101-108.

Castle, Terry. "Lab'ring Bards: Birth TOPOI and English Poetics 1660-1820." *JEGP* 78 (1979): 193-208.

Cohen, Moshe and Margaret Riel. "The Effect of Distant Audiences on Students' Writing." *American Educational Research Journal*, 26 (1989): 143-159.

Costanzo, William V. (1988). "Media, Metaphors, and Models." *English Journal,* 77.7 (1988): 28–32.

Eldred, Janet. "Pedagogy in the Networked Classroom." *Computers and Composition,* 8.2 (1991): 47–61.

Ellmann, Mary. *Thinking about Women.* New York: Harcourt, Brace, Jovanovich, 1968.

Ferrara, Kathleen, Hans Brunner and Greg Whittemore. "Interactive Written Discourse as an Emergent Register." *Written Communication,* 8 (1991): 8–34.

Hawisher, Gail E. and Cynthia L. Selfe. "The Rhetoric of Technology and the Electronic Writing Class." *CCC,* 42 (1991): 55–65.

Lakoff, George and Mark Johnson. *Metaphors We Live By.* Chicago: University of Chicago Press, 1980.

Landow, George. "Changing Texts, Changing Readers: Hypertext in Literary Education, Criticism, and Scholarship." *Reorientations: Critical Theories and Pedagogies.* Ed. Bruce Hendrickson and Thais Morgan. Urbana: U of Illinois P, 1990. 133–161.

Marx, Michael Steven. "Distant Writers, Distant Critics, and Close Readings: Linking Composition Classes through a Peer-Critiquing Network." *Computers and Composition,* 8.1 (1990): 23–39.

Murray, Denise E. "When the Medium Determines Turns: Turn-Taking in Computer Conversation." *Working with Language: A Multidisciplinary Consideration of Language Use in Work Contexts* Ed. Hywel Coleman. Berlin: Mouton de Gruyter, 1989. 319–337.

Ricoeur, Paul. *The Rule of Metaphor.* Trans. Robert Czerny with Kathleen McLaughlin and John Costello. Toronto: University of Toronto Press, 1977.

Schneiderman, Ben and Greg Kearsley. *Hypertexts Hands-On: An Introduction to a New Way of Organizing and Accessing Information.* Reading, Mass: Addison-Wesley Publishing, 1989.

Shiff, Richard. "Art and Life: A Metaphoric Relationship." *On Metaphor.* Ed. Sheldon Sacks. Chicago: University of Chicago Press, 1979. 105–120.

Slatin John M. "Reading Hypertext: Order and Coherence in a New Medium." *College English,* 52 (1990): 870–883.

Thompson, Diane. "Conversational Networking: Why the Teacher Gets Most of the Lines." *Collegiate Microcomputer,* 6 (1988): 193–201.

———. "Interactive Networking: Creating Bridges between Speech, Writing, and Composition." *Computers and Composition,* 5.3 (1988): 17–22.

Walters, Keith. "Language, Logic, and Literacy." *The Right to Literacy.* Ed. Andrea Lunsford, Helene Moglin, and James Slevin. New York: MLA, 1990. 173–88.

Wilkins, Harriet. "Computer Talk: Long-Distance Conversations by Computer." *Written Communication,* 8 (1991): 56–78.

Part II

Looking Beyond Virtual Horizons: Teaching Writing on Networks

Introduction

Computer-mediated communication, and the advent of personal electronic interactivity in general, rank with the alphabet and the printing press as signal developments in cognitive media. (40)

Paul Levinson

Electronic conferencing, or computer-mediated communication, as Paul Levinson refers to it, is currently enjoying the same prominence in writing classes and our professional lives that word processing found earlier in the last decade. Indeed, as Levinson suggests in the epigraph, computer-mediated communication may well be transforming not only our writing classes but also the very fabric of our literate lives. Nowhere, however, is its importance perhaps more evident and more recognized than in those professions that study and teach writing and communication. At the national Computers and Writing Conferences of the past three years, electronic networks have been increasingly featured as technologies for writing instruction, with over 20 presentations devoted to them at the most recent 1991 meeting in Biloxi, Mississippi. But if, as a profession, we have accepted the technology itself, we have been less certain as to what to call it. A name to describe what most of the contributors in this book call the computer or electronic conference is still undecided. In fact, the proliferation of names suggests the newness of the development for the general populace and for us as writing teachers, despite the first system having been created in 1970 (Hiltz).

The most encompassing term seems to be computer-mediated communication (CmC), a term which includes electronic mail (e-mail), along with electronic or computer-based conferences, both asynchronous and synchronous. Asynchronous networks are sometimes called non-concurrent because participants can access the network at anytime and anyplace where there is a computer and modem connection. The asynchronous conference is also called an electronic bulletin board because participants can post messages (e-messages) for others participating in the conference. Synchronous networks, on the other hand, are concurrent; that is, all the participants are on-line at the same time. When this term is applied to class settings, the students are often in the same place, usually a conventional classroom with computers and special software to enable the conference (see Paul Taylor's description of this sort of setting in chapter 8). But the students really don't have to be physically present: synchronous networks are not bound by place, as Hugh Burns demonstrates in chapter 7, anymore than the asynchronous electronic bulletin boards. Sometimes the term "computer conference" is used to specify a more structured environment, and this is the way that William Wright uses it in chapter 6. The "computer conferencing" that Wright describes denotes a virtual space where topics and subtopics branch off and separate from one another but which participants can nevertheless access at will (see, for example, Michael Spitzer's "Computer Conferencing"). When we refer to electronic conferences in the various contexts presented in this book, each of us specifies exactly how we are using the term so that we don't confuse readers any more than the introduction of any new technology necessitates.

The various terms applied to electronic conferences are interesting in that many suggest notions of people working and talking together over networks, sometimes in an attempt to create something new in ways that suggest activities appropriate for students. Even the word "networks" reflects the web of connections with which students and other participants can use the technology to communicate with people from all over the world. "Interactive written discourse," "computerized conferencing," "groupware," and "computer conversation" also suggest a dynamic relationship among network participants. The constant verbal activity of the conference holds special promise for those of us who work in educational settings—so much promise, in fact, that Starr Roxanne Hiltz and her colleagues at New Jersey Institute of Technology copyrighted the term "virtual classroom" to designate a set of electronic conferencing practices they developed for distance learning. For writing instruction, Trent Batson coined the term "ENFI" (Electronic Networks for Interaction). Batson's term again stresses active participation among networked students whereas Hiltz's designation moves us more firmly in the direction of virtual environments where all class communication and interaction take place over computer networks.

To give readers a better idea of how this new technology is influencing writing instruction, this second part of the book first presents an overview of the early research aimed at electronic conferences and then goes on to describe actual networked settings for writing instruction. Gail

Hawisher, in chapter 5, reviews the small base of research that has been conducted on electronic conferences and, in so doing, argues that it reflects the profession's newly adopted social views of writing. Unlike word processing research, however, she notes that studies of the electronic conference are taking place in many different disciplines throughout the university, all of which tends to underscore the interconnectivity of the technology itself. In chapter 6, William Wright describes the ways in which Middlebury College has experimented with computer conferences for high school classes at the Bread Loaf School of English. After presenting a short history of BreadNet, the electronic network at Bread Loaf, Wright shows us how the technology can be used to bridge communities of students that are often kept separate. In its fifth year as this book goes to press, BreadNet is one of the more successful electronic endeavors for English classes, linking not only students but also their teachers across many different communities all over the country. In chapter 7, Hugh Burns presents us with a newer experiment and asks us to explore its implications for writing classes. Using the telecommunications capabilities provided through satellites, Burns and his colleagues linked college writing classes synchronically in Jackson, Michigan, with those in Austin, Texas. Burns was also part of this emerging on-line community and spoke to students from Apple headquarters in Cupertino, California. In presenting the students' dialog and probing the possible benefits of such a "multisited, multinetworked, multimedia, televised class discussion," Burns challenges readers to consider how we might use such virtual environments for writing classes. In chapter 8, the final chapter of this section, Paul Taylor also asks us to consider synchronic conferences but this time in connection with how they might relate to chaos theory. Taylor demonstrates how such conferences result in a "communal text" that ultimately challenges our notions of authorship and coherence. After analyzing examples of such text, he goes on to argue that computer conferences are indeed a new genre and will play an increasingly important role in the discourse of the virtual age. The four chapters presented in this section try to evaluate what we've learned so far about the potential of electronic conferences, all the while challenging us to to look forward with the same sort of critical perspective we have applied to looking back at past technologies: They ask us to engage in serious speculation about the educational potential of electronic conferencing for the future.

Works Cited

Batson, Trent W. "The ENFI Project: A Networked Classroom Approach to Writing Instruction." *Academic Computing.* (February/March 1988): 32–33; 55–56.

Hiltz, Starr Roxanne. "Collaborative Learning: The Virtual Classroom Approach." *T.H.E. Journal.* (June 1990): 59–65.

Levinson, Paul. "Media Relations: Integrating Computer Telecommunications with Educational Media." *Mindweave: Communication, Computers, and Distance Education.* Eds. Robin Mason and Anthony Kaye. New York: Pergamon, 1989. (40–49)

Spitzer, Michael. "Computer Conferencing: An Emerging Technology." *Critical Perspectives on Computers and Composition Instruction.* Eds. Gail E. Hawisher and Cynthia L. Selfe. New York: Teachers College Press, 1989.

5

Electronic Meetings of the Minds:
Research, Electronic Conferences, and Composition Studies

Gail E. Hawisher
University of Illinois, Urbana-Champaign

Over the past decade two electronic innovations have profoundly influenced writing classes. Although each of these innovations had simply been part of the computer programmer's work environment for many years, for writers and for writing teachers they have been revolutionary, changing not only the way we teach but also influencing our research and our understanding of composition studies. I'm speaking, of course, first of word processing and then of the electronic conference, each of which was uncommon to the writing instructor's life before the advent of the first fully-assembled microcomputer in 1977 and each of which entered our professional lives sometime during the eighties.

These two technological innovations, however, did not grow up in isolation; they emerged as our very theories of writing and writing instruction were evolving. Word processing appeared as a classroom technology at the same time that the process paradigm was establishing itself in composition studies. Electronic conferencing has taken hold of the field at the same time that social constructivist views of language have similarly become prevalent in the profession. Such changes in our views of writing and writing instruction have allowed us to prize both these technologies as we have come to understand writing as the active creation of meaning, of knowledge.

Yet if our theoretical perspectives have allowed us—indeed have encouraged us—to accept word processing and electronic conferencing, the new technologies have also influenced the ways we think about writing and writing instruction. From word processing, we have learned that text is fluid, ephemeral, and constantly emerging (Balestri, Catano). From electronic conferences, we have learned that it has all these properties and more: text is made by many and is meant to be shared—it is intrinsically communal (Barker and Kemp). Because of our work with word processing and electronic conferences, we are also able to envision a writing class in which most of the learning matter exists not on paper but on-line; we are able to think about what our classes might be like without printed texts. In other words, as a result of our work with computers over the past decade, we can begin to imagine teaching and writing in a virtual age where a meeting of the minds might well occur without the physical presence of students and teachers.

At the moment, more than any other technology, the electronic conference is leading the way in introducing us to virtual environments. Since, unlike hypermedia, it doesn't require the extensive and time-consuming development of on-line materials, it immediately lets us see how school learning, how literacy learning, *might* take place without print. If we choose, we can conduct a paperless writing class, as Edward Jennings did several years ago, with student and teacher contributions all occurring on-line.[1] Or we can conduct a class in which we use the electronic conference as a supplement to other kinds of writing activities occurring within and outside of classes.[2] Yet despite our having these approaches to writing instruction available to us now, important questions remain to be answered: Why should we sacrifice print? Why should we use electronic conferences in our writing classes at all?

By highlighting the major findings and observations aimed at electronic conferences, this chapter tries to provide a basis for answering these questions. In so doing, it explores the connections between social constructivist theory and the electronic conference. By bringing together recent research from a variety of disciplines, it also seeks to establish a small knowledge base from which we might inform our work in composition studies. After discussing the principal findings from recent research, it then returns to a discussion of electronic conferences and social perspectives on writing. Throughout the chapter, I use the term electronic conference to denote computer-mediated communication and modify it with "synchronous" to denote "real-time" or "chat" programs over which participants communicate at the same time and "asynchronous" to denote electronic bulletin boards or electronic mail that participants can access at any time.

Electronic Conferences and Composition Theory

Both synchronous and asynchronous electronic conferences have become increasingly popular in writing classes as the profession has come to understand writing, and hence writing instruction, in terms of the social or social epistemic theories of writing. As Janet Eldred has pointed out, it wasn't until October of 1986 with Lester Faigley's important article, "Competing Theories of Process," that composition studies began to think seriously of social perspectives on writing; later with Karen LeFevre's 1987 *Invention as a Social Act* and James Berlin's 1988 piece on "Rhetoric and Ideology in the Writing Class" social approaches to writing instruction became more common. Kenneth Bruffee's views of the value of collaborative learning were well known before this, but the term "social construction" doesn't begin to appear with any regularity in composition journals and texts much before 1986. I would argue that until the profession accepted and endorsed a view of meaning as negotiated, texts as socially constructed, and writing as knowledge creating, we were unable to value the kinds of talk in writing classes that electronic conferences encourage. In other words, the adoption of the electronic conference as a pedagogy corresponds closely to the profession's evolving theories of what it means to learn to write in the late eighties and nineties.

But what about our research? Does the research of the past few years reflect this move from a process paradigm to a social view of writing and writing instruction? The answer appears to be a tentative yes, but we need to look at the electronic conference in relation to the small body of research that has been conducted so far.

Electronic Conferences, Research, and Observations

A major difference between research aimed at word processing and the current research on electronic conferences is that the research on the conference is occurring across disciplines whereas the interest in word processing research, with the possible exception of human factors research, remained largely confined to composition studies. One might argue that the composition profession's very interest in multidisciplinary approaches, as well as its willingness to accept findings from other research areas, underscores its growing acceptance of social constructionism. In other words, in viewing knowledge as made, not found, the profession has come to realize the value of multiple perspectives from many different sources and to recognize that studies being conducted across many disciplines can contribute to composition studies. It is also true that although the body of research is growing, as yet there are only a few studies on the electronic conference that have been conducted within composition studies. For a more complete picture, we must look to the studies of those working in distance education, communication research, organizational settings, linguistics, cognitive science, psychology, sociology, and information systems, to mention a few of the fields actively involved.

But regardless of the field, many of the studies converge on similar issues and ask similar research questions. They seek first to identify the characteristics of conference discourse, examine participants' response to such discourse, and then, for those working in educational settings, explore the electronic conference's potential for teaching and learning. Many of the initial findings related to on-line conferences also seem more in the spirit of observations gleaned from experience in working with the medium, not unlike the early exploratory studies in word processing. Many of the interpretations of the findings also seem to reflect social constructivist views of language and learning. Taken together they begin to suggest what writing teachers can and cannot expect when they introduce electronic conferences into their classes.

But questions still remain regarding the advantages and disadvantages of the medium for writing classes. For those working in composition studies the most important findings relate to whether instructors and students can use electronic conferences to accomplish what they want and need to do. Will the medium help teachers teach and students learn? Let me first review the observations and findings that are often construed as advantages and then turn to what some have noted as the disadvantages of the medium, both for synchronous and asynchronous electronic conferences. I'll then come back to discussing how these observations relate to composition theory and writing classes.

Why Should We Use Electronic Conferences in Writing Classes?

Electronic conferences are text-based environments.

When participants in an electronic conference communicate with one another, be the conference synchronous or asynchronous, they are totally immersed in writing. Based on their research on the social consequences of computerized communication, James Chesebro and Donald Bonsall argue that the electronic conference "possesses the advantage of focusing attention upon the written word . . . [and also] allows or forces users to employ words concretely, vividly, and meaningfully" (118). "Concretely," "vividly," and "meaningfully" are all adverbs that call forth the sort of writing that English teachers are thought to want from students. The total immersion in text has also been thought to be a factor that might improve student writing. Because of the heavy emphasis on writing, Starr Roxanne Hiltz and her colleagues working with a writing class at Upsala University are one of the few groups who asked the question that scholars in composition studies asked frequently of word processing environments: Will students' writing improve as a result of this technology and environment? Hiltz and her colleagues could detect no improvement and attributed this finding in part to the short overall time (one semester) spent in the writing environment and to a less than satisfactory holistic scoring system ("Evaluating the Virtual Classroom" 166).[3] Within composition studies, Christine Neuwirth, Michael Palmquist, and their colleagues also saw no improvement in student writing when they used a synchronous electronic conference at Carnegie Mellon.

Others within composition studies have noted other advantages of a totally text-based environment to writing classes. Of synchronous networked settings, Trent Batson argues that "since students and teachers *write* to communicate, they aren't required to move away from the genuine 'feel' of their face-to-face oral exchange and into a seemingly more contrived solo writing exercise" (32). In this setting, students are able to refine their rhetorical skills of persuasion as well as to sharpen their mechanical skills. They are in an environment in which they constantly write and read. Thomas Barker and Fred Kemp have noted that "irrespective of further pedagogical measures, the sharing of text [on-line] easily promotes the power of text, which in turn motivates and directs the writer in instructionally effective ways" (18). The importance of having a classroom environment in which people primarily communicate with one another through writing is difficult to underestimate for those of us who teach and study writing.

Another often cited benefit of the text-based environment is the ability to print out and to use the transcripts of electronic conferences for a variety of purposes. In Jerome Bump's survey of three writing classes, several of the students found that this feature of the conference was a primary advantage: It allowed them to reflect on both their contributions to discussions as well as on those of their classmates. Student writing from transcripts can also be treated as sources, with students citing one another and their views on a particular subject they have discussed electronically in class. Charles Moran, for example, asked students to write what they thought were the important issues facing the United States after the Persian Gulf War. After printing out the entire transcript of conference responses, students used the written text as the basis for a paper in which they discussed college students' views on these issues.[4] Transcripts also allow teachers to review students' work and can be used *diagnostic tool* (margin note)

as a diagnostic tool. In their study of synchronous conferences, Christine Neuwirth and her colleagues found that the writing instructor viewed the written transcript as the most significant advantage of the conference. Using the transcripts, the instructor was able to discern what sorts of help students needed in developing collaborative skills, a prime emphasis of the course. Thus transcripts can function as supplementary print materials in conjunction with electronic writing activities with advantages for both teachers and students.

Electronic conferences provide real and expanded audiences for writers.

Many have noted the importance of both a real and expanded audience that electronic conferences can provide. Linda Harasim, working in distance education, demonstrates this shift in audience when she writes of interactions that can be one-to-one, one-to-many, and many-to-many in face-to-face contexts ("On-Line Education" 50). In writing classrooms despite our best efforts to create an audience that is more than the "teacher as examiner" (Britton), we often don't get beyond the one-to-one (teacher and student or student and student) or the one-to-many (usually teacher to students) and sometimes for good reason. Unless confined to small groups, many-to-many interactions can be loud and chaotic, but with electronic conferences they are considerably less so. They can also be confusing especially in synchronous settings (see Hugh Burns, chapter 7, this volume), but they are certainly not loud and are often workable and interesting for participants.

× groupwork (margin note)

Those working in composition studies have been especially taken with this feature of a real and expanded audience for both synchronous and asynchronous environments. Jeffrey Schwartz demonstrates the benefits for asynchronous settings when he describes the BreadNet[5] electronic exchanges between high school English classes in Pennsylvania, Montana, and South Dakota. Students in these classes were drawn from a private school in suburban Pittsburgh, a public high school in Wilsall, Montana, and Little Wound High School, which is on an Indian Reservation in Kyle, South Dakota. Schwartz notes that having an authentic audience of peers encouraged students "to play the scales of discourse, adjusting language to the reader, the topic, the purpose for writing and the image [the students] want to project" (17). The students were also able to learn a great deal about the different cultures of the students with whom they were sharing their writing. In a very different setting, Delores Schriner and William Rice also note the advantages of a real electronic audience with a group of students in a class at the University of Michigan. "Whenever they wrote," argue Schriner and Rice, "they knew they had an audience beyond the teacher, and as a result their writing emerged as 'real,' 'volunteered,' even urgent" (475).

Electronic conferences encourage a sense of community.

Connected to this idea of a real audience and of many communicating to many is a growing sense among participants and researchers that writer participants perceive themselves as part of a community. Cynthia Selfe and Paul Meyer have documented electronic exchanges which suggest that members of Megabyte University, an asynchronous electronic conference for writing teachers, think of themselves as a closely-knit group who "chat away like old friends" (173). Similarly, Chesebro and Bonsall found that messages in such conferences are often more "socially oriented" than "task related" and that they seem to foster a sense of belonging among participants (5). Harriet Wilkin's research supports similar conclusions. She notes that during three months on the network Presbynet, participants came to think of one another as friends. One participant, for example, stated "I am still constantly amazed at the 'companionship' and warmth one can find on a computer terminal" (71). This affective response to the group is also demonstrated in Lester Faigley's observations of students not wanting to leave class but rather to continue their synchronous online discussions. Schriner and Rice also noted students coming early to class and staying late, and Hiltz similarly reported that one of her asynchronous electronic conferences was still going strong a month after grades had been submitted ("Collaborative Learning" 64).

This sense of belonging and comradeship may not emerge when there are only two participants. Sarah Kiesler and her colleagues found that on a synchronous network pairs of people liked one another less than those who met and talked face-to-face initially (Kiesler et al.). Unlike the Kiesler study, there were 56 participants in the Selfe and Meyers' study and 33 in Wilkins' study. For participants to develop a liking for one another there is probably an optimium group size within a range of possible numbers, but as of yet research has not looked carefully at this issue.[6]

Electronic conferences demonstrate a high degree of involvement on the part of participants.

Another finding across studies has to do with the high degree of personal involvement invested in the communication, a phenomenon that is more common in face-to-face communication than in written discourse. Using linguistic analysis, Kathleen Ferrara and her colleagues documented participants' frequent use of adverbs and direct questions in the electronic discourse, all features of oral language that indicate involvement. Denise

Murray also noted the high degree of "personal involvement . . . characterized by use of active voice and personal pronouns; emotive and informal diction; hedging and vagueness; paralinguistic cues; and direct quotations" (217). Both the Ferrara and Murray studies focused on synchronous communication between two people.

But levels of high interest and involvement in the computer conference have also been noted by others looking at larger groups of participants in educational settings. Hiltz, for example, in her survey of students having participated in the virtual classroom of a management course notes that active participants often used the word "fun" to describe the class, and she ascribes this in part to the participants' high level of involvement ("Collaborative Learning"). Schriner and Rice also note that the "students' engagement was quite astonishing . . . with each student [generating] an average of 50 pages of double-spaced [network] text" (473). They also report that many students often signed onto the network "as often as twice a day, every day" (473).

Andrew Feenberg ("Computer Conferencing") provides an interesting analysis of the sort of social system that arises in electronic conferences and refers to what I'm calling involvement as "absorption" or "engrossment," terms originally introduced by Erving Goffman. Feenberg writes, "The sociability characteristic of conferencing is like that of sports or games in that we are drawn in by interest in the next step in the process of interaction more than by any other motive" ("Computer Conferencing"). Such gaming intrigues participants and probably in part accounts for why students remain after class to continue both asynchronous and synchronous online discussions: They want to see what happens next. Since the entire game consists of reading and writing, we might say that participants are involved in a game of literacy or as Feenberg has noted "a new form of collaborative writing" ("Computer Conferencing" 182). In the context of the writing class, Barker and Kemp call this form of collaborative writing "group knowledge" and view the whole as a communal text that the students have created.

Electronic conferences encourage equitable participation.

Another common finding related to electronic conferences is that because face-to-face cues are eliminated, "charismatic and high status people may have less influence, and group members may participate more equally in computer communication" (Kiesler, Siegel, and McGuire 1125). Marilyn Cooper and Cynthia Selfe used this finding to inform their research for writing classes, arguing that when students adopt pseudonyms in such environments the resulting "egalitarian discourse" enables them to speak and think in ways not characteristic of traditional classrooms. It enables them, Cooper and Selfe suggest, "to form their own opinions of the experts" (853) and to try out "different perspectives and hypotheses" (857). In electronic conferences, students can also open themselves to the divergent views of their classmates. As Diane Langston and Trent Batson have noted in their discussion of synchronous conferences, teaching and learning writing in the virtual age might have more to do with bringing together multiple perspectives and creating new understandings, rather than in producing something that is thought to be original. Electronic conferences foster an openness to other discourses and to multiple perspectives, making the weaving together of such disparate views possible. Kaye of England's Open University writes, for example, that electronic conferences have "the potential to provide a means for the weaving together of ideas and information from many peoples' minds, regardless of when and from where they contribute" (3). He and Robin Mason have called this phenomenon "mindweave," and have gone so far as to use the term as the title of their text about electronic conferencing in distance eduation.

Selfe also explored the potential for equitable participation among conference members in her study with Meyer. Since paralinguistic cues are eliminated and participants can't see or hear those with whom they are communicating, the argument goes, they are less likely to react to other participants' gender, social class, appearance, or other status markers. Yet in the exploratory research with Megabyte University, Selfe and Meyer still found that with and without pseudonyms males and high profile participants (those who had published in the field) tended to dominate the electronic discussion slightly. They suggest further research to explore more fully how gender and power relationships function in electronic discourse.[7]

Although the medium at times may favor some participants over others, student participation does seem to increase in electronic conferences. For both synchronous and asynchronous conferences, teachers and researchers report that a greater number of students take part in discussions and do so more frequently than in traditional classes (Harasim, Faigley, "Subverting" Schriner and Rice). Because electronic conferences obviate the need for taking turns, those who in face-to-face discussions wait patiently for their chance to speak no longer need to hesitate and can contribute frequently to the discussion. Harasim's research also reveals that students tend to cross the traditional time barriers of schooling: Her studies with asynchronous conferences reveal that the only hour students didn't log onto the network was 5 A.M. in the morning. Thus in addition to electronic networks encouraging equitable participation among class members, learning and discussion time can extend virtually to 24 hours a day.[8]

Electronic conferences can encourage a decrease
in leader-centered communication.

Directly related to increased participation on the part of electronic conference members is the decrease in leader-centered and leader-initiated discussion (Kiesler, Siegel, and McGuire; Chesebro and Bonsall; Feenberg "Computer Conferencing"; Hiltz and Turoff). In educational settings, this finding often translates itself into the teacher talking less as students participate more frequently and extensively in electronic class discussions both synchronous and asynchronous. It also has the further benefit of no longer emphasizing the teacher as the sole source of knowledge (Hawisher and Selfe). When students can write to one another and read one another's texts, they become very intent on making this electronic space and place their own. Cooper and Selfe, for example, point out that "once students became used to setting their own agenda for the conference—determining the topics, the pace, the tone, and the direction of the discussion—they resisted any suggestions the teacher made in class designed to influence the nature of the conference. The students had assumed power within this alternate forum, and they did not welcome the intrusion of the power structure of the classroom into the computer conference" (857). By disrupting traditional pedagogical arrangements, in other words, electronic conferences demand that students themselves take responsibility for the communal text as the teacher's role moves from evaluator to moderator to occasional participant. Elaine McCreary has suggested that using students to moderate topics gives students important experience with the medium; it also may help them decide on how best to use the conference for their own learning.

In educational settings, researchers and teachers often react to this decentering of authority by calling for teachers to assume the role of a strong moderator (Feenberg, Hiltz and Turoff, Batson, Kremers) who can lead and facilitate a productive discussion or by viewing the electronic conference as a liberating force for students' resistant discourse in the school environment (Cooper and Selfe; Faigley "Subverting"; Bump). Feenberg takes the first stance, believing that a strong leader is essential to online discussion. He cites, for example, the importance of the "art of weaving" in electronic conferences ("Computer Conferencing" 180). Weaving comments are those that unify the discourse, summarizing major points, pulling together the various threads, and integrating the various participants' contributions. By advocating that the leader judge the purpose of the discussion and then choose a role, such as that of "chairperson," "host," "teacher," "facilitator," "entertainer," and so forth, Feenberg does not advocate that the leader assume a position of authority so much as one of a reassuring moderator. Marshall Kremers sums up this position nicely when he says of his basic writers, "Rather than use the network to dominate my students, then, I use it to help them find ways to channel their energy. The problem is how to help them to work productively—to become authors . . . ("Sharing Authority" 35)." The "synergy," the tremendous amount of group energy generated in both synchronous and asynchronous conferences but perhaps more immediate in synchronous settings, is one of the most cited characteristics of the medium (e.g., Cooper and Selfe, McCreary, Bump); yet it also remains one of the most troublesome. As teachers, we are not always sure as to how we might best use it to the students' advantage—how we might make productive use of this "constantly moving stream of communication" (Faigley "Subverting").[9]

Why We Shouldn't Use Electronic Conferences

Electronic conferences encourage "flaming."

Many of the findings that researchers and teachers interpret as advantageous to learning environments can also be construed as disadvantages. Although Cooper and Selfe, for example, suggest that one reason students thrive in conferences has to do with "the liberating influence of the electronic medium," (857) others find the freedom less desirable. Related to a feeling of liberation is conference members' tendency to sometimes use "emotionally-laden language" and to demonstrate uninhibited behavior, a phenomenon that has come to be known as "flaming" (Kiesler, Siegel, and McGuire 1129; Kiesler, et al.). Flaming can include impoliteness, swearing, charged outbursts, and often a high use of superlatives. An explanation for this type of behavior over networks often focuses either on the sometimes anonymous relationship among the participants or, once again, the lack of paralinguistic cues. (Not seeing someone's physical reactions to your remarks fails to temper the response). Regardless of its cause, however, flaming can be disturbing. Marshall Kremers relates the story of how a group of his writing students mutineed, so to speak, and took over the synchronous electronic conference ("Adams Sherman Hill Meets ENFI"). The students' behavior was not only rude and rife with sexually offensive comments but also abusive to women.[10] Although Bump noted that some of the language in the electronic conferences of the students he surveyed paralleled flaming, he viewed it more as "emotional honesty" and saw it as an asset to class discussion rather than as a deterrent (57). There seems to be a range of flaming behavior as well as a range of teacher acceptance of its potential danger or worth. The phenomenon itself, however, has been documented in both synchronous and asynchronous settings and in the workplace as well as in educational contexts (Sproull and Kiesler).

Some contend that the more focused the task, the less flaming is likely to occur. In their research looking at synchronous communication, Ferrara and her colleagues observed no inflammatory language, a finding that might have something to do with the communication being focused very narrowly on the services of a travel agent. Denise Murray in a study of synchronous and asynchronous communication in a business environment also found no evidence of flaming ("The Context of Oral and Written Language"); nor did Neuwirth and her colleagues in their study directed at the writing class. In each of these cases, however, the activity was goal oriented, with the roles of participants being clearly defined.

Electronic conferences contribute to "communication anxiety."

For those of us in computers and composition studies who are already familiar with "writing anxiety" and "computer anxiety," it should come as no surprise that there is also "communication anxiety." In some respects such an anxiety seems to be the exact opposite of the kinds of feelings that lead to flaming, grounded as it is in fear rather than in freedom. Yet communication anxiety, a term coined by Feenberg ("Computer Conferencing"), is every bit as real among participants as the uninhibited behavior of flaming. Feenberg explains that to comment in an asynchronous conference "is a minor but real personal risk, and response is generally interpreted as signifying success while silence means failure" (175). Whether or not participants interpret others' comments as important or interesting enough to respond to, then, causes anxiety and may lead to the "lurking phenomenon." That is, a conference member may refrain from participating—from contributing his or her ideas on a particular topic under discussion. When one doesn't lurk, when one participates, electronic conferences foster an intense need for response and to be ignored is to be rejected. In educational settings, communication anxiety caused by fear of rejection can be as detrimental to learning as phobias associated with writing and computers in that it can lead students to avoid the opportunity to learn interactively.

Electronic conferences can cause sensory overload.

When participants do contribute their share to a conference, a great amount of text is generated, so much in fact that James Levin and his colleagues warn researchers that studies in electronic communication result in "a massive number of pages of messages" (186). So while it may be advantageous to have printed transcripts for both research and teaching purposes, the sheer bulk of the printed text can be daunting. It is also daunting in electronic form. In addition to great quantity, there are many different strands or threads of discussion for participants to hold in their minds at the same time. Langston and Batson, in describing a synchronous setting, note that the medium encourages multiple perspectives on many issues from many participants. In trying to give readers a feel for it, they portray the participants as "prowling wolves" wandering around ideas. The ideas themselves, Langston and Batson argue, are "immediately evident in the seemingly chaotic computerized display of multiple and disparate written contributions. . . . It is as if many of the thoughts in one social context were present at once" (156). How to process this huge amount of informaton while at the same time making sense of it is one of the challenges of both synchronous and asynchronous settings.

Electronic Conferences can be every bit as ineffective
as traditional forums for learning.

Despite the enthusiasm that has greeted electronic conferences during the past few years, they are not always successful. Harasim notes that Haile in analyzing a distance education course found "that the activities were teacher-centered and [showed] little evidence of student interaction" ("On-line Education" 52–53). Hawisher and Selfe have suggested that instructors sometimes use networks to keep tabs on students and, inadvertently perhaps, end up creating as oppressive a learning space as might occur in traditional classrooms. Neuwirth and her colleagues found that students perceived the on-line conference only as somewhat helpful in improving their writing compared with face-to-face encounters. And Annette Lorentsen, reporting on her research at Jutland's Open University in Denmark, reminds us of the importance of integrating the conference fully into coursework, or students will not use it. It's that simple. She also reminds us that training teachers for this new environment is essential. As Cynthia Selfe has argued in this volume, it is not enough to prepare teachers as we have in the past: We must, in addition, educate them to be critics of the virtual spaces in which they conduct their writing classes.

Electronic Conferences, Research, and Social Constructionism

As with the research on word processing in the last decade, these early studies on electronic conferences reveal an array of findings that have, for the most part, been interpreted in a positive light. I found many more reasons why we should use electronic conferences than why we shouldn't. Like the early word processing research, there are also several surveys that query students for their opinion of the value of the new technology (e.g., Hartman, Neuwirth et al., Neuwirth, Palmquist, et al., Bump, Hiltz). The surveys, along with the studies and more informal observations, point to researchers, teachers, and students seeing electronic conferences as holding great promise for writing classes and for educational settings in general. The research itself, primarily exploratory in emphasis, is also sensitive to the context into which electronic conferences are being introduced: The studies in the main seek to examine the conference as a contextual change that ripples through the whole of the environment rather than as a treatment that creates a particular effect.

The studies and the interpretations of the studies also tend to reflect social perspectives on writing and learning. One of the hallmarks of social constructivist theory is the notion of intertextuality, "the principle that all writing and speech—indeed, all signs—arise from a single network . . ." (Porter 34), that no text exists totally independent of another. As James Porter argues in his important article, "Intertextuality and the Discourse Community," this view of text allows those of us in composition studies to shift our emphasis from the individual to the "the writer [as] simply a part of a discourse tradition, a member of a team, and a participant in a community of discourse that creates its own collective meaning" (35). Although Porter wrote his article before the widespread introduction of electronic conferences to composition studies, his words call forth the dynamics of the conference, with its text-based environment making intertextuality almost visible at a glance—indeed almost palpable. In synchronous and asynchronous conferences, students view one another's networked words at the same time that they are borrowing and using one another's ideas and writings to create their own contributions, their own syntheses (Langston and Batson, Kaye, Feenberg). In this way, the notion of intertext corresponds closely with some of the research findings that are emerging from computers and composition studies as well as from other fields studying the conference.

And certainly the social constructivist view of the "discourse community" relates to early research findings on electronic conferences. Kenneth Bruffee notes that "social construction understands reality, knowledge, thought, facts, texts, selves, and so on as community-generated and community-maintained linguistic entities . . . that define or 'constitute' the communities that generate them . . . " (774). Over time, as members participate in an electronic conference, linguistic norms and conventions come to be established by conference members (Wilkins). The corresponding feeling of community that arises, the fact that participants perceive themselves as a closely-knit group of friends (Selfe and Meyer) who create their own intellectual spaces (Cooper and Selfe), parallels a social understanding of the power of language. Bruffee also points to the importance of the notion of community knowledge to social constructionism. In citing Thomas Kuhn's conception of scientific knowledge as "intrinsically the common property of a group or else nothing at all" (201), Bruffee echoes recent observations of the conference. Barker and Kemp have used these views to help them make sense of their observations of synchronous conferences and have coined the term "group knowledge" (15) to describe the textual contributions of a networked class. This idea of group knowledge demonstrates such a striking correspondence to what happens in electronic conferences that Mason and Kaye, using other words, also draw our attention to it. Their concept of "mindweave," where the ideas of many are brought together in an electronic environment, is in fact one way to depict this notion of community knowledge, a hallmark of social constructionism.

A view of language as socially constructed also tends to see the teacher as one learner among many within the writing class rather than as the prime authority among the members of the class. In describing a class informed by Ira Shor's notions of critical teaching and one that James Berlin believes to be congruent with social epistemic rhetoric, Berlin writes, "This is a place based on dialectical collaboration—the interaction of student, teacher, and shared experience within a social, interdisciplinary framework—and the outcome is always unpredictable" (492). In such a class, there is a decentering of authority where the students' contributions are as valued as the teacher's and, like Porter's and Bruffee's social views of language, Berlin's words evoke the feel of the electronic conference that teachers and researchers continue to document. The majority of the studies of conferencing in educational environments see learning as the result of active engagement and interaction among the participants where no one person or instructor dominates the discussion (Feenberg "Computer Conferencing," Hiltz, Kaye). It is also interesting in the context of Berlin's statement that researchers have remarked on the "serendipitous" nature of the medium where nothing is predictable but many things possible (McCreary, Feenberg "Computer Conferencing"). All these observations seem to support a strong connection between research findings dealing with electronic conferences and social constructionism.

I don't want to imply from this discussion, however, that social constructionism or social views of composition studies are fixed phenomena that can be described as succinctly as Maxine Hairston earlier described process approaches to writing instruction. As Faigley has noted, the social view "is less codified and less constituted . . . because it arises from several disciplinary traditions" ("Competing Theories" 534). Among these traditions, Faigley identifies poststructuralist theories of language and ethnography, all of which have influenced the work of those of us in computers and composition studies. Using poststructualist theory to inform observations and thinking about electronic conferences (e.g., Cooper and Selfe, Hawisher and Selfe, Barker and Kemp), employing a "situated evaluation" to examine writing classes that use synchronous conferencing[11] (e.g., Bruce and Peyton), and examining the social processes through which participants negotiate meaning (e.g., Faigley "Subverting," Langston and Batson, George), compositionists continue to choose the lens of the social constructivist through which to examine electronic writing classes. As teachers immersed in the social theories of writing, we have come to understand the conference as an electronic meeting place of the minds where—with our students—we move ever more steadily toward the virtual age in our thinking and our teaching.

Patricia Bizzell, in a 1986 review of research on composing, notes that when a particular theoretical perspective prevails in a discipline, research results are interpreted in light of the assumptions that the particular view embraces. (At this time she was arguing that research was persistently interpreted with expressive—what she called "personal-style"—pedagogical assumptions or with an emphasis on what goes on within the writer's head, the cognitive assumptions.) In arguing that this sort of interpretation is unavoidable, she writes: "Scholars writing up their research, like students struggling with their first essay assignments, must work within the language-using practices of a particular community, which are in turn shaped by its social, cultural, and political circumstances" (68). As social constructivist views have taken hold in composition studies, this argument is perhaps more readily accepted today than it was five years ago. Yet even when we accept this argument and also acknowledge that theory and technology are interactively dynamic—that correspondences between a predominant theory of language and an electronic technology, an artifact of our culture, are inevitable—the similarities remain striking. As the decade progresses, it will be interesting to see the ways in which we continue to study electronic conferences and to interpret the observations, findings, and conclusions that other scholars report. How we go about this work—how we adapt our teaching and research to meet the demands of electronic writing spaces—will largely determine the success with which we are able to serve coming generations of students in the virtual age.[12]

Notes

1. Edward Jennings might well be the first writing instructor to conduct such a paperless class in the field of composition studies in the spring of 1985. It was, in any case, the first experiment in a virtual environment to be *published* in composition studies. Andrew Feenberg points out that David Hughes of Colorado College was the first to use electronic mail for a writing course in 1981 ("The Written World"). See the Works Cited section for a complete citation of Jennings's article "Paperless Writing: Boundary Conditions and Their Implications."

2. In another early experiment, Mark Mabrito used electronic conferences for peer group work. See his dissertation for a complete description.

3. For an interesting discussion of how electronic technology is transforming our understanding of writing to the extent that our definitions (and hence evaluation) may no longer be valid, see Nancy Kaplan's "Ideology, Technology, and the Future of Writing Instruction."

4. For a more complete description of this writing assignment, see Moran, "Using What We Have," *Computers and Composition*. 9 (1991): 39-46.

5. See William Wright's chapter in this volume for additional descriptions of the BreadNet electronic exchanges.

6. This is an issue that is especially important for classroom settings. For an interesting discussion of Paul Levinson's desire to teach a class "with as many people in the world as were willing to register" (34), see Harasim's *Online Education: Toward a New Paradigm for Distance Education*.

7. In an unpublished study in which she tried to replicate the findings in a graduate class, Selfe and her colleagues found that gender and status did not predict dominance (Selfe, Pellar-Kosbar, Meyer). She also found that three foreign-born students participated significantly more in the electronic conference than in face-to-face discussions. Karen Hartman, Christine Neuwirth, and their colleagues found in their study of undergraduates that the less able students reported communicating more with teachers over the network than did other students. These last two findings hold promise for us who as writing teachers hope to encourage all our students to participate as equals in class discussions.

8. See Charles Moran, chapter 1, in this volume for a description of how current classes might evolve into 24-hour on-line environments.

9. Although I have tried to distinguish synchronous from asynchronous conferencing, at times I have treated the two as though they were one form of computer-mediated communication. Those working with electronic conferencing know that there are many differences. Synchronous or real-time exchanges are very fast and provide for less reflection than the asynchronous environments. Some might argue that they also need stronger or at least different leadership, if indeed leadership is possible or desirable. I am not aware of any articles that suggest ways in which one type of conference should be used in contrast to the other.

10. For an excellent feminist perspective on electronic conferences, see E. Laurie George's "Taking Women Professors Seriously: Female Authority in the Computerized Classroom," 7 (Special Issue): 45–52.

11. A thoughtful ethnographic investigation that focuses on writing and learning as social activities is the "situated evaluation" that Chip Bruce and Joy Peyton carried out for ENFI, Electronic Networks for Interaction. (ENFI, a synchronous approach for using electronic conferences for writing instruction, was developed by Trent Batson at Gallaudet University in 1985.) For their evaluation, Bruce and Peyton recognized that the introduction of a synchronous electronic network is "but one small addition to a complex social system" (5). Their intent wasn't so much to assess ENFI per se but to observe what happens when teachers try to implement an innovation.

12. I am much indebted to many colleagues who continue to help me understand more about teaching and learning in the virtual age. Among those whose comments and insights have been invaluable are Paul LeBlanc, Springfield College; Ron Fortune, Illinois State University; Patricia Sullivan, Purdue University; Janet Eldred, University of Kentucky; Robert Yates, Central Missouri State University; and Charles Moran, University of Masssachusetts at Amherst.

Works Cited

Balestri, Diane Pelkus. "Softcopy and Hard: Wordprocessing and Writing Process." *Academic Computing* (February/March 1988): 14–17, 41–45.

Barker, Thomas T., and Fred O. Kemp. "Network Theory: A Postmodern Pedagogy for the Writing Classroom." *Computers and Community.* Ed. Carolyn Handa. Portsmouth: Boynton/Cook, 1990. 1–27.

Batson, Trent W. "The ENFI Project: A Networked Classroom Approach to Writing Instruction." *Academic Computing.* (February/March 1988): 32–33; 55–56.

Berlin, James. "Rhetoric and Ideology in the Writing Class." *College English.* 50 (1988): 477–94.

Bizzell, Patricia. "Composing Processes: An Overview." *The Teaching of Writing.* Eds. Anthony Petrosky and David Bartholomae. Chicago: University of Chicago Press, 1986. 49–70.

Britton, James et al. *The Development of Writing Abilities* (11–18). London: Macmillan Education, 1975.

Bruce, Bertram, and Joy Peyton. "A New Writing Environment and an Old Culture: A Situated Evaluation of Computer Networking to Teach Writing." *Network-Based Writing Classes: Promises and Realities.* Eds. Bertram Bruce, Joy Peyton, and Trent Batson. New York: Cambridge UP, forthcoming.

Bruffee, Kenneth. "Social Construction, Language, and the Authority of Knowledge: A Bibliographical Essay." *College English.* 48 (1986): 773–90.

Bruner, Jerome. *Actual Minds, Possible Worlds.* Cambridge, MA: Harvard University Press, 1986.

Bump, Jerome. "Radical Changes in Class Discussion Using Networked Computers." *Computers and the Humanities* 49: (1990), 49–65.

Catano, James. "Computer-based Writing: Navigating the Fluid Text." *College Composition and Communication* 36 (1985): 309–16.

Chesebro, James W., and Donald G. Bonsall. *Computer-Mediated Communication: Human Relationships in a Computerized World.* Tuscaloosa: The University of Alabama Press, 1989.

Cooper, Marilyn, and Cynthia L. Selfe. "Computer Conferences and Learning: Authority, Resistance, and Internally Persuasive Discourse." *College English* 52 (December 1990): 847–69.

Eldred, Janet. "Computers, Composition Pedagogy, and the Social View." *Critical Perspectives on Computers and Composition Instruction.* Eds. Gail E. Hawisher and Cynthia L. Selfe. New York: Teachers College Press, 1989. (201–18)

Faigley, Lester. "Competing Theories of Process: A Critique and a Proposal." *College English* 48 (1986): 527–42.

———. "Subverting the Electronic Network: Teaching Writing Using Networked Computers." *The Writing Teacher as Researcher: Essays in the Theory and Practice of Class-based Research.* Eds. Donald A. Daiker and Max Morenberg. Portsmouth: Boynton/Cook, 1990. (290-311)

Feenberg, Andrew. "Computer Conferencing and the Humanities." *Instructional Science* 16 (1987): 169–86.

——— . "The Written World." *Mindweave: Communication, Computers, and Distance Education.* Eds. Robin Mason and Anthony Kaye. New York: Pergamon Press, 1989. (22-39)

Ferrara, Kathleen, Hans Brunner, and Greg Whittemore. "Interactive Written Discourse as an Emergent Register." *Written Communication* 8 (January 1991): 8–34.

George, E. Laurie "Taking Women Professors Seriously: Female Authority in the Computerized Classroom" *Computers and Composition* 7 (Special Issue, 1990): 45-52.

Goffman, Erving. "Fun in Games" *Encounters.* New York: Bobbs-Merrill, 1961.

Hairston, Maxine. "The Winds of Change: Thomas Kuhn and the Revolution in the Teaching of Writing." *College Composition and Communication.* 33 (1982): 76–88.

Harasim, Linda. "On-Line Education: A New Domain." *Mindweave: Communication, Computers, and Distance Education.* Eds. Robin Mason and Anthony Kaye. New York: Pergamon Press, 1989. (50-62)

——— . *On-line Education: Perspectives on a New Environment.* New York: Praeger Press, 1990.

Hartman, Karen et al. "Patterns of Social Interaction and Learning to Write." *Written Communication* 8 (January 1991): 79–113.

Hawisher, Gail E. "Research and Recommendations in Computers and Composition." *Critical Perspectives on Computers and Composition Studies.* Eds. Gail E. Hawisher and Cynthia L. Selfe. New York: Teachers College Press.

Hawisher, Gail E., and Cynthia L. Selfe. "The Rhetoric of Technology and the Electronic Writing Class." 42 (February 1991): 55–65.

Hiltz, Starr Roxanne. "Collaborative Learning: The Virtual Classroom Approach." *T.H.E. Journal* (June 1990): 59–65.

——— . "Evaluating the Virtual Classroom." *Online Education: Perspectives on a New Environment.* Ed. Linda M. Harasim. New York: Praeger, 1990. (133-83)

Hiltz, Starr Roxanne, and Murray Turoff. *The Network Nation.* Reading: Addison-Wesley, 1978.

Jennings, Edward M. "Paperless Writing: Boundary Conditions and Their Implications." *Writing at the Century's End: Essays on Computer-Assisted Composition.* New York: Random House, 1987. (11-20)

Kaplan, Nancy. "Ideology, Technology, and the Future of Writing Instruction." *Evolving Perspectives on Computers and Composition Studies: Questions for the 1990s.* Eds. Gail E. Hawisher and Cynthia L. Selfe. Urbana and Houghton: NCTE and Computers and Composition Press, 1991. (11-42)

Kaye, Anthony. "Computer-Mediated Communication and Distance Education." *Mindweave: Communication, Computers, and Distance Education.* Eds. Robin Mason and Anthony Kaye. New York: Pergamon, 1989. (3–21).

Kiesler, Sara, Jane Siegel, and Timothy W. McGuire. "Social Psychological Aspects of Computer-Mediated Communication." *American Psychologist* 39 (1984): 1123–1134.

Kiesler, Sara, David Zubrow, and Anne Marie Moses. "Affect in Computer-Mediated Communication: An Experiment in Synchronous Terminal-to-Terminal Discussion." *Human-Computer Interaction* 1 (1985): 77–104.

Kremers, Marshall. "Adams Sherman Hill meets ENFI: An Inquiry and a Retrospective." *Computers and Composition* 5 (1988): 69–77.

———. "Sharing Authority on a Synchronous Network: The Case for Riding the Beast." *Computers and Composition.* 7 (Special Issue 1990): 33–44.

Langston, M. Diane, and Trent Batson. "The Social Shifts Invited by Working Collaboratively on Computer Networks: The ENFI Project." *Computers and Community.* Ed. Carolyn Handa. Portsmouth: Boynton/Cook, 1990. (160–84)

Levin, James, Haesun Kim, and Margaret Riel. "Analyzing Instructional Interactions on Electronic Message Networks." *On-Line Education: Perspectives on a New Environment.* New York: Praeger, 1990.

Levinson, Paul. "Media Relations: Integrating Computer Telecommunications with Educational Media." *Mindweave: Communication, Computers, and Distance Education.* Eds. Robin Mason and Anthony Kaye. New York: Pergamon, 1989. 40–49.

Lorentsen, Annette. "Evaluation of Computer Conferencing in Open Learning." *Mindweave: Communication, Computers, and Distance Education.* Eds. Robin Mason and Anthony Kaye. New York: Pergamon, 1989. (196–97).

Mabrito, Mark. Writing Apprehension and Computer-Mediated Peer-Response Groups: A Case Study of Four High- and Four Low Apprensive Writers Communicating Face-to-Face Versus Electronic Mail. Unpublished Dissertation. Illinois State University, Normal, Il, 1989.

McCreary, Elaine. "Computer-Mediated Communication and Organisational Culture" *Mindweave: Communication, Computers, and Distance Education.* Ed. Robin Mason and Anthony Kaye. New York: Pergamon, 1989. (101–14).

Moran, Charles. "Using What We Have." *Computers and Composition* 9 (1991): 39–46.

Murray, Denise. "The Composing Process for Computer Conversation." *Written Communication* 8 (January 1991): 35–55.

Neuwirth, Christine et al. "Why Write—Together—Concurrently on a Computer Network?" *Networked-Based Writing Classes: Promises and Realities.* Eds. Bertram Bruce, Joy Kreeft Peyton, and Trent Batson. New York: Cambridge University Press, forthcoming.

Porter, James. "Intertextuality and the Discourse Community." *Rhetoric Review* 5 (Fall 1986): 34–45.

Schriner, Delores K., and William C. Rice. "Computer Conferencing and Collaborative Learning: A Discourse Community at Work." *College Composition and Communication* 40 (December 1989): 472–78.

Schwartz, Jeffrey. "Using an Electronic Network to Play the Scales of Discourse." *English Journal* 79 (March 1990): 16–24.

Selfe, Cynthia L. and Paul R. Meyer. "Testing Claims for On-Line Conferences." *Written Communication* 8 (April 1991): 163–98.

Selfe, Cynthia L., Christine Pellar-Kosbar, and Paul R. Meyer. "Computer-based Forums for Academic Discourse: Testing the Claims for On-Line Conferences, Redux." Paper presented at the Conference on College Composition and Communication. 21–23 March 1991.

Sproull, Lee, and Sara Kiesler, "Reducing Social Context Cues: Electronic Mail in Organization Communication." *Management Science* 32 (1986): 1492–1512.

Wilkins, Harriet. "Computer-Talk: Long Distance Conversations by Computer." *Written Communication.* 8 (January 1991): 56–78.

6

Breaking Down Barriers:
High Schools and Computer Conferencing

William W. Wright, Jr.
Bread Loaf School of English

The grandmother in one of James Thurber's stories "lived the latter part of her life in the horrible suspicion that electricity was dripping invisibly all over the house. It leaked, she contended, out of empty sockets if the wall switch had been left on" (Thurber, 186). Teachers arriving at Bread Loaf (a six-week summer graduate program of Middlebury College in Vermont) were not that suspicious of technology in July 1984, when the UPS man slid boxes of Apple computers out of his truck onto the Inn porch—but almost. Many high school English teachers arriving at the mountain campus reacted to the gadgets as one would to a foaming-at-the-mouth bull terrier. Why put your hand on the thing if you don't have to?

Now (as I write this in 1991) we are into the eighth summer of computer-related late-paper excuses (the cat ate my floppy disk), and there is a well-worn path down to the bottom of the library wing—the lab which someone dubbed the "Apple Cellar" and someone else more accurately labeled the "Apple Seller." English majors, and other people who write, like these machines simply because they make it easy to change things. They are here to stay.

But there is another way—maybe the most powerful way—to use a personal computer, and that is as a communications device. Some of the projects that I have directed over the last five years have been looking at how new technologies can help with the teaching of writing—especially

102

when schools are linked to other schools by modem. Students do seem to write better when it is easy for them to revise. And when they know that a peer audience in London or Montana or New York will read their personal narrative, it (to borrow loosely from Dr. Johnson) concentrates the mind wonderfully. One teacher in a red-clay and textile-mill region in the South said that her students were "just tearing up the dictionary."

To back up a little, Bread Loaf is a six-week summer graduate program where K-12 English teachers and others can take graduate courses at Vermont, Santa Fe, or Oxford and, if they wish, work towards a master's degree over four or five summers. In 1978, Bread Loaf began offering a Program in Writing and started by bringing in, as instructors, people like Ken Macrorie, Peter Elbow, James Britton, Nancy Martin, James Moffett, Shirley Heath, and Dixie Goswami. At the same time, grants for tuition encouraged teachers from isolated parts of the country to attend.

In 1983 Bread Loaf proposed to set up a computer writing lab in the summers and to link teachers by modem in the school year. Our proposal to Apple Computer, Inc. cited James Britton, Donald Graves and the early work of James Levin and colleagues. We felt that this might be a new way to provide audience and purpose for young writers. In the project, which began in early 1984, we wanted to see if:

- students at rural schools would revise more and write better if they used personal computers
- students would write differently if they wrote for an audience of readers other than the teacher (by sending writing over a network)
- teachers could share ideas on a distance network

Do computers and networks make a difference? We don't have quantitative evidence, but practice has shown that technology can help students and teachers. Computers let them write more freely and allow them to link to other worlds. Networks make active learning possible and can help bring life to the classroom.

Teachers do share ideas. Some topics on BreadNet have become interactive journals with teachers discussing topics such as portfolio assessment in Vermont and educational reform in Kentucky. Here are a couple of excerpts:

92 (of 98) PMCGONEGAL Apr. 13, 1991 at 17:57 (2203 characters)

Dear Assess Mentors,

Remember Vermont's Portfolio Assessment project? Want an update?

To recap, VT is asking a few dozen "sample schools" to collect portfolios of student writing and math in 4th and 8th grades.

(Hereinafter I will address myself to the writing; you can get your math info from some other busybody.)

This winter we have been thinking a lot about criteria. A bunch of teachers who advised the setup from the start has articulated 5 criteria for the assessors to think about: organization, purpose, detail, voice and mechanics. (These are clarified in descriptors which I will furnish on request.) The leaders of the program last week borrowed 600 student portfolios to take "benchmark" samples from.

This week several of us assembled at a White River Junction hotel for two-day stints to benchmark pieces of writing. This was a tough but, for me, a very educational and satisfying job. What we came away with . . .

Tish

ACTION on "ASSESSMENT" 92 (of 98) = = >

READ, KEEP, WRITE, JOIN, LEAVE, PROFILE MEMBERS, PROFILE BRANCHES, FIND "text", OTHER

Enter a command or press < RETURN > for: (Next)

93 (of 98) SWOOD Apr. 14, 1991 at 9:04 (1372 characters)

Tish, I appreciate very much hearing about Vermont's progress with portfolio assessment. Please do continue to keep us posted. And if it is not too much trouble, please send me the criteria description.

Did you see the article in NCTE's COUNCIL-GRAMS about the port-folio plan at Miami University in Ohio? Incoming freshmen are being given a choice. They can take the timed essay test writing to a limited prompt, or they can submit a portfolio containing their best edited high school writing, verification from the teacher, working notes and drafts for one paper, and a writing biography.

All teachers—not just those in small towns in Montana or on reservations in Arizona—are isolated. Barriers come down when a teacher can ask peers across the country how to teach *Hamlet* or how to work with small writing groups in the fifth-period writing class. But teachers on the net-work do much more than share recipes. There is talk of how learning the-ory applies to the classroom and constant self-examination of what we are doing. A question that Christa McAuliffe Educator Carol Stumbo asks is, "Are we simply using expensive gadgets to do what can be done just as easily some other way? Does technology make a difference?"

We asked Carol's question after our first efforts on the network. Early e-mail projects between two classes may have been expensive ways to do what could have been done more easily with the U.S. Mail. When we moved to computer conferencing we felt that we were having groups of classrooms do things that could not be done any other way.

What is a Computer Conference?

Computer conferencing is an unfortunate term for one kind of computer-mediated communication—unfortunate because many confuse it with real-time video conferencing or real-time electronic mail. A computer conference makes use of a central computer's ability to store, retrieve, and display information. More elaborate than electronic mail and electronic bulletin boards, computer conference systems make it easy for a group of people in different locations to read about and comment on a topic in an on-going, sustained way. There is also a permanent record of "conference proceedings." The best thing is that people in different time zones with busy schedules can communicate about an immediate issue. Since users don't have to be on at the same time (this is not a "real-time" electronic meeting), they can take part when it is convenient.

In 1986 BreadNet moved from electronic mail (and rather stagnant distribution lists) to computer conferencing. The latter works something like this: Carol Stumbo, a teacher in McDowell, Kentucky, might get up and read a comment on the "assessment" conference that Jan Lowman in Jakarta, Indonesia, put up several hours earlier. Carol can respond at her convenience. John Forsyth, in Livingston, Montana, might get up a few hours later and react to what Jan and Carol said. A computer conference is not like sitting around a table, cup of coffee in hand, talking to group of people, but it is the closest thing that—during the school year—we can get to right now, short of jetting people back and forth.

Because a computer conference lets groups of people share ideas, it is more dynamic than one-to-one electronic mail exchanges, and the results are sometimes greater than the sum of the parts. An idea sparked in Bethel, Maine, might be added to in Lower Greasewood, Arizona. The important difference between this and electronic mail is that groups of people work together and continue one of the best reasons for going to Bread Loaf: They talk to each other. This sort of collegial support in sometimes lonely classrooms is important for most teachers, not just Bread Loafers.

How BreadNet Structures Activities

We have had a range of projects on BreadNet—from electronic writing workshops for students, to online guests, to global conferences about the environment. Here I will tell a little about a few of them. For a project to be effective we have found that it needs to have a definite beginning and ending, a good moderator, and guidelines so that you won't have too much writing. For example, we do not encourage "pen pal" projects between classrooms. These can become management nightmares for the teacher and usually fall apart when plans for matching students don't work out. We encourage teachers to set up small groups—both in the classroom and online—an arrangement that can provide more benefits than the one-to-one links. We also think it important for teachers and students to be involved with the planning of an online activity from the beginning. Teachers have resisted projects dreamed up by those who do not know the realities of the K-12 classroom, projects that might not fit into the curriculum.

The following box shows what you see when you first log on to the host (central) computer and go to the computer conferencing software that we use (in this case, a system called Participate). You first go to the INBOX. There, the system shows you any topics or conferences that have new activity. In the example that follows, the main conference called "BREADNET" (where we post brief announcements) has five messages that I have not seen.

SEGMENT NAME (# OF NOTES)
        1 Urgent Notes (3)
        2 Personal Notes (29)
        3 "BREADNET" (5)
        4 "BARN" (14)
        5 "BT" (3)
        6 "COLLEGE" (14)
        7 "PLAN" (8)
        8 "GATEWAY" (35)
        9 "NA" 12)
        10 "ASSESSMENT" (20)
        11 "WORLD TRADE" (10)
        12 "WORKSHOP" (3)
        13 "SOCIAL ACTION" (5)

ACTION on 161 Notes = = >

If you are having a busy week and don't have time to read other conferences, you might check the first one for news from time to time. Someone might post an announcement about an upcoming face-to-face conference or an especially good article that appeared in the *English Journal*. We do not allow long discussions on this main conference.

There is an informal discussion on "barn." The Bread Loaf campus is located in the Green Mountains on what was once a horse farm. The main meeting place is a converted barn. One side is where classes meet;

the other is where people sit around in small groups and drink coffee between classes. The electronic "barn" is more like the gambril-roofed one where people share ideas—on any topic—over coffee.

In "workshop," a moderator might post a schedule and five classes might sign up. The first class might have the first two-week slot and put up pieces of writing that others respond to. We limit the writing to five or so pieces which can be either selected pieces or pieces written collaboratively. A problem with networks is dealing with information overload. Even if a class puts up only a few pieces of writing, we must remember that most of the good work goes on before information is uploaded. The network serves as a catalyst.

We also have an international writing workshop called "world trade," where the classes are from different parts of the world. The writing here describes the community the writer lives in so that the readers "out there" can understand. Here is an example:

2 (of 139) LIMA Dec. 3, 1988 at 11:25

> Peru is a third world country that is trying to keep up with the times. The papers make it sound a lot worse than it is, not that it doesn't have its problems. It's extremely unstable politically. . . .
>
> The predominant Terrorist group, the "Sendero Luminoso" (The Shining Path) will often bomb power plants, causing blackouts in various areas of the city. These blackouts are known as "apagones." They terrorize the smaller cities and will do periodic raids either killing or torturing people. The Indians in these cities are caught between the government and the terrorists because the terrorists will kill them if they don't join their 'cause' and the police will kill them if they do. It's common to see armored cars and men with machine guns, as well as an occasional tank.
>
> But that's the bad part; there are a lot of advantages we have here that you can't get in the States, like the beach resorts, the discotecs, the pubs and just learning about a new culture. . . .
>
> Peru's economic situation is extremely poor. The poor class represents over 90% of the people, there is virtually no middle class, and the rich, who make up about 5% of the people are wealthy beyond belief. Lima itself is a pretty dirty city, as there are over seven million people. The reason for the population being that high is that the Indians in the mountains who have a hard life hear about Lima and how wonderful it is, come here, then end up on the streets. Watching those people live on the street with absolutely nothing is the hardest part of living here.
> Nicole Beck
> The American School of Lima

Some of the other activities we have tried include

- an international reading group (moderated from Peru)
- online guests (Al Gore's office, Margaret Riel, WorldWatch)
- interactive journalism (online reports from an NCTE conference)
- "book talk" (an informal place to talk about what you are reading)
- "world class" (a discussion of environmental issues)
- a network of teachers of Native Americans
- "college" (college students answer questions from high school students)

Three projects that linked K-12 with college

The Native American project has been especially exciting. A Georgetown University graduate course in Native American literature is linked to K-12 schools on reservations around the country—and also to a class at Berkeley. Lauren Muller, the instructor at Berkeley, said that her college students were learning about good story-telling from the K-12 Indian students. She says that the network projects are working well because her students are writing for an audience of readers outside the classroom and writing honestly about what matters. A benefit is that the writing of the K-12 students on the reservations echoes what the college students are reading in literature. They quickly learn that the literature is not from a dead culture, not a culture only described in museums and movies (Muller). The K-12 Indian students are seeing models of good writing and hearing from reservation students who made it to college. The Georgetown instructor, Lucy Maddox, now head of the English department, says that it is one of the most energizing things to happen to her in many years of teaching (Griffith and Maddox).

Another way that the K-12 world has linked with higher education is on a conference called "college." Here, students in high school get to see writing of those in college, and K-12 students get to learn what life is really like on campus. The notes read like a wonderful journal of college life.

In a third conference called "gateway," we started by trying to have a technical link between a group of college composition teachers on BIT-Net and secondary teachers on BreadNet. The programmer's first try did not work and the college composition teachers, in the middle of a discussion of rhetorical theory, suddenly got hundreds of error messages. We will work out this technical snag in the future. Gateways to other networks do exist. We will see more and more. However, so that we could carry out this meeting of the two worlds, we invited representatives from the two networks to join a computer conference. It was good for the K-12 teachers to hear what people like Trent Batson (Gallaudet) and Fred Kemp (Texas Tech) were doing in their writing classrooms—and for them to find out the constraints and triumphs of high school teachers like Carol Stumbo in eastern Kentucky.

This meeting of the two worlds (K-12 and college) will continue. There are initiatives underway (such as those by EDUCOM and the National Science Foundation) to give more K-12 schools access to the Internet, e-mail, and computer conferencing. While the electronic mail discussion groups on these systems don't offer the more-evolved features of computer conferencing, it is a step in the right direction and a way for barriers to come down. Everyone benefits when the teachers at both levels can talk with each other.

We do hope that the NSF, EDUCOM, and those who run the emerging National Research and Education Network (NREN) will test the emerging, dominant e-mail systems and develop systems easier to use and more conducive to group work. Until easier-to-use systems (systems more like the evolved conferencing packages) are in place, the ideal arrangement is for teachers to have access both to the Internet *and* to computer conferencing. There are ways for some individuals to use Internet connections to get to conferencing systems. Another low-cost option is parallel or distributed conferencing. You can set up, for example, a conference called "assessment" on a host computer in Austin, Texas, and one by the same name on a host computer in New York. Using very-high-speed, error-checking modems, you "port" notes back and forth in such a way that all the participants feel that they are part of the same discussion (Wright, "Conference").

Where Are We Going From Here?

In Nicholas Lemann's book, *The Promised Land*, he talks about how the mass production of the mechanical cotton picker led to the migration of more than five million African-Americans from the fields and farms of the Deep South to big cities. Technology, especially the emergence of networks linked to networks, may now be causing a migration of a different sort. Just as that well-worn path to the computer room appeared at Bread Loaf's bucolic mountain campus in Vermont, there we are slowly changing the way that we work and teach. Local- and wide-area networks allow for more egalitarian communities of writers. Rather than a face-to-face seminar dominated by the more-vocal student or two and the teacher, we are seeing the emergence of a more democratic electronic "classroom."

Indeed, this is not the first time that technology has had an impact in our field, one, we must not forget, that was made possible by technology. Alvin Kernan aptly summarizes the history of print culture in his book, *The Death of Literature*:

> Western Europe was also transformed conclusively, three centuries after the appearance of the printing press, from an oral to a print culture. Mechanical and democratic print brought the pressures for change being exerted everywhere directly to bear on the old court-centered aristocratic poetry and belles lettres that had lasted from Dante and Petrach to the days of Swift and Pope. Print created an open marketplace for books and ideas, made censorship and patronage uneconomic, transferred literary power to an increasingly literate public of "common readers," as Samuel Johnson styled them, and fostered a new type of professional writers who made their living and reputation by providing what the market would buy. (12)

Among Kernan's lists of evidence that there is a decline in literacy is one development that should, instead, give a spark of hope:

> As people write and read less, while watching television and using telephones, computers, and other visual and aural electronic modes of communication more and more, reading books is ceasing to be the primary way of knowing something in our society. As the number of expensive journals in the sciences continue to increase, "scientists rely on them less and less. The latest ideas in science are typically exchanged well in advance of formal publication, at conferences and through advance copies of papers distributed by fax machines and computer networks." (140)

An increase in the use of the Internet, the network of networks that people in academia and the government use, should please those of us who shake our heads over the decline of literacy. A free exchange of writing on computer networks is a livelier use of words and brainpower than having our scientists labor over deadly prose for a journal. However, at a December 1990 seminar at the Congressional Office of Technology Assessment (OTA), Steve Cisler, librarian for Apple Computer, Inc. (and avid user of grassroots networks such as the Well) pointed out that librarians and scholars are frustrated by this movement to the networks. It is becoming more and more difficult to document ideas.

If "groupware" (computer conferencing is one kind) lets more people work together to solve the world's problems, the librarian's lament should be one of our happier concerns. The OTA meeting was one of the many to discuss the building of a national data highway, an infrastructure for the online world. These highways exist and will become more powerful. If current legislation is approved by the U.S. Congress, we will have a supercomputer network that will operate at speeds of gigabits per second.

Raymond Williams, a high school English teacher from Virginia (not the cultural historian), recently, in a computer conference note, justified the small expense for letting him and his class use BreadNet by pointing out that using networks will be the way that his students work in the world. But even the small amount of funding (he and his class could get by on $250 a year), is keeping rural teachers out of the network world. In this time of diminished budgets, even urban teachers, who pay much less than rural teachers do to connect, are having to rule out networks because of the connect-time costs.

Most of the other writers in this book have access to BITNet, a computer network paid for by higher education institutions (usually free for users in academic communities). Some have local-area networks, classrooms full of computers wired to each other. Many have their students "talk" to each other in "real-time" on the computer and hope this is how all writing classrooms are set up in the near future. Others say that the age of print is dead, that hypertext and multimedia are here to stay, and project that students will "hand in" multi-media presentations—rather than papers—in a few years.

The reality of high school budgets right now is that most schools will not have funds for local-area networks for writing or for multimedia tools. Alexander Coleman recently wrote in *Education Week* about some of the unfortunate uses of technology in South Carolina schools that do manage to come up with equipment. He pointed out that some schools let only the advanced students use the computers they have managed to acquire. On the brighter side, he pointed out the impact a low-end computer hooked to a modem can have.

> But if we want to, we can give all students access to powerful technology that is not expensive. Several interactive educational networks, such as BreadNet, a network for teachers and students sponsored by the Bread Loaf School of English, require only the cheapest machines (I use a $500 clone.) And though on-line time is not free, teachers who have been given the time and the support necessary to learn to use networks wisely themselves can give their students inexpensive experiences, rich in reading, writing, and thought.
>
> BreadNet supports, for students and teachers, what is called asynchronous computer conferencing, which simply means that a number of sites send writing to a central "conference" to be read by all members of the conference at their convenience. Unlike electronic pen-pal systems, such conferences allow a great deal of collaboration, among classes and

groups within classes, before writing is sent—and a great deal of communication, oral and written, for the amount of writing actually transmitted. (26)

Unfortunately, some schools, in their push to get some equipment, are
letting companies "give" them television sets and VCRs if they agree to
show students news highlights. Students stare passively at images—
"news" which is interspersed with commercials for such items as soft
drinks and expensive athletic shoes. It is also alarming to hear about the
amounts of money some states and federal programs spend in order to
bring in satellite images. In some cases, it solves a problem. It might
allow, for example, one German teacher to cover several schools in a big
rural state. On the negative side, it brings more passive learning, more
"talking heads" to the classroom, more of the wrong kind of spoon-fed,
skill-and-drill teaching that bores students to tears. We have to think that
low-cost networks like BreadNet or Big Sky Telegraph in Montana
(another network of schools) could bring active learning—and some life
to classrooms—at a fraction of the cost of some of the video "solutions."

That is not to say that all experiments in video are bad. We would
love to see hypertext and multimedia tools in every school. We simply
question the justification for spending large sums only for video tools
when lower-cost networks seem to engage students in a way that video
does not. We also see low-cost ways to combine video and text experiences. For example, in some projects we had classes view videotapes then
write (in online groups) about them on the network.

It is now possible to combine low-cost graphics with the text being
sent over networks. Telecommunications pioneer Dave Hughes recently
demonstrated (at the Bread Loaf School of English in Santa Fe) what he
calls a "word dance." This form uses the computer screen as more than
an electronic printed page; it allows for colorful artwork to appear and
for text to appear or disappear when the writer wants it to. The writer
also can have words move or change shape in ways that make the presentation more meaningful. The emerging NAPLPS graphics format that he
works with takes up less memory and lets the user send creations through
networks quickly. As NAPLPS software improves, we envision students
creating low-cost, interactive "word dances" using text and graphics, and
sharing them with peers around the globe. This use of NAPLPS graphics
with text and group work on the networks are ways that people are beginning to reimagine composition.

Summary

We have pointed out the benefits of this medium. For example, isolated
teachers share ideas, students write for new audiences, busy professionals

make "online visits" to the classroom, and students collaborate with distant peers on projects that have a meaning and a purpose.

The convenience of asynchronous communication and the design features of many computer conferencing packages open up many possibilities. An online written transcript of the "proceedings" allows users to come in at any point and catch up. There is also the more subtle, but probably most important feature, the aspect of "groupware" that makes it different from any medium we know of. This allows the spark that comes only from a good brainstorming session, the notion that the total (of the ideas) is greater than the sum of parts. As groupware improves with the addition of graphics and other decision support tools, we should be able to transcend age and discipline categories and become interdisciplinary problem solvers.

We, as writing teachers, say that there must be a real audience out there and a purpose for a piece of writing. When a high school student writes (as she did on a global BreadNet conference) about what she and her colleagues did to to change the recycling policy in a small town in Kentucky, she is writing with honesty and for a purpose. In describing what she and her schoolmates did and what her class and others around the globe accomplished on the network, she ended by saying "we did something important together" (Stumbo, 1991). Call it "televirtuality" (Keizer) or just group work, we must use these new tools to transcend traditional writing instruction and do something important together.

Works Cited

Cisler, Steve. Discussion at seminar held at the Office of Technology Assessment (OTA) in December 1990.

Clement, John. "K-12 Networking benefits for higher education." EDUCOM Review 26.2, Summer 1991.

Coleman, Alexander. "Managing Information in the Information Age," *Education Week,* April 17, 1991.

Coleman, Ike, and Leslie Owens. "Touching the World." *Bread Loaf News* 5.1 (1991): 5.

Griffith and Maddox. "Letting them teach each other: An experiment in classroom networking," *Studies in American Indian Literature* 3.2 (1991): 41.

Hughes, David. Presentation at the Bread Loaf School of English at Santa Fe. July 11th, 1991.

Keizer, Gregg. "As Good As There." *Omni.* 13 (April 1991): 39.

Kernan, Alvin. *The Death of Literature.* New Haven and London: Yale University Press, 1990.

Lemann, Nicholas. *The Promised Land.* New York: Alfred A. Knopf, Inc., 1991.

Maddox, Lucy. Note on BreadNet, 1991.

Muller, Lauren. Conversation in Berkeley, California, March, 1991.

Stumbo, Carol. Note on "social action" conference on BreadNet, 1991.

———. "The World Class Environmental Conference." *Bread Loaf News* 4.1 (1990): 7.

Thurber, James. "The Car We Had to Push," in The Thurber Carnival. New York: Harper and Row, 1945.

Walker, Susan. "BreadNet: An Online Community." *Bread Loaf and the Schools* 1.1 (1987): 12.

Williams, Raymond. Note on BreadNet, 1991.

Wright, William W., Jr. "Conference Addresses International Education Links." *Link-Up.* (September/December 1989).

———. "International Group Work: Using a Computer Conference to Invigorate the Writing of Your Students." *The English Classroom in the Computer Age.* Ed. William Wresch. Urbana: NCTE, 1991.

7

Teaching Composition in Tomorrow's Multimedia, Multinetworked Classrooms

Hugh Burns
The University of Texas at Austin

Prologue

I only had one class tomorrow. No sweat. All I had to do was lead a writing workshop. But this composition lesson would be radically different in an awesome postmodern chaotic virtual kind of way. So technically virtual, in fact, that I could hardly sleep that night, 23 January 1991. If I fell asleep, would visions of actual technology crash in my head?

I was tired. We had spent the day rehearsing for tomorrow's broadcast in Apple's television studio on the "Apple campus" in Cupertino. Apple Higher Education was producing a television series entitled "Imagine: The Apple Education TV Series" which featured educational technologies in general and Macintoshes specifically. The essential theme for the entire series was imagining how computers and associated high technologies were transforming the future dimensions of education.

Apple had invited me and several of my colleagues to do something "extraspecial." Using the "breakthrough" electronic technologies of synchronous networking, distance learning, and satellite television, we were to have a class discussion about the future of distance learning collaboration on networks for writing instruction. We would have live television in the studio in Cupertino and in a computer-networked writing classroom at Jackson Community College in Jackson, Michigan. Standing by in Jackson would be Paula Ashley-Harris, Michael Joyce, and six of their students. In addition, we would have Shiva netmodem connections from these two sites with the English Department's Center for Humanities and Liberal Arts Computing at the University of Texas at Austin where some of our students would be standing by with my colleague and the Center's director, John Slatin. Using the Daedalus Group's software package, we would converse on InterChange, a new Macintosh version for local area network and wide area network "real time" conferencing. The file server was a new Macintosh IIci in Cupertino. Burt Cummings, Apple's Director of Higher Education, would be interviewing the participants during two separate live segments during the sixty-minute broadcast. Up above us was a communications satellite waiting to transmit the pictures of snowy Michigan in between CNN images of the Desert Storm ground war which had been initiated the week before.

The task would be to conduct a multisite, multinetworked, multimedia, multicommentary, multipersonality class discussion among strangers in this strange new setting—some brave new world. We were feeling brave and nervous. So?

Sleep? Piece of cake.

I only had one class tomorrow. No sweat. Solar flares? Quark storms? A blizzard in Michigan? New equipment in Austin? Real students? Oh no, not real students!

The Challenges of "Show"

There's no business like show business. I can assure you that the sixty-minute broadcast happened. I can also assure you that while the show was going on, the three sites were communicating with each other about matters of technology, about writing, about fame, about nerves, about altered state goggles, about being on-line with the world. I can assure you that 219 messages were sent successfully among the participants. I cannot assure you that every participant read each of the 219 messages, for sometimes they were on camera, sometimes they were off camera. The set at Cupertino was active to say the least, as two other feature stories were being told. But on the network transcript, the collaboration took its own shape as the personalities of the participants were empowered by the technology. As I reflect back on these events and "reimagine composition in the virtual age," I see vast potential here. What happened was experimental; we wanted and felt education needed to take some of the hype and "magic dust" away. Some software and hardware could be integrated well enough to transform a virtual classroom into an actual classroom. We knew enough technology to use satellites, video, telephones, netmodems, and software to establish a text-sharing, text-constructing community of writers. Would it be common? No. Would it be "as easy as pie"? No. Would it be possible? Absolutely. Would we be especially critical about realizing a significant educational gain in the hour? Never. We educators are too tough-minded when it comes to technology assessment. We believe in being shown rather than told; there is NO business like SHOW business. This program and the many people who participated wanted to meet that challenge of SHOW. Did we learn something? I hope so. What follows here is my testimony. What's important to understand, however, is that this was a first attempt and what follows illustrates both the strengths and weaknesses of doing something for the first time. Here are three groups who had never talked to one another before. Yet we were asking them to form a "discourse community" in a one-hour broadcast.

Four challenges were apparent to me after the show was beamed and on the tape for this Imagine broadcast. Each challenge raises some important issues and suggests directions for establishing future and more effective distance learning courses and curriculums.

- *Yes, we can do it, but why should we?* For the expense of buying and learning the technology, are we able to realize educational gains?

- *Yes, it takes many resources and talents, but exactly how can we learn to manage all of these components?* For the energy and diverse talents required, will we be able to organize our classrooms and train ourselves in the ways of innovation, and, will we learn to call the corresponding innovative organization the "school without walls"?

- *Yes, people wrote a lot, but exactly what writing instruction occurred?* For all of the chaos being created and stimulated on these networks, what can we point to as the bright and shining moments of writing instruction?

- *Yes, people were openly challenged during the experience, but what challenges did they leave with?* For all of the excitement of being a participant in the wizardry of modern communication, what positive changes happen in learners and would such changes last?

On "Yes, we can do it, but. . ."

We could do it; the virtual age had ended for multisited, multinetworked, televised class discussions and writing workshops. Virtual ages end suddenly. Like that. Initially commotion, then whoosh: actuality where once was virtuality. But let's reflect for a moment on the whole idea. Why were we doing this?

Are we satisfied with the way we teach today? Could we improve? Could we reach more students? Are we satisfied that we are giving each student enough individual attention? Are we satisfied that our students are learning to learn in our courses? Are we satisfied that our students have enough access to the information in their interests and in our world? Are we satisfied that we have enough access to information in our world? Are we satisfied that our students have enough opportunities to talk with experts? Are we satisfied with the social and motivational settings for learning in our schools? Are we satisfied with the way our communities interpret our effectiveness as educators? Are we satisfied with our educational and training opportunities as professionals? I hope not. I hope we see better ways of doing business, and in fact I hope we are all vigorously engaged in the profession of teaching.

Certainly, we want to know what the technology is good for, what differences it will make, and whether or not it works satisfactorily. How does technology satisfy the yearnings for something better? Fair questions. But obviously, we are never going to find out the answers to such questions unless we try to create situations in which to explore the issues.

Technically, we arranged for live two-way television between Jackson Community College and the television studio in Cupertino. We also had audio return with common telephone lines. For the interactive portion of the program, we used six Shiva netmodems (two at each site for incoming and outgoing transmissions). A Macintosh IIci was the file server in Cupertino. The Macintoshes at each of the sites were Macintosh IIsi machines.

I suppose there is artifice in such an integration of all of these technologies. In order to show what education might become in the future, it is important to remember this: Technology is a means not an end. While the technology enabled, the people empowered. Any "significant change" would occur among the participants not the technology. The impact of innovative technology is only beginning to be discussed and interpreted; studies such as Terry Winograd and Fernando Flores's *Understanding Computers and Cognition: A New Foundation for Design* (1986) are stimulating the discussion of futures. In such studies, we are seeing a design philosophy which emphasizes the human dimensions of being and understanding. Multinetworked, realtime communication among learners is providing such transcripts and artifacts. "Interactivity" is the real strength of and hope for computers. This set of communication tools in a local network configuration provides a mini-forum for stimulating the "knowing" processes. The design of the systems is moving toward learner-centered, reactive learning environments. Local Area Networks (LAN) solutions may help such users by working collaboratively, thus being able to negotiate the meaning and the construction of the parts together. As the students would comment on the "assigned" topic, the global village aspects of such learning environments were readily apparent and perhaps far, far away. What is also apparent is a social chatting which has been very common in such networked settings. How chatting becomes "learning" is another interesting phenomenon which this paper only barely skims. Turning to the transcript, we saw and heard the participants' amazement as well as a few critical comments on the theme of "now what?"

Hugh @ Apple:
IMAGINE! Here I am in Cupertino, California. There you all are in Jackson and Austin. But we are together in this electronic web. This will really be fun. . . . Your assignment is to imagine what such technologies will bring us in the future. What do you think? Let's *INTERCHANGE* about the processes of writing, thinking, and learning. Let's reflect on how we do what we do. And what we can be. Let's speculate on how new, innovative technologies are changing education.

Stan @ Austin:
An environment such as Interchange empowers everyone in the classroom—rather than the traditional classroom which allows only one student to converse with the instructor at a time, networked discourse encourages multiple, and equally valid discussions.

Kristi @ Jackson:
Some of us are nervous, anybody else? I'm so-o-o impressed!

Kevin @ Austin:
We all hope that everyone is exposed to new ideas, and that could most certainly be true within a group that has a ground of understanding. But being in an expanded environment also can lead to a few misunderstandings, not everyone uses the same lingo.

Stan @ Austin:
Kevin—that's where hypertext could come into play. I could link a pop-up field to any terms that I may think others might not "get.". . . Let's say we're having an Interchange, and I use some terms from my information science classes that I think other people in the discussion may not know. Hopefully, I could link a definition of these terms, and send the annotated message into the interchange.

Deborah @ Jackson:
Okay, here's my two cents worth—so many of us view the world around us in a very limited way. Technology like this makes it practically impossible!!! (But with this gang maybe that's not such a great thing, ha ha)

Kristi @ Jackson:
I agree with Deb, technology opens up so many new worlds and views!

Stan @ Austin:
I would love to see a combination of networked discourse and virtual
reality. Probably a few years down the line, but how would the possibility of an infinite number of identities (make your own face, essentially)
affect communication?

Hugh @ Apple:
That's worth more than two cents, Deborah. Boy, the limitations are off
for sure. Kristi, I am sooooooooo impressed too. . . .

Ben @ Jackson:
I think we are just beginning to realize how the mind really works
through this stuff. Maybe hypertext therapy?

John @ Austin:
Hi. Couldn't resist taking a turn here-my students will tell you I can
never keep my "mouth" shut during InterChange. I have found again
and again that students feel free-er to join the class discussion. Sorry to
be so dull, and glad to be on-line with the world.

Is this a case of using technology for the sake of technology? I think not.
There is more than two cents worth of speculation here as these writers
began to find their shared "lingo." Although only fourteen writers are
really participating in the discussion, the feeling at each of the three sites
seemed to reflect "being on-line with the world." There was also a serious
sense of being at the beginning of something new in education as Ben
expressed in his desire to seek out hypertherapy or Kevin's worry that
such environments may allow for misunderstandings when "common
experiences" are not well understood or poorly articulated.

Was this more of an experiment? Yes, this program was an experiment. However, we should expect to see such experiments in education.
Such an experiment in itself provides data and information—that's valuable. We cannot learn what works if we do not try. This experience was
done in the service of learning.

Theoretically, the technology should be invisible, but computers will
probably not be invisible for the immediate future. Although I have
already made the point that a technology should be a means not an end,
the "real" process of innovative technology transfer does not make that
humanly possible. We humans are curious, and we are always concerned
about revealing too much about what makes us human in the first place—
imperfection. The following sequence illustrates how the "serious" transcript changed when "lights, camera, action" took over at Jackson Community College. Deborah is about to be asked a question or two over the
satellite television hookup; meanwhile, here's what happens on Inter-
Change:

Deborah @ Jackson: We are famous!!!

Alice @ Jackson:
Famous for what?

Kristi @ Jackson:
Your involvement in things and bravery to be on TV, and your dedication . . . it all fits with what I know. COOL, I HAVE ALWAYS WANTED TO BE FAMOUS

Deborah @ Jackson:
Our roles are interchangeable as teacher and students, they just said. [*Deborah is watching the monitor and listening to the "live" feed from Cupertino.*]

Kristi @ Jackson:
Hey Deb, what's goin' on in your ear?

Skiz @ Jackson:
Deb is talking. shhhhhh! [*Deborah is "live" coast to coast.*]

Bill @ Jackson:
I don't know what is going 'round me but intend to act as though I do.

Kristi @ Jackson:
Is she talking too loud?

Deborah @ Jackson:
They just pulled questions out of no where. [*It's over.*]

Hugh @ Apple:
Deborah, John: Your comments are right on. The role of the teachers and the role of students are becoming *INTERCHANGEABLE*! [*I'm responding to Jackson and Austin on-line while answering Burt's studio questions in Cupertino. Meanwhile back in Jackson. . . .*]

Alice @ Jackson:
Congratulations Deb—good job—well done!

Kristi @ Jackson:
Deb is awesome Deb is awesome

Deborah @ Jackson:
feedback feedback feedback....

Bill @ Jackson:
This overwhelming caring for Deb is all a ploy to get on my (Bill's that is) bad side.

Kristi @ Jackson:
You are so full of dookey!

Deborah @ Jackson:
They are just being caring because they realize that everyone downstairs who saw that is going to laugh hysterically every time they see me now.

Deborah @ Jackson:
Kristi you are now an "interchange" star!!!

Kristi @ Jackson:
Besides, Bill, I think you are awesome, too, and so do a few others I know of. Stop being a pile!

Deborah @ Jackson:
Do you realize this awesome demo of us talking to ourselves!!

Bill @ Jackson:
Why couldn't we have school during the broadcast? The idea of chatting nationwide seems like a waste except for the fact that we are even able to do it is amazing.

Is this a community or what? The idea of chatting nationwide is amazing, indeed. The novelty of these experiments will undeniably affect what is being said and done and thought in the enclosed circle of the participants, even though this enclosed conversation is being broadcast nationwide. If I had a regret about the demonstration on the broadcast itself, it was simply that this social construction of community could not be adequately conveyed in the two, short "live" segments.

Yes, we can do it. Why should we? A "why not?" is too glib, especially when most of us know that we are not satisfied with the state of our educational systems. If we are not, then let's be active, relentless, and enthusiastic about defining what we need in order to provide better instruction.

On "Yes, it takes many resources and talents, but. . ."

Who are we fooling—every teacher a multisite, multiskill, multimedia expert? What are we really saying about the realizable future?

Multimedia. Multisite. Multinetwork. That *multi* prefix creates predictable and problematic reactions among educators. While most will grant that the promise of rich learning environments could be more effective and challenging for students, most agree that the cost in time and energy to learn everything is just too staggering. If the only choice is learning more, do not expect much to change. If, however, the technology becomes more integrative, then we can expect more acceptance.

One of the most obvious advantages of tomorrow's technology implementation will be simply having more technically prepared people. That more general literacy, more scientific literacy, more technical literacy is necessary in our society is not a surprising observation. While social technology for "just plain folks" allows some skills to be more and more common (e.g., playing videotapes, using a word processor, withdrawing money from automatic tellers), depending on technical assimilation alone is a poor way to design instruction and to prepare teachers for their new roles as creators of robust learning environments. As our society introduces more technology into our social workscapes, we should derive opportunities for re-imagining our schoolscapes.

The student-writers on *Imagine* had already figured out some of the new "rules." They brought with them mental maps and seemed to me to be rather comfortable in knowing what they were doing, where they were going, and what they were communicating about. The artificial boundaries we had delineated in our academic worlds apparently had not been subscribed to in any large way. In fact, they seemed intuitive about the need to focus discussion and the need to get on with their educations. I did not sense that they had necessarily bought our distinctions between arts and sciences, pasts or futures. As Bill points out, "Of all the computer classrooms in the world, you had to walk into mine." Gosh, Bill, sorry.

Bill @ Jackson:
Of all the computer classrooms in the world, you had to walk into mine.

Kevin @ Austin:
I think we would all need to become poets pretty quick, or at least confine our comments and emotions to a single and accessible piece of literature.

Skiz @ Jackson:
Future is never, Ben. We think we are so advanced. This technology will not be common for another 5 to 15 years; if that quick.

Bill @ Jackson:
This could make it into the past, these talks and conversation could very well be forever.

Ben @ Jackson:
This place where I come to speak my piece is perhaps the most forgiving environment I have ever known. I can always take it back. As children

we sometimes demanded that others "take it back," as adults we should allow each other the chance in this place we make.

The metaphors for describing tomorrow's teachers and tomorrow's learners will be larger in scope and, as Ben suggests, electronic communications settings will become "perhaps the most forgiving environments." These new metaphors will also incorporate notions of navigating in a world of ideas and of doing so without horrible consequences. Of course, we will need to develop "sails" or "engines" or "energizers" or "toolkits" which will help us all create more possibilities.

Can our communities work together? Certainly. Who can work the VCR? The video camera? The digitizer? The scanner? Anyone who is trying to improve education can attest that the more time spent with students, the greater the likelihood that learning will improve. These production opportunities are becoming more and more available for teachers, especially as local school districts, states, and federal agencies explore instructional methods for realizing the full flexibility of advancing educational technologies, and provide access to an even vaster array of technological tools for insuring well-written products.

Most teachers will expect, in fact demand, more control over instructional technologies to help them meet their students' individual needs. Tomorrow's solution is to design in flexibility. More opportunities for communication among the community of learners, more avenues for teachers to modify the design where they see fit, more tools for creating a robust instructional and performance environment, and more accessible knowledge and expertise—all of these needs exist. As the *Imagine* broadcast demonstrated, such well-designed environments are being demonstrated in local area networks and distance networks which incorporate multimedia. Such instruction requires rich, focused, "feature presentation" learning occasions in which teams of "learners" become more like producers, directors, choreographers, and even saints in order to make occasions for learning.

On "Yes, people wrote a lot, but. . ."

Why should we write in community? What are the goals of communicating in electronic networks? Answering this question perhaps calls for the most "re-imagining" of the virtual writing classroom. We have been so caught up in theoretical models of text and of product and process that we may be missing several key points about how we learn to write. The literature has illustrated our renewed and recent concerns with establishing socially constructive territories for building writing and reading communities. The bald fact is that writing itself is a technology, an agreed upon though frequently debated set of symbols which when arranged in linear patterns stand for meaning. The tension is one of making meaning in words or in pictures when it comes to producing electronic images so our students can learn. Would it be heresy to suggest that we may be able to learn something about "writing" without writing as we know it today. We are on the verge of actually teaching the language arts—reading, writing, speaking, listening—in one immense language rich environment.

During the broadcast, the participants worried about the effects of their communication, about the benefits of so-called face-to-face communication, and about the sincerity of what they were writing/saying/feeling/thinking. When writers work alone, these concerns do not as readily surface. Look at the nature of the feedback these participants want from each other? Is that what we provide now when we evaluate their writing? Neither was this personal tutoring, although we might claim some personal tutoring moments, especially when participants speak directly to each other by name.

Kristi @ Jackson:
Are we going too fast for the Austin peeps to Interchange with us? Us Jacksonians seem to be the only ones here.

Deborah @ Jackson:
Could we "meet" face to face through interchange and virtual reality?

Stan @ Austin:
Sorry, Kristi, didn't mean to make you feel alone.

Ben @ Jackson:
We have had some really in depth discussions here in jacktown that probably wouldn't have happened face to face. I think it strips away inhibition.

Kevin @ Austin:
link to pop . . . wouldn't it be great if there was a visual linkup with the same interference [interface?] . . . new and different paths of evolution. . . .

John @ Austin:
Deborah, "face to face" gets pretty complicated in this environment. So does meeting. But we could try. I expect the tech people say we need more bandwidth for that, though.

Deborah @ Jackson:
Could we achieve peace if the world leaders could "interchange"? People seem much more open and friendly this way.

Kristi @ Jackson:
That would be cool, Deb, I just wanted to make sure we weren't being overpowering. Hey, we could form relationships here, and never meet

face to face! Would be cool, takes away the inhibitions of "the first meeting"!

Joan @ Austin:

One way that this is better than a conference *phone* call is that we are free to take our time to think and respond.

John @ Austin:

Nice thought, Deborah. I heard former President Carter talk about taking a laptop into negotiations between leaders on different sides of civil wars around the world.

Ben @ Jackson:

Hussein and Bush on interchange with pseudonyms would probably be good friends

Kevin @ Austin:

information is only useful if its timely, as Gn. Powell tells us, but I'm not sure where that puts us,

Deborah @ Jackson:

Okay, I know my comment was corny but I meant it from the heart! (How do you convey sincerity over this thing?)

Joan @ Austin:

Deborah, I don't think your comment was corny at all!

John @ Austin:

You just did, Deborah (convey sincerity). Students often express that concern, but as a teacher I think it actually makes for better, clearer writing. People have to try harder to make themselves clear.

Bill @ Jackson:

We must guard depending on technology like this considering the length of dilithium crystals.

Stan @ Austin:

Ben—a recent collection of abstracts in cyberspace technology and theory included several papers discussing the use of virtual reality in working with people suffering from emotional trauma.

Stan @ Austin:

Deborah, that's a good point. As someone suggested here, offline, that's where improved writing comes in.

Sometimes in a network, respect is discovered in surprising ways: in monolog (writer-to-self), dialogue (writer-to-one other), and polylogue (writer-to-many others). How does one privilege another writer's remarks through negotiation strategies? In the context of transforming words to ideas, such radical new settings invite more in the way of respect for ideas and feelings. And then there is creativity, language play, and imagination:

Skiz @ Jackson:
Attention all planets, attention all planets; I have assumed control.

Hugh @ Apple:
Hey, Skiz—Thanks for beaming in.

Skiz @ Jackson:
Metaphysically yours. . . . Greetings! Nefarians.

Kristi @ Jackson:
Helloo there!

Joan @ Austin:
Hi, Deborah. Hi, Skiz. Just for openers, how's the weather there? It's rainy here.

Kristi @ Jackson:
This is so exciting! Skiz, isn't that Rastafarians? It is SNOWING!!!

Skiz @ Jackson:
My feet are freezing, but maybe I should buy some real shoes!

Joan @ Austin:
What do you have on your feet, anyway, Skiz?

Kevin @ Austin:
It's a pleasant 53, the birds are singing and the clouds have all moved away to shine on our noble experiment. . . .

Skiz @ Jackson:
lime olympid green the second scene the fights between the blue you once knew

Skiz @ Jackson:
floating on the ground the sound surrounds the icy water on the ground

Skiz @ Jackson:
jupiter and saturn oberon they're on the run titania

Alice @ Jackson:
If these remarks are found by the archaeologists of 3000AD I wonder what they will make of them?

Kristi @ Jackson:
They will think we are crazy!

Skiz @ Jackson:
Hey, I'm here, does anyone need any electronic altered-state goggles?

In the communication parlance of "sender-message-receiver," the receivers—readers, audiences, participants, the interpretative community—seem to me to be receiving more of the emphasis. Any lessons should exploit the advantages of the diversity of audience. The voices of audience should be amplified. Let the audiences venture thesis and antithesis. The voice of a traditional teacher should show restraint, patience, waiting for the moments of synthesis. Where does community begin? Around here somewhere. Sorry to be so vague. But I am thinking about it? *Olympid?* Would you give it some thought too?

On "Yes, people were openly challenged, but. . ."

"Lessons" in such an environment should be even more open-ended. They should challenge participants to think hard and to question. Staying open versus "doing" open is the issue.

The mass in the mass media should be energized and allowed to become the creative force behind such composing instruction. Again, on the television program, students in a substantial writing component course at the University of Texas at Austin deliberated on-line with students from Jackson Community College in Jackson, Michigan, and a "teacher" in Cupertino, California, about how computers can extend the reach of the classroom, how computers allow us to reflect in 1991 on writing about writing, on learning about learning, and on communicating about communicating. What of that? There was, of course, the question of existence:

Skiz @ Jackson:
I don't know about you "people", but we were promised pizza for being here and I'm feeling malnourished.

John @ Austin:
Skiz, why did you put "people" in quotes? Don't you think we really exist?

Kristi @ Jackson:
Do you really exist?

Kevin @ Austin:
What I meant to say was that we were promised hardware.

Stan @ Austin:
No, I don't exist at all. Believe me I'm lying.

Stan @ Austin:
Don't read this message.

What is so compelling about being asked not to read that last message? Of course, these tools themselves must be assessed, but there are many signs of intelligent life here. Quite often, this environment seems to spawn its own topics, and, therefore, the environment may have to also create the instruments and performance standards by which to judge itself. Paradoxically, if done well, then technology assessment initiates new designs and new developmental agendas. The knowledge in our heads and hearts is not always the precise knowledge that we take from such experiences. What issues should be raised on such global networks? Had we made the most of this grand experiment? Probably not. Yet I still believe that tomorrow's renaissance classrooms will need renaissance learners using renaissance methods. Our sophisticated planning and sophisticated instruments are not enough to understand precisely what is appropriate or well understood or agreed upon in this multisited, multi-networked demonstration. Where was there agreement?

Joan @ Austin:
Well, we can't agree on what the weather is here in Austin. (We're in the basement). Better not ask us anything very *hard*?!

Alice @ Jackson:
Does nervous come after numb or before?

Skiz @ Jackson:
Skiz, your licensed Hypnotherapist, at your disposal.

Deborah @ Jackson:
Are there any agents in the audience???? I think nervous is before numb!!

Kristi @ Jackson:
Who all are we Interchanging with? I think it comes after, Alice. OOH, hyper-text therapy! What a concept!

Stan @ Austin:
Hi Alice. I think nervous comes after numb. And don't believe what these guys are saying about the weather in Austin. We are sitting in a basement room with no windows.

Deborah @ Jackson:
If you had hypertext therapy, could you virtual reality the bill?

Whereas virtual consequences are wonderful; actual consequences are full of wonder.

Technology is never content for long, with either its form or its function. While educational technology evolves more toward a social construction in collaborative settings, the future of multisite, multimedia, multinetworked computers in classrooms is bright because the outlook for connectivity in the future is so promising. How promising? Global. Soon local area networked classrooms will focus attention on fundamental skills such as writing well, reading well, and thinking critically—in many languages, in many nations. The "invisible colleges" Vallee once predicted will be anything but invisible as such environments multiply and are demonstrated to be useful. Not all of these environments will be in schoolhouses either. Many learning needs and opportunities will be in corporate training settings and throughout communities in libraries and in community centers.

Epilogue

We did fine. Kudos for all, and all for one. We certainly did not portray the power of the interactions during the live shots. The participants would compose and send 219 messages during the program, but I would show only eight "live." Debbie @ Jackson was relieved. Stan @ Austin was hypereloquent. Hugh @ Cupertino was determined to try all of this again. Soon.

A virtual age becomes an actual age once we stop talking about it and do it. Hugh's First Law of the Virtuality? Thus, for me, the virtual age of multinetworked, multimedia composition classes would end for me in just a few hours after the broadcast when I pried open the cork on a bottle of Stag's Leap Chablis the evening of January 24th, 1991, and had a second helping of a dessert Ruth and Dean Whitlow, *Imagine's* director, called "Death by Chocolate."

Works Cited

Bump, Jerome. "Radical Changes in Class Discussion Using Networked Computers. *Computers in the Humanities* 24 (1990): 49–65.

Costanzo, William. V. *The Electronic Text: Learning to Read and Reason with Computers.* Englewood Cliffs: Educational Technology, 1989.

Winograd, Terry, and Fernando Flores. *Understanding Computers and Cognition: A New Foundation for Design.* Norwood: Ablex, 1986.

Turkle, Sherry. *The Second Self: Computers and the Human Spirit.* New York: Simon and Schuster, 1984.

Vallee, Jacques, Robert Johnansen, and Kathleen Spangler. "The Computer Conference: An Altered State of Communication?" In *Intercom: Readings in Organizational Communication,* ed. Stewart Ferguson and Sherry Devereaux Ferguson, eds., Rochelle Park, New Jersey: Hayden Book Company, Inc., 1980: 290–300.

8

Social Epistemic Rhetoric and Chaotic Discourse

Paul Taylor

Texas A & M University

Late in the sixteenth century, a young man named Galileo stood in a church and watched a lamp swinging slowly back and forth. He began to investigate bodies in motion, and legend has it that he started dropping weights from the Leaning Tower of Pisa to see how quickly they would reach the ground. Soon he extended his observations to include the motions of planets and stars, and in 1632 he published the *Dialogue on the Great World Systems* in support of the Copernican theory of celestial motion. The following year, he was brought before the Inquisition and forced to recant his assertion that the earth moves around the sun. After the trial he was placed under house arrest, where he remained until his death in 1642.

Why did Galileo's investigations lead him into such conflict? Certainly not because his theories profoundly altered daily life. For centuries farmers had moved stones out of their plowed fields and dropped them in unused corners; the farmers never noticed or cared whether the large stones fell to earth faster than the small ones. But when Galileo claimed that small things fall as fast as large things, he did much more than overturn an obscure point of Aristotelian reasoning—he challenged the *method* by which truth was determined. Galileo, along with other scientists of the sixteenth and seventeenth centuries, suggested that truths about the physical world could be determined by experimentation rather than faith in the divine authority of the Church. Galileo, in effect, was offering a new way of structuring knowledge, and that new structure did not privilege the prevailing power structure. Conflict was inevitable.

The lesson to be learned is that new theories often reach beyond their original scope and precipitate a larger examination of how we know what we know. With that lesson in mind, I wish to consider a relatively new body of scientific theory and its potential impact on how we structure knowledge through language. The theory is called *chaos theory,* or the study of complex dynamical systems. Chaos theory has emerged over the last three decades as a powerful paradigm for investigating physical phenomena that have been poorly understood through traditional methods of inquiry. Examples of chaotic phenomena include the populations of ecological systems, the fluctuations of the weather, and the shapes of coastlines; to this list I am adding textual interaction—specifically, the dynamic electronic texts that appear in computer-based conferencing. Chaos theory suggests that we should be asking different kinds of questions about these texts—that our traditional notions of authorship, coherence, and style are changing along with our scientific theories and the technology of communication.

In order to explain the relationship between chaos theory and electronic discourse, I will first need to explain what chaos theory is. Next I will consider the similarities between the science of chaos and current theories of social epistemic rhetoric. Finally, I will examine a specific example of electronic conferencing to show how its features respond to an analysis based on chaos theory.

The Science of Chaos

Traditional scientific inquiry has attempted to investigate nature in its purest forms—to strip out as many variables as possible and look at the simplest cause-and-effect relationships that can be identified. It is a science of hierarchy and linearity. But the scientists of chaos have argued that these simplifications tend to hide other structures and relationships. The mathematician Benoit Mandelbrot expresses the problem in geometric terms: "Clouds are not spheres, mountains are not cones, coastlines are not circles, and bark is not smooth, nor does lightning travel in a straight line" (1).

The complexity of natural forms makes even simple questions surprisingly difficult. For example, in 1967 Mandelbrot published an article with the disarming title "How Long is the Coast of Britain?" Following up on the earlier work of the English scientist Lewis F. Richardson, Mandelbrot found that standard reference works revealed substantial discrepancies in the reported lengths of various borders and coastlines. He concluded that the differences arose not because the geographers made physical errors in measurement, but because it is theoretically impossible to measure a coastline's length. Here is why.

Suppose that, in order to measure the length of Great Britain's coastline, you took a measuring stick 1000 meters long and flipped it end-over-end all the way around the coast. As you proceeded, you would inevitably cut across small inlets and peninsulas; consequently, your final answer would be somewhat shorter than the actual length. To remedy the situation, you might try using a measuring stick 100 meters long, or 10 meters, or 1 meter. Each measurement with a shorter stick would result in a longer coastline, but the measurement would still be less than the actual length because the coastline exhibits an irregular shape at even the smallest scale, as illustrated in Figure 8-1. Mandelbrot reasoned that, since measurements with shorter sticks would never converge on a finite length, coastlines are actually infinite in length though they circumscribe a finite area. (Incidentally, you might be wondering why you couldn't simply stretch a long string around the coast for an accurate measurement; the answer is that, unless the string were infinitely thin, it would still involve essentially the same kind of over-simplification as the stick.)

Of course, it is counter-intuitive to declare that two obviously different islands (for example, Great Britain and Australia) have coastlines with the same (infinite) length. But Mandelbrot and the scientists of chaos have created a genuine paradigm shift—they have changed the fundamental questions that are theoretically valid. Instead of worrying about the length of a coastline, the scientists of chaos consider its "fractal dimension" (basically how rough or smooth the contour is). They have brought about this change by challenging the premise that complex physical phenomena can be described in linear, hierarchical terms.

Such mathematical explorations have led to quite practical applications. For example, the meteorologist Edward Lorenz, another pioneer in the science of chaos, began modeling weather patterns on computers in the 1960s. He demonstrated that weather forecasting is inherently impossible for the long term because the weather is determined by the dynamic interaction of innumerable components. This finding has been called the Butterfly Effect after the whimsical (but useful) notion that a butterfly in China could, by the beating of its wings, disturb the air so that thunderstorms in the United States eventually would be affected. Since it is impossible for anyone to know the precise movements of all the butterflies in the world, let alone all of the other factors affecting the weather, prediction becomes impossible. Paradoxically, however, Lorenz has actually assisted weather forecasting by providing a better model of the self-organizing process by which recognizable structures (storms, pressure systems, the passing of the seasons) arise out of chaotic interactions (Gleick 11–31).

Because self-organization depends on dynamic interaction, structures are often most clearly defined in terms of their borders—the border

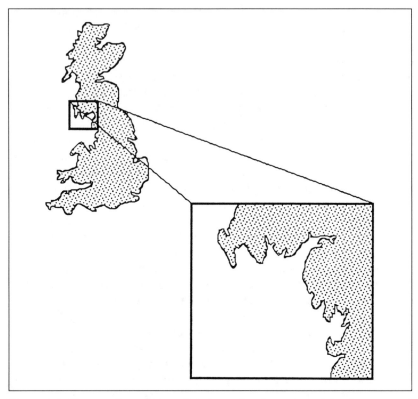

Figure 8-1: The coastline of Great Britain, and a closer view of the shore around Solway Firth. At finer levels of detail, the coastline displays irregular contours not visible at a larger scale.

between land and sea (coastlines), between cold air and warm air (storms), or between adequate and insufficient food supplies in an ecosystem (animal populations). In the following sections I will attempt to show that texts (particularly electronic texts) similarly arise out of dynamic interactions at the borders between speaking individuals.

Social Epistemic Rhetoric

In 1982 Maxine Hairston compared contemporary changes in writing instruction to the "paradigm shifts" that Thomas Kuhn had described in *The Structure of Scientific Revolutions.* Her article "The Winds of Change" outlined the characteristics of current traditional writing programs and described the goals and procedures of the new process-based curriculum. Drawing on Aristotle's emphasis on democratic persuasion, Hairston explained the need for writing programs that help to build a sense of community and thereby prepare students for audiences and purposes beyond those represented by traditional English classes.

This movement toward collaborative process-based learning has been accompanied by a theoretical emphasis on social construction—an epistemology that locates reality in social consensus achieved through language. James Berlin's historical work *Rhetoric and Reality* helps to situate current rhetorical practices in terms of three epistemologies, which he calls objective, subjective, and transactional. The dominant objective rhetoric in this century has been the current traditional model, which emphasizes grammatical correctness and the final written product; the process for achieving the final text is relatively unimportant because language is assumed to correspond to an objective reality. In recent years, objective rhetoric has been enriched by behaviorists such as Robert Zoellner and Lynn and Martin Bloom, who argue for changing empirically verifiable behaviors in students—an approach which involves students in a social process (Berlin 139–45).

Subjective epistemologies, by Berlin's reckoning, have led to the rhetorics of Ken Macrorie, Donald Murray, Peter Elbow, and other expressionists (145–55). Expressive methodology encourages the student writer to enter a dialectic relationship with language in order to gain self-knowledge. The practitioners of subjective discourse range from the intensely individualistic (emphasizing the need to break traditions and confound expectations) to the intersubjective (emphasizing a cooperative effort toward individual selfhood).

The third epistemology, which Berlin labels *transactional,* provides the basis for a rhetoric in which knowledge is *generated* through language, rather than *represented* by language. Kenneth Bruffee is one of the better known implementers of transactional rhetoric, but Berlin also mentions several others who might not be considered social constructionists at first glance. For instance, Berlin includes the tagmemicists Young, Becker, and Pike. Tagmemic theory, though clearly based in cognitive science (and hence subject to categorization as objective and/or subjective), encourages the understanding of different individual perspectives; if a rhetoric emphasizes this multiplicity of viewpoints rather than the distinctiveness of a particular perspective, it stimulates interactive discourse and thus counts as "transactional" or "social epistemic" in Berlin's terminology (155–79).

Berlin's work illustrates that many different rhetorics have existed and continue to exist simultaneously, but transactional rhetoric currently appears to be gaining dominance. The concept of knowledge as a social construct can be a powerful tool for those who wish to change or influence society. However, one of the problematic issues in social construction is the notion of consensus. Consensus, particularly as implemented by Bruffee in his collaborative approach to writing instruction, often emphasizes a final state in which all participants agree—either two (or more) viewpoints compromise dialectically into a third, higher viewpoint, or else everyone is eventually won over to one of the original viewpoints. I wish to suggest, however, that consensus is more like an uneasy truce in which individuals with conflicting interests and values agree to cooperate for a period of time in order to achieve some goal. Their cooperation means that the group actually gets something done, but it does *not* mean that their opposing perspectives disappear. As I hope to show, the science of chaos provides a tool for understanding how individuals can create a communal text that exhibits a coherent consensus while actively incorporating dissenting viewpoints. Before moving on to electronic discourse, however, it will be helpful to examine text-based interaction from a related viewpoint: the work of the literary intertextualists.

In the 1960s Julia Kristeva gave the name "intertextuality" to the field that studies the relationships between texts, and in the 1980s Gerard Genette developed a useful taxonomy for the field. In his book *Palimpsestes: Literature at the Second Degree,* Genette introduces the term *transtextuality* to describe "all which puts [a text] in relation, manifest or hidden, with other texts"(1). Under this broad definition he outlines five kinds of transtextual relationships: intertextuality, paratextuality, metatextuality, hypertextuality, and architextuality. The first of these, intertextuality, is the least abstract of the five; Genette applies it only to the specific cases of citation, plagiarism, and allusion. The second term, paratextuality, refers to the things that accompany a text: title, preface, epigraphs, marginal notes, illustrations, book jackets, and other paraphernalia supplied by the author, publisher, or various readers. The third area, metatextuality, encompasses commentary and criticism, including criticism that does not actually cite the text upon which it is based. The fourth transtextual relationship, hypertextuality, is Genette's primary concern; he defines it provisionally as "every relationship uniting a text B (that I will call *hypertext*) to an anterior text A (that I will call, of course, *hypotext*) on which it is grafted in a manner which is not that of a commentary" (5). The fifth term, architextuality, is the most global and abstract in the classification; this area includes studies of textual archetypes or genre.

Two problematic issues are evident even in a relatively straightforward description of Genette's taxonomy: the relationship between individuals and language, and the definition of a "text." The theory of transtextuality emphasizes texts, not people. In fact, Kristeva specifically sought to unseat "the bourgeois idea of an autonomous and intentional subject"—to replace intersubjectivity with intertextuality (Pfister 12). And yet Genette's explanations certainly seem to suggest an individual intentionality: citation and plagarism, for example, imply specific authorial purposes in the production of texts and the linking of ideas.

In its most extreme form, intertextuality asserts that there is only one text—the intertext. "There is no first or last discourse" (Mikhail Bakhtin, qtd. in Todorov 110). As Manfred Pfister points out, however, this statement is a rather obvious one with limited meaning. Every text has connections of some kind to other texts; each unique text (however one chooses to define the word) represents, in some sense, the intersection of all the previous texts that a writer has experienced. But there seems to be little we can say about the universal intertext until we consider it in more manageable quantities—finite texts produced by individuals and analyzed in terms of specific manifestations of transtextuality, such as the categories outlined by Genette.

Both Genette and Kristeva have based much of their work on the writings of the Russian language theorist Mikhail Bakhtin. In a passage that echoes my own concern for borders and dynamic interaction, Bakhtin explains how individual writers appropriate the language of other texts in producing their own specific utterances:

> Language, for the individual consciousness, lies on the borderline between oneself and the other. The word in language is half someone else's. It becomes "one's own" only when the speaker populates it with his own intention, his own accent, when he appropriates the word, adapting it to his own semantic and expressive intention. Prior to this moment of appropriation, the word does not exist in a neutral and impersonal language (it is not, after all, out of a dictionary that the speaker gets his words!), but rather it exists in other people's mouths, in other people's contexts, serving other people's intentions: it is from there that one must take the word, and make it one's own. (293–94)

As noted above, Bakhtin does argue against the notion of discrete, self-sufficient texts, but this passage makes clear that intertextuality is a dynamic process with intentional speakers, not an unlimited "play" of language. Speakers take the words that are rich in others' contexts and proceed to make them their own. In appropriating the language of others, a speaker becomes a participant in a discourse community; the speaker's meaning arises out of interaction with the other members of the community.

This multiplicity of voices is a central component of Bakhtin's literary theory. He reacts against traditional poetic genres because those forms value a movement toward isolation and stasis: all language within a lyric poem, for instance, is tightly crafted to assert one vision—that of the speaker. In contrast, Bakhtin argues that the novel (the most recent literary genre to evolve) reflects the dynamism of living language because it incorporates many voices—the voices of the diverse characters who populate the novel and reflect the culture within which the work was written: "The novel must represent all the social and ideological voices of its era, that is, all the era's languages that have any claim to being significant; the novel must be a microcosm of heteroglossia" (411). He uses the term *heteroglossia* (literally, different tongues or languages) to emphasize the profusion of voices within a single text. The word is useful because, like social epistemic rhetoric, it focuses on meaning as the product of interpersonal discourse—except that *heteroglossia* avoids the emphasis on (narrowly defined) consensus and explicitly celebrates diversity. It is this term, I believe, which most accurately describes the kind of discourse that has evolved in electronic conferences.

Electronic Conferencing

What is electronic conferencing, and where did it come from? In its broadest sense, electronic conferencing refers to any computer-based system that allows people to send messages to each other. Included in this definition are both electronic mail and "real-time" discussion software. Electronic mail enables a user to compose a message and send it to a particular individual or group; the recipient will receive and read the message the next time she checks her "in-basket" in the mail system. "Real-time" conferencing, on the other hand, requires the simultaneous participation of several members of a group; it is more like a text-based conversation than a postal service. Since my particular interest is this second form of interaction, I will be using the term *electronic conferencing* to refer only to real-time interaction.

The earliest computer conferencing systems appeared in the 1960s for strictly pragmatic reasons. Murray Turoff, a physicist with the New Jersey Institute of Technology, is credited with designing the first one for the President's Office of Emergency Preparedness. It enabled government officials to confer in times of crisis without necessarily being in the same place at the same time—all they needed was access to a mainframe computer terminal that could tie in to the conferencing system (McKendree 15). Soon scientists scattered across the world began to use computers to send messages to each other in order to keep up with the most recent developments in their respective fields; the electronic messages were faster and less expensive than other means of sharing information (letters, telephone calls, formal papers, or presentations), and they provided a public, written record of current research. Some of the conferences actually became alternatives to traditional professional meetings: they lasted for a specified period of time (usually several months) and addressed an announced range of topics (Bamford and Savin 13).

With the introduction of personal computers and local area networks in the 1980s, educators began to consider possible classroom applications for electronic conferencing. At Gallaudet University, Trent Batson used a communications package called CB (developed through the ENFI [Electronic Networks for Interaction] project) to improve the writing skills of deaf students, and Diane Langston of Carnegie-Mellon worked with Batson to extend the use of the program to hearing students in traditional writing courses. In 1987 Fred Kemp (then a graduate student at the University of Texas) attended presentations by Batson and Langston and subsequently directed the development of a similar conferencing program called InterChange; the following descriptions and analyses are based on this particular program.

InterChange allows students to hold a conversation that is written rather than spoken. Each student sits at a separate work station. The student's computer screen displays both a public "window" (an area in which all the messages appear as they are sent) and a smaller personal window (where the student can compose messages before sending them). Since messages often arrive faster than students can read them, the program allows the students to scroll through the public window in the same way that they can scroll through a single document in a word processor. After the discussion is over, the text of the discussion is saved in a simple text file that can be printed out or viewed electronically.

The use of conferencing software in the classroom has been accompanied by a pedagogical shift toward student-based, active learning. Instead of listening to a lecture about a subject, students are actively engaged in exploring a topic. Electronic conferencing empowers students in several ways that have been impractical or impossible without computers—most notably by increasing the level of participation, by improving individual facility with language, and by promoting an understanding of discourse communities. The most obvious of these is the significant increase in participation. Spoken conversation allows only one speaker at a time, but written discussion allows every student to contribute ideas; the electronic medium "levels out" many of the differences between dominant, outspoken students and quiet, reticent ones (Bump 55).

A second benefit to students is the development of facility with written language (the classical concept of *facilitas*). Participants in computer-based forums write much more than they are accustomed to, and this low-pressure practice makes the students more confident in their ability to communicate effectively through writing (Bump 56).

A third empowerment of the students takes place as they learn that they can create and participate in different discourse communities. They determine the rules by which their conversation will proceed even as they pursue academic goals supplied by the instructor. They see a living demonstration that written arguments that are appropriate and effective for some readers are not appropriate and effective for others. It should be noted, however, that broad participation does not automatically result in a democratic process leading to consensus. Internal power structures can still develop along traditional lines; for example, participants tend to give more attention to messages sent by the teacher and by students with stronger verbal skills. Still, an important transformation has occurred—everyone participates, and everyone has the opportunity to witness and review *how* the power structures develop.

Transcripts of electronic conferences are valuable for students who want to look over the discussion later, but they are also quite valuable resources for researchers. Analysis of electronic conferencing transcripts shows that the text as a whole has a coherent structure—but the structure is not the hierarchical organization one might expect in a traditional written document. Using M.A.K. Halliday's functional grammar, I have examined a number of electronic conferences and found that the cohesive ties are much stronger for the text taken as a whole than they are for any individual's comments. The text thus displays a coherence that is not the result of hierarchical planning or explicit collaborative decisions. The coherence, in fact, rises spontaneously as the result of dynamic interaction among the individual participants (a feature of chaotic phenomena). And while this coherence does represent a kind of consensus, the consensus incorporates a multiplicity of independent voices rather than constructing a final, authoritative position. The conferences thus appear to represent an example of Bakhtin's heteroglossia.

Previous studies of electronic conferencing have been dominated by researchers in the social sciences. Information scientists and social psychologists have concentrated on the quantifiable features of the messages and participants: the number and length of messages, the frequency of participation by different users, the amount of time necessary for groups to arrive at decisions. These studies have generally concluded that computer communication exhibits a smaller total quantity of text than oral discussion, requires more time for groups to arrive at a consensus, and encourages greater equality among the participants (Hiltz, Johnson-Lenz, Kiesler). However, many of the researchers state explicitly that interdisciplinary cooperation is necessary to understand adequately the processes involved in computer-mediated discourse. The following analysis, although continuing to deal with quantifiable features, concentrates on how the participants work together to construct meaning.

In *Spoken and Written Language*, Halliday argues that written language tends to treat phenomena as products, while spoken language shows them as processes. Thus, written language is typically more densely packed with lexically significant nouns, and spoken language is more complex in the clausal structures that relate different processes. This difference between written and spoken language has often challenged students who are learning to participate in academic discourse; the spoken language they know best does not use exactly the same rules as the written language expected of them in school. Halliday does say, however, that computer technology appears to be reducing the differences between written and spoken language: the simple fact that computer displays are not static (like the printed page) reinforces the notion of reading as a process:

> So the period of our semiotic history which began with the invention of printing in the Tang dynasty in China, and reached Europe just in time for the Renaissance, a period in which speech and writing were pushed very far apart by the application of technology to writing, may now be coming to an end. At least one of the factors that has led to the difference between spoken and written language, the effect of the medium on the message (to hark back to McLuhan's formulation in the 1960s), may now be disappearing; not that the medium will cease to have an effect, but that in both cases—both speech and writing—the nature of the medium itself has begun to change ("Spoken Language" 81-82).

I believe that the transcripts of computer-mediated conversation—and not just the physical manifestation of the discourse—show that language is in the process of changing. To illustrate these changes, I have examined messages sent by students using InterChange at the University of Texas. In terms of lexical density, clausal complexity, thematic emphasis, and the representation of processes, the messages show an interesting mixture of spoken and written features, particularly when compared with relevant passages from written papers.

Karen, one of the students in a computer-assisted course, wrote a paper based on Roger Schank's book *The Cognitive Computer*. In the process of writing the paper, she discussed her ideas with other students using InterChange. An analysis of lexical density reveals that Karen was relatively consistent across both media in the ratio of lexically significant words to purely grammatical terms (pronouns, conjunctions, prepositions): the focal passage from InterChange shows a density of 46 percent, while the passage from her paper has a density of 53 percent. The difference is probably too slight to be significant (especially since the ratio of lexical items to clauses is almost the same for both passages), though what difference there is supports the expected conclusion that the InterChange message is more like oral discourse, and the paper is more like written discourse.

In terms of clausal complexity, however, Karen's two passages show fairly substantial differences. As this sentence demonstrates, the computer message reflects the intricacy of spoken speech:

> If there were a certain "script" in a program to explain to the kids
>   that when you walk into the store
>   you get a cart, walk up and down the aisles, make selec-
>   tions, pay for your food, etc.,
>   the kids could learn what to expect while grocery shopping.

The clauses descend through several hypotactic relationships before the final clause jumps back up to a relationship with the first clause. The clauses throughout this message are connected primarily through subordination and conjunction. In contrast, the sentences in the paper are less involved; when they do include multiple clauses, they often use the clauses as nominal structures:

> These programs could even incorporate a section
>   which would tell the child about why
>   certain situations are unavoidable
>   and what exactly
>   their purposes are.

This particular sentence is not necessarily less complex than the one above (though most of the others are), but the clausal relationships are different. The clauses "certain situations are unavoidable" and "their purposes are" act as static representations of processes: They stand as the "facts" that would be told to the child. They could, of course be further nominalized; for instance, "why certain situations are unavoidable" could become "the impossibility of avoiding certain situations." But they are already significantly removed from the active representation of process seen in the InterChange message.

In addition to the clausal differences between the message and the paper, the thematic emphasis differs from one medium to the other. Sentences in the messages frequently thematize the actual participants in the dialogue—either the writer or the reader, or sometimes both. Many of the sentences represent mental processes of the writer: "I think" or "I'm not sure." Others directly address the reader and his own concerns: "Peter, your paper sounds really interesting."

The thematization of the participants reflects nothing so much as an acute awareness that the messages are written to communicate to living, responding readers. This becomes humorously apparent near the beginning of an InterChange session when Karen finds that she is talking to herself. She sends the message, "Is anybody else in this conference?"—here making another person's mere existence the thematic portion of the message. When she follows that question with another short message ("I guess not, so I'll see if I can't join a different conference!"), Karen is also tacitly acknowledging another audience. There is no immediate reason to send this message when no one is listening, but she realizes that others may join the conference later. Students who stumble on her messages will know what happened to her. And in addition, the teacher—this is, after all, a classroom exercise—will be able to see that Karen has done her academic duty even though she was alone.

In order to expand the examination of the texts beyond the short passages above, I have written a computer program to analyze much longer texts using techniques suggested by Halliday's functional grammar. The computer-based analysis is not as discerning as a human reading of the passages because the computer has not been programmed to understand language; it simply sorts the words in the texts by comparing them to different wordlists. However, what this approach lacks in delicacy, it makes up in numbers: I have used the program to analyze 8 complete InterChange sessions (totaling approximately 34,000 words) and 88 student papers (totaling approximately 72,000 words). In addition to this "bulk processing" approach, I also examined separately the work of three different students in order to make more specific distinctions between a writer's participation in InterChange as opposed to more formal written work. The comparison is particularly significant because this close analysis covered an InterChange session and a paper assignment on the same topic.

The primary calculations made by the computer program focus on Halliday's distinction between lexical and grammatical terms. I created a database of 181 grammatical terms in five categories: conjunctions, determiners, prepositions, pronouns, and existential/auxiliary verbs. The program checked each word in the texts, classified it as either grammatical or lexical, and recorded its specific category. Then the program figured simple lexical density—the total number of lexical words divided by the total number of words in the text. The analysis showed a small but consistent difference: The students' papers exhibited a higher lexical density (characteristic of written language, according to Halliday) than the InterChange sessions.

	Karen	Andrew	Sharon	Overall
InterChange messages:	49.5%	55.3%	48.3%	52.4%
Papers:	53.3%	57.8%	52.8%	54.5%

The difference in lexical density is primarily due to significant changes in the use of pronouns. The other four categories of grammatical terms remained relatively stable between InterChange messages and written papers, but the InterChange messages contained many more pronouns than did the students' papers:

	Pron.	Conj.	Determ.	Prep.	Verbs
InterChange messages:	13.9%	7.0%	10.9%	11.2%	7.6%
Papers:	8.8%	7.7%	11.9%	12.5%	6.8%

This large shift in the use of pronouns apparently results from a change in tenor: if students believe that their papers have an audience at all, they usually limit that audience to the teacher, but in InterChange they are constantly aware of immediate reader reactions to their writing. They communicate directly with each other, and they use pronouns freely to refer to themselves and their classmates.

In addition to lexical density and grammatical categories, the program also quantified lexical cohesion—albeit in very broad terms. Halliday observes that texts cohere through simple repetition of words, through the use of synonyms, and through collocation (the tendency of related words to co-occur). Since the computer is not programmed to understand the semantic values of words, I considered only the number of times that specific words are repeated in a text. Mere repetition is not a highly sophisticated concept, but it is one way in which writers unify their texts.

Halliday does not quantify cohesion, so I am introducing the term *cohesive density* to refer to the amount of repetition in a text. I have figured cohesive density in two ways. The first, which we may call "general cohesive density," is simply the total number of words divided by the number of unique words in a text; this gives the average number of times each word is used. General cohesive density does not distinguish between lexical and grammatical terms. Since lexical words may be a better guide to the subject of a text, I have also computed "lexical cohesive density." Lexical cohesive density is the average repetition of lexical words (the total number of lexical words divided by the number of unique lexical words).

	Karen	Andrew	Sharon	Overall
General Cohesive Density				
InterChange messages:	2.2	1.7	2.1	4.5
Papers:	2.8	2.3	3.0	4.0
Lexical Cohesive Density				
InterChange messages:	1.5	1.2	1.5	2.3
Papers:	1.9	1.5	2.0	2.1

The figures on this chart represent the average number of times each word appears in the text; a higher number means that more words have been repeated. This is the only analysis where the results obtained from the individual students' writing are different from the overall results—but there is a good reason for the seeming discrepancy.

In each individual case, for both "general" cohesion and "lexical" cohesion, the student's formal paper contains more repetition of words than the corresponding InterChange messages. When writing papers, therefore, the students unify their work to a greater extent by repeating words. When all the InterChange messages and all the papers are considered as a whole, however, the InterChange sessions show a higher level of repetition. The reason? Each student paper is a discrete work. It has its own internal coherence; there is no reason it should reflect the vocabulary of any other paper in the class. An InterChange conference, on the other hand, is a communal activity—the participants share common topics and common goals. Their sense of a shared task shows up when they repeat words that others have used.

And what broader lessons can we learn from the study of Inter-Change? I would like to suggest that computer conferencing is evolving into a new genre, a new form of communication that has not been possible before now. Carolyn Miller gives three criteria for identifying a genre in rhetorical terms (163–64). First, the associated texts must exhibit similarity in form. Although computer-based messages are not yet exceptionally uniform, they do display several common features: They regularly appear in a single medium (computers), the individual messages are usually relatively short, and, most importantly, they are unusual in their incorporation of grammatical features from both written and spoken discourse. Second, Miller states that the genre must be based on all the rhetorical elements in recurring situations. Do computer conferences arise from a genuine exigence relative to a specific audience? Only if we begin to narrow the terms somewhat—if we begin to see computer conferencing not as a single genre, but as a collection of related genres. For instance, scientific conferences conducted through computers satisfy the need of the individual scientist to keep abreast of recent developments while maintaining personal status within the scientific community; a separate audience and purpose are served by conferences held in writing classrooms. Miller's final criterion is that a genre must be clearly pragmatic as a form of social action. This requirement is the most interesting for computers because electronic discourse is a decidedly social phenomenon; it cannot succeed or even exist without the explicit decision of individuals to pursue a common goal.

But why would a new genre happen to come along just now? Because our current scientific and rhetorical theories are reshaping our knowledge structures. Just as Galileo's musings on a swinging lantern led to new ways of thinking about (and writing about) the physical world, so is our modern world being changed by simple questions like "How long is the coast of Britain?" We are beginning to value texts that are produced communally—texts like the transcripts of electronic conferences, texts which are structurally self-organizing much like thunderstorms or Jupiter's Great Red Spot.

Am I arguing that non-linear, chaotic texts are inherently better than traditionally structured and authored texts? No. I am *not* saying that chaos theory somehow proves the superiority of non-linear, non-hierarchical knowledge structures. I *am* saying that the world is changing, with or without us. Computers are transforming the nature of texts, and some forms (such as the expository essay) may not figure prominently in computer-based discourse of the (near) future. Certainly, rhetoricians should use what we have learned to help shape the future. But we must also be prepared to reevaluate our old assumptions about how texts communicate. Otherwise, we will simply become the old guard that, according to Thomas Kuhn, will literally have to die off while the winds of change sweep past us.

Works Cited

Bakhtin, Mikhail M. "Discourse in the Novel." *The Dialogic Imagination.* Ed. Michael Holquist. Trans. Caryl Emerson and Michael Holquist. Austin: U of Texas P, 1981.

Bamford, Harold E., and William Savin. "Electronic Information Exchange: The National Science Foundation's Developing Role." *Bulletin of the American Society for Information Science* 4.5 (1978): 12-13.

Batson, Trent. The ENFI Project: A Networked Classroom Approach to Writing Instruction. *Academic Computing,* 2(5)(1988), 32 + .

Batson, Trent, and Joy Kreeft Peyton. ENFI Project Report 1985-1986. November 1986. Unpublished manuscript available from the ENFI Project, HMB 120, Gallaudet University, 800 Florida Ave. NE, Washington, DC 20002.

Berlin, James A. *Rhetoric and Reality: Writing Instruction in American Colleges, 1900-1985.* Carbondale: Southern Illinois UP, 1987.

Bloom, Lynn Z., and Martin Bloom. "The Teaching and Learning of Argumentative Writing." *College English* 29 (1967): 128-35.

Bruffee, Kenneth A. "Collaborative Learning and 'The Conversation of Mankind.'" *College English* 46 (1984): 635-52.

———. "Liberal Education, Scholarly Community, and the Authority of Knowledge." *Interpreting the Humanities.* Princeton: Woodrow Wilson Foundation, 1985. Rpt. in *Liberal Education* 71 (1985): 231-39.

———. "Social Construction, Language, and the Authority of Knowledge: A Bibliographical Essay." *College English* 48 (1986): 773-90.

Bump, Jerome. "Radical Changes in Class Discussion Using Networked Computers." *Computers and the Humanities* 24 (1990): 49-65.

Elbow, Peter. *Writing Without Teachers.* New York: Oxford UP, 1973.

Genette, Gerard. *Palimpsestes: Literature at the Second Degree.* Paris: Editions du Seuil, 1982. Chapters I–VII, unpublished translation by James Wimsatt.

Gleick, James. *Chaos: Making a New Science.* New York: Viking, 1987.

Hairston, Maxine. "The Winds of Change: Thomas Kuhn and the Revolution in the Teaching of Writing." CCC 33 (1982): 76–82.

Halliday, M. A. K. *An Introduction to Functional Grammar.* Baltimore: Edward Arnold, 1985.

————. *Spoken and Written Language.* Language and Learning 5. Geelong, Austral.: Deakin UP, 1985

Hiltz, Starr Roxanne. "Annotated Bibliography: Publications on Computer-mediated Communication and Education." *Teaching in a Virtual Classroom: Volume 2 of Final Evaluation Report, A Virtual Classroom on EIES.* New Jersey: New Jersey Institute of Technology, 1988.

Kristeva, Julia. "The System and the Speaking Subject." *The Kristeva Reader.* Ed. Toril Moi. New York: Columbia UP, 1986.

————. "Word, Dialogue, and Novel." *The Kristeva Reader.* Ed. Toril Moi. New York: Columbia UP, 1986.

Kuhn, Thomas S. *The Structure of Scientific Revolutions.* 2nd ed. Chicago: U of Chicago P, 1970.

Langston, Diane M. "Invention Aids for Computer-Based Writing: Expanding the Horizons through Collaborative Invention." Conference on College Composition and Communication. Atlanta, GA, March 19–21 1987. ERIC ED 280 055.

Macrorie, Ken. *Telling Writing.* 3rd ed. Hasbrouck Heights: Hayden, 1980.

Mandelbrot, Benoit B. *The Fractal Geometry of Nature.* New York: W. H. Freeman, 1983.

McKendree, John D. "Project and Crisis Management Applications of Computerized Conferencing." *Bulletin of the American Society for Information Science* 4.5 (1978): 13–15.

Miller, Carolyn R. "Genre as Social Action." Quarterly Journal of Speech 70 (1984): 151–67.

Murray, Donald. "The Interior View: One Writer's Philosophy of Composition." *College Composition and Communication* 21 (1970): 21–26.

Pfister, Manfred. "Concepts of Intertextuality." *Intertextualitat: Formen, Funktionen, anglistische Fallstudien [Intertextuality: Forms, Functions, Studies of English Examples].* Eds. Ulrich Broich and Manfred Pfister, with the collaboration of Bernd Schulte-Middelich. Tubingen: Max Niemeyer, 1985. Unpublished translation by James Wimsatt.

Schank, Roger C. *The Cognitive Computer: On Language, Learning, and Artificial Intelligence.* Reading: Addison-Wesley, 1984.

Todorov, Tzvetan. *Mikhail Bakhtin: The Dialogical Principle.* Trans. Wlad Godzich. Minneapolis: U of Minnesota P, 1984.

Young, Richard E., and Alton L. Becker. "Toward a Modern Theory of Rhetoric." *Contemporary Rhetoric: A Conceptual Background with Readings.* Ed. W. Ross Winterowd. New York: Harcourt, 1975.

Zoellner, Robert. "Behavioral Objectives for English." *College English* 33 (1972): 418–32.

———. "Talk-Write: A Behavioral Pedagogy for Composition." *College English* 30 (1969): 267–320.

Part III

Navigating Virtual Waters:
Where Do We Go
From Here?

Introduction

In asking what computers can do, we are drawn into asking
what people can do with them, and in the end into addressing
the fundamental question of what it means to be human. (7)
                              Terry Winograd and Fernando Flores

One of the strongest themes running through the rhetoric of virtual age literacy is that of overcoming long established obstacles to teaching and research. The contributors to this volume speak to that dynamic again and again. Charles Moran argues for a virtual writing class that crosses the boundaries of time and space; Janet Eldred and Ron Fortune urge us to transcend the constraints of our metaphorical thinking; William Wright, with his work on BreadNet, and Hugh Burns, with his telecommunications project, pull down barriers between teachers and students, video and text, high school, community college, and university; Cindy Selfe, Gail Hawisher, Paul Taylor, and Elizabeth Sommers all call for an end to disciplinary barriers in training, research, and politics. Yet, as we have seen at the end of the last decade, when national barriers have ceased to exist in places like East Germany, Poland, and Romania, bold initiatives are often followed by confusion, mistakes, and the need for hard thinking and clear-sightedness.

A significant part of the problem we face as a profession attempting to account for dramatically different media, genres, and conventions for written discourse is the speed and breadth of the change and the degree of its impact. In just ten years, we have gone from expensive, underpowered personal computers (Remember the days of 64K memory?) to less expensive, high-powered machines that provide desktop publishing, access to remote databases, e-mail connections to other writers and researchers, on-line dictionaries, handbooks, and editing programs, and most recently, the use of multimedia for teaching and presentations. The use of such systems in both school and business settings is pervasive. Compared to the adoption of other communication technologies and the time it took for their impact to be felt, writing and the printing press for example, the pace at which modern industrial culture is appropriating the microcomputer is breathtaking.

We have entered new uncharted waters and navigation can be difficult and dangerous, as we have already seen in some uses of technology. Software that replicates old drill and practice workbooks (Thiesmeyer), style checkers every bit as eccentric as the stereotypical English teacher (Collins), and prepackaged instruction intended to remove the teacher as a classroom presence (Apple)—all suggest some of the mistakes of the past decade. Yet the newer electronic software may be no better. There now exists network software that allows a teacher or network manager to secretly examine the onscreen text of students connected to the network, to take over the screens, and to broadcast the onscreen text to everyone else on the network. Although we can think of pedagogically effective uses for such technology, we can also see the dangers inherent in software that puts some, even if conscientious writing teachers, in control over others (Hawisher and Selfe). We should also note that electronic mail in some work settings can actually diminish the quality of communication and decision-making and may also result in self-absorbed, ill-conceived, and unclear messages that the senders might never consider sending as print memos (Sproull and Kiesler). Neither we nor our students are exempt from this sort of "messaging" and electronic writing in the educational settings we inhabit. Many writing teachers would also argue that computers have made their professional lives worse as they have become saddled with lab and computer repair responsibilities, and with the added duties of monitoring facilities and training new faculty (Hawisher). As teachers and researchers, then, we must cast a critical eye on the careless and unthinking use of computer technology. Regardless of the potential benefits that computer technology may offer us, we are not immune from misapplying it to both our teaching and our research.

Our best tools for helping us remain vigilant are, in fact, our research and our practice. We can, after all, conduct the kind of research that suggests sound pedagogy for our writing classes. In the third and final section of this volume, contributors point to concrete ways in which we might come to a better understanding of the virtual age. In Chapter 9, Marcia Curtis and Elizabeth Klem criticize the "technocentrism" that has characterized much of the research in computers and composition and that fails to account for the larger socio-political phenomenon that is the computer-based classroom. They argue for more ethnographic research and urge a more complete vision for the profession that is both inherently democratic and skeptical. In Chapter 10, Christine Neuwirth and David Kaufer move us away from the now irrelevant question, "Should we use computers?" to the vital question, "What should the computers we use look like?". To help answer that question they outline a research methodology, a mode of inquiry that unites the strengths of cognitive science with the potential of software design as a research tool in composition studies. In so doing, Neuwirth and Kaufer describe a way for us to help guide the direction of the software market in the creation of better computer tools for writing instruction. In Chapter 11, Paul LeBlanc looks at the potential impact of a relatively new technology, hypermedia authoring software. He argues that the new authoring programs, which allow non-programmers to create complex hypermedia software, can revive faculty-based software development in composition studies and be a powerful tool for helping writing teachers and their students enter the virtual age. In Chapter 12, our final chapter, Richard Selfe offers the newcomer a useful glossary of terms for virtual age technology. With ten years of practice with the computer terminology of word processing and computer-assisted instruction now behind us, we look to Selfe's glossary for the essential terms and concepts of the next ten years.

Taken as a whole, the four chapters, like those before them, argue for the breaking down of barriers and the building of bridges. We see these perspectives in the scope of ethnographic study and its ability to account for literacy within a wider social context. We see it in the bringing together of cognitive research methodologies and software design, and the building of a closer link between research and the marketplace. The technology barrier between writing teachers and software designers begins to weaken with the introduction of hypermedia authoring programs and the resultant hypermedia software that teachers can create. Implicit in this section, then, is an answer to the question "Where do we go from here?". The firm answer is forward, as teachers and researchers, equipped with effective methodologies and tools, navigating the virtual waters of the future.

Works Cited

Apple, Michael W. "Teaching and Technology: The Hidden Effects of Computers on Teachers and Students." *Crisis in Teaching: Perspectives on Current Reforms.* Eds. Lois Weis et al. Albany: SUNY Press, 1989.

Collins, James L. "Computerized Text Analysis and the Teaching of Writing." *Critical Perspectives on Computers and Composition Instruction.* Eds. Gail E. Hawisher and Cynthia L. Selfe. New York: Teachers College Press, 1989.

Hawisher, Gail E. "Reading and Writing Connections: Composition Theory and Word Processing." *Computers and Writing: Theory, Research, Practice.* Eds. Deborah Holdstein and Cynthia L. Selfe. New York: MLA, 1990. 71-83.

Hawisher, Gail E., and Cynthia L. Selfe. "The Rhetoric of Technology and the Electronic Writing Class." 42: (February 1991): 55-65.

Sproull, Lee, and Sara Kiesler. "Reducing Social Context Cues: Electronic Mail in Organizational Communication." *Management Science* 32 (November 1986): 1492–1512.

Thiesmeyer, John. "Should We Do What We Can?" *Critical Perspectives on Computers and Composition Instruction.* Eds. Gail E. Hawisher and Cynthia L. Selfe. New York: Teachers College Press, 1989. (75–94.)

Winograd, Terry, and Fernando Flores. *Understanding Computers and Cognition: A New Foundation for Design.* New York: Addison-Wesley, 1987.

9

The Virtual Context:
Ethnography in the Computer-Equipped Writing Classroom

Marcia Curtis and Elizabeth Klem
University of Massachusetts at Amherst

More than any other methodologies, current critical and feminist ethnographic practices, as Anne Herrington writes, "stress documenting one's own values, reflecting on how they shape the research," and thus locate the research itself, in Sandra Harding's words, "in the same critical plane as the overt subject matter" (quoted in Herrington). From this we understand that who we are shapes our view of others' research and the outlook for future research which we will sketch here, too. We therefore begin our examination of ethnography in the computer-equipped writing classroom by identifying ourselves for you, at least insofar as the characteristics we identify affect our project.

We are two women—one, a graduate student in her early thirties; the other, a non-faculty staff member, forty-something—who, having come out of backgrounds in post-structuralist literary criticism, now identify themselves first as teachers of composition, more specifically of basic writing, and secondarily as writer-researchers. We both teach and conduct our research in our writing program's networked classroom. The research questions we ask and the means by which we choose to answer them have been informed by ethnographic methodologies as well as by our personal histories as teachers and students.

By each of these identifying factors—that we are women, that we teach first and secondarily conduct research, that our teaching takes place in a computer-equipped writing classroom, that the research is not "hard" or quantifiable—we see ourselves as, in the current parlance, "marginalized," in relation to our institution and the larger "Academy." Lisa Gerrard, speaking for and to "compositionists" and "computerists," recently summarized our situation well:

> As instructors of composition, we occupy the bottom of the academic hierarchy, and as compositionists whose main interest is pedagogy (as opposed to theory and research), we occupy the bottom of the composition hierarchy as well. Thus as teachers who devote their energies to computer-based learning materials, we may be triply stigmatized: as computerphiles, as teachers, and as compositionists. (9)

In relation to many of our colleagues, on the other hand, especially those teaching in secondary school or two-year college settings, we must admit our own privilege: ours is a large, research university; though each of us has other professional responsibilities—one, her studies; the other, her administrative duties as assistant Writing Program director—we teach just one course a semester and are given personal encouragement, if not institutional reward, for writing and research; the networked classroom in which we do teach, set aside for just a fraction of the University's freshman composition sections and their teachers, is generously appointed and equipped with work stations enough for all of our twenty students; finally, of our program's twenty computer-composition teachers—most of them graduate student instructors—we are two of the three-person network management team with the knowledge and "rights" to configure the computer system, the "virtual environment," within which we all work.

Like most people's, then, our own positions within our professional authority structures are complex, being in some ways "marginalized" and in others privileged. But it seems to us that our association with computers in large part embodies, perhaps exacerbates, the complexity, even the conflict, of our positions: privileging us in the eyes of some, yet for others establishing us more squarely in marginal "tech" and "service" fields. We believe that attention to our own acute self-consciousness, our awareness of our shifting place within the total, as well as the particular instructional setting is of value; we also appreciate the ability of ethnographic methods to reveal the complex relationships we all constantly negotiate.

Hence the opening focus on our own situations. We will return again and again throughout this chapter to other questions of positioning, to questions regarding the teacher's and the teacher-researcher's place in and, just as often, absence from past computer-and-composition studies; we will urge, again and again, a new reflexive stance, repositioning teacher and researcher alike within the scope of investigation, and teacher, student, and technology together within the larger social situation that is ethnography's province.

What Is Ethnography's Place in the Current Research Field?

Contemporary theories and pedagogies situate writing in a social context: current interests in the writer-audience relationship, "discourse communities," and the social construction of discourse, all bespeak an understanding, by teachers and theorists alike, of our subject as socio-political in nature. Yet despite this fact, and despite an almost pervasive acknowledgement of the potential benefits of research focused, not on "texts" exclusively, but on the "contexts" in which writers produce them, relatively little ethnographic—that is, true contextual research—has appeared, in composition studies generally and computerbased-composition studies especially (Durst; Hawisher). Russell Durst notes that in the five years between 1984 and 1989, just 100 studies of writing contexts appeared in *Research in the Teaching of English* bibliographies, out of nearly 1,000 studies surveyed. Of these 100 ethnographic projects, Durst does not cite any devoted to computer-assisted writing or instruction. However, in her survey of research related specifically to computers and covering approximately the same time period, Gail Hawisher does: four. Of these four, two are published pieces and therefore readily available at this time (Dickinson; Herrmann); two are dissertations (Curtiss; Reid). We should add that, while just four of the studies Hawisher surveyed can be categorized as ethnographies, a number of other qualitative studies classified as "case studies" have appeared, and most of these do explore, according to Hawisher, "how word processing in combination with a process-oriented teaching methodology" affects composing (47).

We nevertheless must agree with Hawisher's broader observation that, in fact, surprisingly few studies—qualitative or quantitative—have investigated ways in which computer use affects or is affected by the wider instructional environment (Hawisher 45). Durst similarly reports that of the 48 computer focused studies categorized as "writing instruction studies," most still stop short of delineating just "how a specific teaching approach might promote" growth in writing (396). Our own readings have found a corresponding absence of *teachers* and actual *teaching* from the bulk of computer research, even from examinations of the computer's relationship to teaching methodology; the focus, rather, seems inevitably to shift to the presence of the machines. We fear that this shift denotes a somewhat odd substitution of computer for teacher as locus of influence, instruction and motivation among student writers, a phenomenon which

Hawisher, following Seymour Papert, calls "technocentrism" and suggests is fostered by the formulation of such questions as "What is *the* effect of *the* computer on cognitive development?" or "What is *the* effect of the computer on *the* composing process?" (Hawisher 45).

Centralizing the technology carries a high price for our field, one which can be seen in the past research on computers and composition. We have all felt the frustration caused as research claims have wavered between heady expectation and subsequent disenchantment. Let us look for a moment at the expectations we have, as a community, shared. In questioning his own motivations for introducing computers into the composition classroom, Charles Moran reviews them thus:

> Computers will, we think, give students authority and control over texts (Elder, Bowen, Schwartz, & Goswami, 1989, p. 7); computers will encourage student writers to take risks (Schwartz, 1984, p. 245); computers will give new authority to voices now marginalized (Selfe, 1988); and the presence of computers in our classes will exert pressure on us to make our writing classes more student-centered, more writer-centered (Sudol, 1985; Stine, 1989, p. 30). Recently, we have heard that local area networks (LANs) will further decenter our writing classes, permitting us, or even causing us, to further empower our student writers (Batson, 1989). (Moran 61)

Against each of these happy expectations, we could easily set a sadder discovery: that students do not make more substantial revisions on computers; that hegemonies existing in traditional classrooms reappear in network systems; that students left to their own devices on LANs may regress into anti-social, even overtly hostile, behavior (Collier; Daiute; Harris; Kremers; Sirc; George). The optimism of the '80s has been discredited to such a degree that Hawisher and Cynthia Selfe, speaking in a recent edition of *College Composition and Communication* from their influential post as editors of *Computers and Composition,* have explicitly called for restraint among potential contributors. "This rhetoric—one of hope, vision, and persuasion—is the primary voice present in most of the work we see coming out of computers-and-composition studies, " they write. And they add: "This same rhetoric, however, may also be dangerous if we want to think critically about technology and its uses" (Hawisher and Selfe 57).

We would suggest that what really may be needed is not so much restraint as a fuller vision, that these alternating waves of anticipation and disappointment simply replicate the essential paradox of technocentrism out of which they arise; that is, questions that address only *the* effect of *the* computer on cognitive development or *the* effect of the computer on *the* composing process simultaneously delimit, artificially, research's field of inquiry and generalize, both prematurely and just as artificially, its potential findings. Hence research itself may resist change when, for example, "*the* writing process" is viewed but not questioned: when writing processes and products arising out of the traditional context become both measure and model and hence dictate the limits of the new computer-based "culture" (Curtis; LeBlanc). We see this most easily in the pioneering studies of students' unguided revising activities on word processors, studies like those done by Collier, Daiute and Harris, which, in judging *drafts* done in longhand against those done on computers, inadvertently imposed on the potentially "fluid text" of word processing the limitations of sequence and segmentation required by pen and paper. Similarly, research may fail to encompass the comparable counter-force exerted by teachers when, as creatures of culture as well as professional axiology, we unwittingly resist the very changes we hope to install. We see this in the more current reviews of students using synchronous and asynchronous conferencing software. In many of these pieces, the teacher/researcher enters with the best intentions to witness the democratizing force of this software, only to watch "helplessly" as the class devolves into the sort of sexualized and aggressivized "wilding" behaviors reported by Kremers and George. In fact, none of these investigations show enough of the context for the reader or, reflexively, the writer to assess other factors—including such overt catalysts as the topics introduced for discussion or, as likely, the teacher's own attitudes and subtler behaviors—possibly contributing to this phenomenon.

It is crucial to realize, before discussing the ways in which ethnography as a research method can accommodate the computer-based composition classroom as a cultural phenomenon (in other words as a sociopolitical phenomenon), that it is not the methodology that politicizes the subject. As can be seen in Moran's brief summary, the introduction of computers into writing classrooms has already been conceived, throughout the literature, as a political event involving shifts in authority from teachers to students and the further "democratization" of intra-student on-line discussions. We as a field intensely focused on these political issues so that, in his introduction to *Evolving Perspectives on Computers and Composition: Questions for the 1990s,* Edmund Farrell ranks the issue of political power as the key concern of the coming decade. Yet in looking at the impact of computers we seem to have been treating them as discrete, essentially "democratizing" entities. Until we examine the entire context—the teacher, students, and technology as they interrelate in the formation of a new educational culture and, just as importantly, as they all carry with them the traditional values, mores, and motivations of the larger culture out of which they all develop—we will continue to partition this complex and evolving structure into contradictory parts and find ourselves either naively elated or inordinately disappointed in the results we find.

What Is Ethnography?

Ethnography can itself be characterized as an essentially democratic form of inquiry, in principle and methodology. We might even suggest that it represents, in the domain of research, a point of view represented in the classroom by the movement toward student-centered pedagogy. Seeded in postmodern, contructivist soil, they have each developed alongside the physics of relativity, literary deconstruction, Kohutian self-psychology, and even punk rock.

First and foremost, ethnography stands in almost direct opposition to the positivist assumption underlying much other, traditional empirical research in composition studies, that human thought and action can be extracted from their contexts—that is, from the particular situations in which they occur—and that, accordingly, the findings of research can be reckoned generalizable (Herrington 5–6). Demonstrating its shared roots with phenomenology, ethnography holds, on the contrary, that the *significance* of any phenomenon is historically and situationally bound: It is constituted in the beholder's perception of it, a perception correspondingly determined by that person's own historical and cultural experiences.[1]

From the very start, then, ethnography makes us skeptical. It makes us question the impulse to apply findings derived from one study to other—much less *all*—situations and occasions, however apparently similar they may be. So, too, it makes us resist narrowly focused research questions, questions like those implicit in the previously mentioned revision studies, which are derived from prestructured research designs and preset assumptions—from previous contexts—rather than developing naturally from present data and their emerging patterns. But at the most fundamental level, ethnography's relativist view calls into question the researcher's hegemony. Her position as Knower shifts: she joins her subjects as constructors of knowledge and as constructs of the cultures in which they individually and together reside. As Stephen Doheny-Farina and Lee Odell write:

> Researchers and subjects are engaged in similar tasks. Both the researcher and subject interpret their worlds and attribute meanings to the persons, events, and objects in those worlds. Both construct realities, or ways of looking at the world. Both are capable of taking on the perspectives of the others. The researchers differ in that they are interested in doing the latter. (507)

In fact, if we push Doheny-Farina and Odell's understanding a bit further and acknowledge that the subjects of ethnographic research are, in many respects, as knowledgeable about the particular situation as the researcher, then the researcher's interpretive advantage can indeed be lost when subjects, and even readers of published research, are encouraged to become "interested" in the construction of meaning. The ethnographer's findings then become valid subjects of further scrutiny, and in many cases the "subjects" themselves can provide the most cogent interpretations.[2]

It also follows from the relativist view that as the researcher's position within the field of knowledge shifts, the actual field of investigation must correspondingly change. The researcher's task, as Doheny-Farina and Odell further explain, turns to investigating "phenomena in the social contexts in which these phenomena routinely occur" (506), rather than in any artificial, experimental setting. It does so for two principal reasons: 1) by removing her "subjects" from their natural/social context, the researcher eliminates from her own sphere of observation related phenomena that are key to interpreting those particular phenomena under study, and 2) "having separated people from their social resources . . . the researcher substantially alters the very behavior that he or she is trying to isolate in an experimental setting" (507). In other words, both the researcher's observations and the phenomena observed are distorted by the removal of "subjects" from the contexts in which they normally function or even by the isolation of a few functions—be they a student's composing of "drafts" on the computer or the "drafts" themselves—for scrutiny. Key elements of understanding are missed. And true significance is lost because the conclusions derived under artificially limited conditions cannot be assumed transferable to the natural context.

For ethnographers generally, these principles imply the need to accumulate data from a variety of sources using a variety of collection methods (including direct observations, interviews with subjects, and examination of documents), to examine these data from a variety of theoretical perspectives, and offer them up to a variety of interpreters—subjects as well as other researchers. It is only by creating this "thick description" that the researcher can begin to discern meaningful behavioral and rhetorical patterns, patterns of interpretation really, which, though closed to generalization and open to continual revision, can nevertheless generate new hypotheses and questions, new lenses through which other phenomena can be explored.

For teachers in computerized composition classrooms, especially for those of us who have assumed the role of researcher too, these three basic principles—of open questioning, full contextualization, and reflexivity—imply the specific need to see—and to investigate—our own involvement in the complex social act our students perform when they write. To see, for instance, that while as teacher or researcher we may be more knowledgeable than our students about traditional composing techniques and traditionally composed products, it may well be from our students—less encumbered than we by old habits—that insights into the computer's potential for novel procedures *and even products* will come.[3] To see, conversely, that the resistances we meet in our students—to technology, composing, or even the investiture of authority we want for them—may indeed be our own. Finally, these principles may lead us to rest content, not with false and fluctuating "answers," but with more revealing questions of how a specific community of teachers and students together negotiate new rules and roles for themselves within a particularly configured "virtual" community; how these teachers and students, together and apart, navigate between the shared environment and their own individual computer-based or noncomputer-based "homework" environments; how this particular community comes to develop common and individualized composing processes *and* products, "community discourse patterns," within their particular computer-based setting. After such questions have been explored in localized settings, and after the information gathered has been used to direct subsequent questioning, then we can begin still wider explorations across settings and over time, with a view to discerning the emergence of more universal "behavioral and rhetorical patterns" within the whole computers and composition "culture."

What Do the Currently Available Ethnographies Reveal?

Examining how researchers have begun to address questions like those above can help us not only appreciate where we have been but discover areas that next demand exploration. To date, two ethnographic studies of the computer writing environment are readily available, with a third forthcoming, and the findings from these exemplify the benefits that this research methodology can have for the field of computers and composition.[4]

Andrea Herrmann's "Ethnographic Study of a High School Writing Class Using Computers" represents an instructive illustration of a teacher/researcher's inquiry into a course essentially developed to provide both a teaching and research setting. As Herrmann herself describes it:

> During the 1983–1984 academic year, I introduced the word processor into my high school writing class of eight students. I designed the course around it to permit close observation of students, and I studied my class using ethnographic techniques: videotape, audiotape, teacher/researcher journals, student journals, students' writing, and interviews. (79)

Because of her dual intentions, she acknowledges, the setting was, in some respects, artificial: To allow for in-depth research, she restricted the class size to eight, and those eight comprised sophomore, junior, and senior level volunteers from a range of tracking levels.

The design of the course curriculum, on the other hand, was driven by "teacherly" motives, motives we have seen shared by most computers and composition instructors:

> Educators often view their roles as promoting opportunity, reform, and change. . . . This was essentially my view of things as I introduced the computer into my classroom. I hoped it would provide my students with new opportunities to develop as writers, perhaps even as readers and thinkers. (79)

Specifically, Herrmann attempted to present her students with a free and appealing learning environment, "the class less rigidly structured and the teaching style less teacher-centered than that of conventional high school classes" (80). They were explicitly asked only "to spend their time on writing-related activities, either on or off the computer, to maintain a daily writing-process journal outside of class, and to do their best. There were no assignments (initially), no deadlines, and no minimum amount of writing required" (80).

What Herrmann discovered in the progress of her teaching was the full gamut of success and failure we have seen recorded in composition and computer research, and in her report she classifies her students thus: "marginal" learners who had problems with both word processing and writing; "technically proficient" students who easily mastered the word processing but made little progress as writers; and "productive" learners who were "successful on both fronts" (80). What she found—and reveals—through the course of inquiry into the social dynamics of her class and into the relationship between both teaching and learning styles, however, takes us beyond the student-computer partnership. In fact, she argues, the computer itself proved but a minor determinant of individuals' relative achievements. Despite technology, student as well as teacher enthusiasm, and an innovative course structure, "strong continuities with past arrangements" prevailed (83), "arrangements" with which computer and teacher conspired:

> The new demands made by the computer and the course design, along with the research process and the mixed-ability tracks, exacerbated the class divisions made by the larger society and mirrored by the school. . . . Most students who were accustomed to experiencing alienation in school . . . "failed"; most students who were accustomed to getting by "got by"; and the students who were accustomed to doing well "did well." (83)

In interpreting her findings on "marginal learners," Herrmann attributes some of their difficulties to the "face-to-face competition" produced by unaccustomed mixed-tracking, some to the embarrassment resulting from the computer's "public display of writing," some to the self-consciousness heightened by her own invasive research activities (85).

Most significant, however, for these learners and for the "productive learners" was the relative mismatch or match of her own teaching style.

Drawing on the work of Kathleen Wilcox and Melvin Kohn, Herrmann presents a parallel between educational tracking levels and socio-economic classes, contending that while upper-middle class children are taught to internalize academic and behavioral standards in preparation for future professional roles, their lower-middle class counterparts are left to rely on the sorts of external sanctions—rules and directives—that will regulate them later in non-professional occupations. She concludes:

> It seems likely that one reason my students from the lower tracks had difficulty learning was the lack of correspondence between the teaching style they were accustomed to and the style I was using. My course design and teaching manner essentially demanded that students internalize the course goals, especially the implicit notion that they were to be independent, self-directed learners and writers. Rather than imposing an explicit, authoritarian, rule-sanctioned structure, I created an environment that inadvertently assumed students were socialized to an upper-middle-class value system. . . . I had unwittingly created a situation of unequal opportunity that gave upper-track students a distinct advantage. (84)

For teachers of computers and composition, as well as for researchers, Herrmann's findings resonate with meaning: about the dangers inherent in our faith in technology's power to democratize our classrooms, and, also, about dangers inhering in our own efforts to counter-act larger social forces of hegemony by constructing increasingly "free" and unstructured, "student-centered" learning environments within computer-based settings. For most of our students, as Herrmann argues, the challenge will be to master two complex skills—word processing and writing—and we cannot automatically assume that the "new" setting will radically reconfigure our students' learning patterns. As she reminds us, because our classrooms are embedded in the larger society, they can become a site for radical change, or, as likely, provide a new setting for the replication of the old order.

We may well object to aspects of Herrmann's interpretation of her own experience. Sensing in its presentation just the sorts of resistance to change she means to expose, we may question, for instance, her insistent separation of writing from word processing—her advice that one "distinguish 'writing' activities from 'word processing' activities" (82), even separate the teaching of the two (87)—and wonder to what extent that very partitioning of process and means might have effected the division she observed among students. Yet, these questions in themselves do not confute Herrmann's basic argument. On the contrary, they support her counsel: that as teachers and as researchers both, we must "become sensitive to the social dynamics in [our] classrooms and to the compatibility of [our own] teaching style with the learning styles of [our] students"(88) if we are to effect the kinds of transformations and repositionings we claim to value.

David K. Dickinson's study, "Cooperation, Collaboration, and a Computer: Integrating a Computer into a First-Second Grade Writing Program," provides a complement to Herrmann's work as sweet as it is illuminating. Like Herrmann, Dickinson was interested in the use of a computer as a writing tool in a process-oriented writing program and the ways in which teacher attitudes affected that use. And like Herrmann's class, the class observed by Dickinson was mixed in terms of age, gender, race, and ethnicity. Unlike Herrmann's group, however, these first and second graders had not yet been acculturated to the school setting or to its traditional forms of writing. Thus, in observing this classroom over the months following the acquisition of a computer and by relying on field notes, interviews with students and the teacher, the teacher's log, and audiotapes of students' writing sessions, Dickinson was able to show how the computer came to figure at the center of a complex interrelationship between the teacher, who viewed the computer primarily as an editing tool, and the students, who, unrestrained by old writing strategies and assumptions, pushed to use it to compose collaboratively.

The teacher introduced the computer for two initial purposes: the children were instructed in LOGO, a drawing program, at which they worked in pairs, and, working individually, they were taught to enter hand-written stories into a simple text-editing program, in the hopes that computer use might "highlight that phase of writing" (365). Technical problems, however, including lost files and aborted executions, altered use; and selected children were allowed during writing and social studies time to compose, not simply to edit, at the computer instead of at their desks.

Over the next two months, Dickinson watched as the children, on their own initiative and despite the teacher's articulated resistance, began transferring collaborative skills learned in art and social studies projects to computer composing. He recorded their progress:

> In early March, two girls, Sonja and Deborah, asked to write at the computer about dolls they had brought to school. Jean [the teacher] acquiesced and they worked for two periods on this topic. In early April, Ellen and Deborah wrote about a class trip. A week later, Sonja was told she could work at the computer and Ellen asked permission to work with her. Jean at first refused and then relented. They wrote about Ellen's father. (367)

Dickinson continues: "Despite the apparent success of this and subsequent sessions, Jean continued to be uneasy with collaborative writing"

(368); her belief that "young children did not work well when writing collaboratively" (368) persisted until consultation with a writing specialist revealed that the sort of "planning and self-monitoring talk" she wished to foster among these young writers was heightened during collaborative sessions in ways unseen outside of them. In fact, during other occasions, adult presence tended to suppress the youngsters' expression:

> Talk among children about writing may have been limited by an implicit assumption that such talk was to occur between teachers and children. This assumption was fueled by the considerable availability of teachers [including assistant teachers and teachers' aides] for conferences, children's occasional negative responses to each other's work, and teacher efforts to limit irrelevant talk during writing time. (370)

Collaboration on the computer, on the other hand, "placed different communicative demands on the children" (376), providing an impetus for reflective discourse and social cooperation as well. Dickinson ultimately discovered students—forced as they were to articulate both plans and objections to their partners, and thus to "become aware of what they implicitly knew" (376)—exchanging ideas about word choice and pronoun reference, about style as well as punctuation and spelling, at a level of sophistication seldom found even among much older students. And he concludes:

> A computer equipped to do word processing can be integrated into a process-oriented writing program as early as the first grade. In such a classroom, collaborative computer writing may add an important dimension to the writing program. . . . We need to learn more about the effects of encouraging collaborative writing in classrooms where other approaches to writing instruction are being used and more about how older children interact when writing together. (376)

While appreciating Dickinson's conclusions, we would emphasize his method itself, as it demonstrates the worth of both contextualization and reflexivity. The ethnographer's attention to the larger class environment let Dickinson see—and reveal to us—that, despite the teacher's initially narrow vision of the computer as a tool for text-editing, "collaborative writing developed out of the context of a classroom where sharing of ideas was valued" (368) and where an over-arching goal of instruction was "to help children learn to relate to other children" (367). We may therefore appreciate, too, this teacher's willingness to learn from her students and come to understand with her a fundamental lesson of their shared experience: that little children—like these first and second graders, who, as Hawisher notes, have "not yet developed writing strategies with pencil and paper" and so "are not trying to adapt old strategies to a new technology" (56)—may lead us into the "virtual" age.

From Elizabeth Klem and Charles Moran's forthcoming "Teachers in a Strange LANd: Learning to Teach in a Networked Writing Class-room," our third and final picture of the sorts of resistance Herrmann and Dickinson detected among veteran writers begins to emerge.[5] Klem and Moran's semester-long study of two teaching assistants as they adapted to a newly-networked computer writing classroom documents the changes they found these teachers making—and resisting—as they taught their freshman-year writing course in a changed environment.

The researchers followed the teachers as they navigated the transitional semester and found that, despite the teachers' best intentions, the technological capabilities were only marginally used by the students and teachers alike. Observational notes taken over the course of the 15-week semester, transcripts of interviews with the teachers at the beginning and end of the semester, and final surveys of the students in the two classes led the research team to identify three factors contributing to this limited use: the teachers' knowledge of the hardware and software, their preparedness to manage the constant shifting between screen and print text, and the teachers' own beliefs about how writing is best taught.

Klem and Moran found that the two teaching assistants were consistently enthusiastic about the new networked setting, extolling its capabilities to empower their students. Yet, the teachers were just as consistently at odds with the setting, initially through lack of familiarity with the technology. More importantly, however, their study identifies two other factors—revealed through the ethnographic methodology chosen by the researchers. First, both teachers had difficulty moving between the print world in which they had always operated and the impermanence of the screen world in which the students were working: they tended subtly to privilege print text over the more fluid text of the screen. Beyond this, however, the researchers found that "the way a person teaches is much more a function of that person's sense of 'good teaching' than it is of the definition of 'good teaching' that may be built into a particular teaching environment." Finding that the teachers' models for teaching writing clashed with the model of teaching built into the computerized classroom, they conclude that

> making the change to a computer-equipped classroom environment may challenge a teacher's models in ways more deep and more subtle than we have heretofore recognized. Here, a larger conceptual shift is required than is involved in, say, moving student desks into a circle. In the computer-equipped classroom, the instructor must have enough familiarity with the new information, and, more importantly, must have a high degree of self-awareness in order to match the new environment's capabilities to her own goals. Our study has let us see that instructors are restricted by two kinds of limits: limits to their available energy,

which will dictate how much preparation time they will be willing to devote to the shift; and, limits to their ability to examine their own teaching styles—and the implicit assumptions about learning and writing these contain—in order to effect a successful match to the new setting. These limits need to be understood and respected—seen as predictable, comprehensible human behavior and not as a personal failure on the part of the teacher.

Ethnographic methods allowed these researchers to gain a new awareness of the complex connections—shrouded in issues of identity, access, and power—that dictate how much change can reasonably be expected to take place during these transitional times and with how much speed we can reasonably expect to enter the virtual world ahead.

Conclusion, and Points Beyond

Durst attributes the dearth of ethnographies not to want of support in the composition community but to the community's "relative unfamiliarity with ethnographic methodologies" (401). It may be, however, that factors other than unfamiliarity militate against ethnographic research. True ethnographic research obviously makes enormous demands on the researcher's time and resources: it encompasses a "community," not just select subjects; it must extend over time, months and sometimes years; it must be conducted in the subjects' field, not the researcher's laboratory; optimally, it involves more than one researcher. True ethnographic research, in other words, moves us beyond texts and the sort of textual interpretations to which most of us are accustomed; it demands we explore the terrain of "contexts," so much less clearly defined, delineated, and easily grasped. In ethnography's province, we are, we might say, out of our professional element.

Still other less tangible, less practical factors, too, may militate against ethnography, or at least *for* more traditional forms of inquiry. It may well be that some of the very factors contributing to the demand for more ethnographic studies of computers and composition simultaneously contribute to our hesitancy, as a community, to produce them. That is, ours is a new, perhaps more, a still nascent "culture," without established rules, without traditional roles, without even shared artifacts to unify us. As John M. Slatin observes, the technology itself is "changing at an exponential rate" and is "perhaps perpetually immature" (870); consequently the culture driven by it is in constant flux, with each individual "community" comprising the computer-culture at a different point of development along the way. If we look at sites across our culture at a single moment in time—that is, at computer-based classrooms as they currently exist in educational settings nationwide—we see as many differences in equipment and expertise as similarities. If we look at the culture as a whole, as it evolves from one year to the next, we discover apparently endless transition.

For many of us, the newness and change we face every day in our own computer classrooms may, indeed, feel overwhelming. And in our vertigo, it is natural for us to desire to secure ourselves both in and through research: to enter inquiry armed with hypotheses and ready to "test whether," rather than to suspend expectation and simply ask "how"; to seek generalizable "findings" and to apply others' findings to our own experiences, despite how inapplicable they may feel; perhaps most of all, to remove ourselves from the field of questioning altogether and comfort ourselves instead with our rhetoric of persuasion and hope. As we enter the potentially all-text world of tomorrow's virtual classroom—whatever form that text might take—the temptation to retreat into customary textual readings and to make ourselves literary critics of our students' high tech artistry may become for many of us increasingly great. But as Hawisher and Selfe believe the current computer rhetoric to be dangerous to our full understanding of computer technology, we believe all these desires potentially harmful to teaching as well as research ("Research"). Ethnography represents a method of inquiry. But for us, as is no doubt clear by now, it also represents a way of seeing ourselves, our students, and the work we together do.

The end now brings us back to the beginning. At the start we wrote that our own positions within our professional authority structures are complex, being in some ways "marginalized" and in others privileged; and that it seems to us that our association with computers in large part embodies, perhaps exacerbates, the complexity, even the conflict, of our positions. This, we think, is true for most of us in the computer-and-composition field. We think, too, that it is, in many respects, the sense of our own marginalization as much as our privilege that prompts us, in identification with our students, to call for their empowerment, their authorization, through student-centered pedagogy and computer-assisted learning. But we must also beware that in seeking to authorize them we are not simultaneously re-establishing authority in us, that it is not this contradiction that has given our rhetoric of persuasion and hope its particularly hollow ring. By removing ourselves from the center of pedagogy, we may well moderate our power over students; but by removing ourselves from the center of research, we can only make the authority that we do exert unquestionable.

Notes

1. Here we turn to the thoughtful overview provided by Stephen Doheny-Farina and Lee Odell, establishing five factors as constitutive of ethnography:

1) socially significant and constructed, "facts"; 2) a "naturalistic context"; 3) shifting "research roles"; 4) theoretical, investigative, and methodological "multiplicity"; and 5) perhaps the bulwark of ethnography, "thick description"—in terms of detailed observation as well as interpretation—of the full context.

2. Drawing on the work of anthropologist Clifford Geertz, Elizabeth Chiseri-Strater adds still another dimension to Doheny-Farina and Odell's presentation, suggesting that it is neither "thick descriptions" nor the researcher's interpretive powers alone that afford ethnographic research credibility. She writes:

> The credibility of ethnography comes from the reader's acceptance of the ethnographer's ability to depict having been there, having captured the drama of the participants' everyday scenes. (xxii)

Finally, the "credibility of ethnography" resides in its reader's willing suspension of disbelief and in a description full enough to provide the matter for his or her own interpretive act. Unfortunately, because "thick description" requires a monograph-length publication, the little ethnographic research on computers and composition that is available is not available in true ethnographic form, but rather in the form of more typical research articles. The full flavor of the research is therefore missing, as is the opportunity for the reader to participate in the research as alter-interpreter.

This emphasis on the role of the reader reminds us as well of Simon & Dippo's call for "Critical Ethnographic work" which would require the researcher, not only to historicize her work consciously, but also to enter the public sphere to address an audience beyond the standard "scholarly" reader and thereby to effect real change.

3. We are thinking here of the changed product of composing represented in hypertext. It may be, it seems to us, that at least some of our disappointment with student revising patterns on computers may come from our own expectations, not only of *drafts*, but also of the finished products themselves. In other words, our process-centered pedagogy has, in some real ways, forbidden the questioning as well as the privileging of the written product. Hypertext shows that the products appropriate to reading as well as writing on computers may be indeed very different from those produced in traditional fashion and for traditional print. Our students' "failure" to revise on word processors may not be failures at all, but modes of production quite appropriate to new ends as well as means.

4. The two dissertations mentioned earlier take the changes brought to the classroom context by the introduction of the new writing tools as their focus. Reid acted as a participant-observer in a fourth grade classroom and, additionally, used four children for in-depth study. The researcher theorizes from the data that:

> (a) the impact of the computer is determined by its interactions with writer, task, and context; (b) the computer is a catalyst which changes the context in which it is used; (c) the computer creates a new writing environment which transforms writing from a private to a public activity, with important consequences for teachers and children.(817–A)

A similar focus on the interaction of elements in the computerized classroom is found in Curtiss's research project. This researcher followed fifty-three high school seniors through an eighteen week composition course to discover those elements the students identified as important to their own writing progress. The students identified word processing as a positive part of the nurturing context, along with factors such as "a meaningful writing topic," "time to think and write," and "dialogic feedback" although the researcher cautions that not all the student writers preferred the machines as writing tools.

5. In order to maintain strict contextualism, while hoping at the same time not to violate our principle of reflexivity, we refer to one of us here in the third person. As Elizabeth Klem contends, the "Klem" in the context of "Klem and Moran" is different from the "Klem" who writes with Curtis.

Works Cited

Chiseri-Strater, Elizabeth. *Academic Literacies.* Portsmouth: Boynton/Cook, 1991

Collier, Richard M. "The Word Processor and Revision Strategies." *College Composition and Communication* 34, (1983):149–155.

Curtis, Marcia S. "Windows on Composing: Teaching Revision on Word Processors." *College Composition and Communication* 39, (1988):337–344.

Curtiss, D. H. "The Experience of Composition and Word Processing: An Ethnographic, Phenomenological Study of High School Seniors." *Dissertation Abstracts International* 45 (1984): 1021–A.

Daiute, Colette. "Physical and Cognitive Factors in Revising: Insights from Studies with Computers." *Research in the Teaching of English* 20 (1986):141–159.

Dickinson, David K. "Cooperation, Collaboration, and a Computer: Integrating a Computer into a First-Second Grade Writing Program." *Research in the Teaching of English* 20. 4 (December 1986): 357–78.

Doheny-Farina, Stephen, and Lee Odell. "Ethnographic Research on Writing: Assumptions and Methodology." In *Writing in Non-Academic Settings,* Eds. Lee Odell, and Dixie Goswami. NY: Guilford Press, 1985. (503–535).

Durst, Russell. "The Mongoose and the Rat." *College Composition and Communication* 41 (1990): 393–408.

Farrell, Edmund J. "Foreword" to Hawisher and Selfe, *Evolving Perspectives* . . . ix–xii.

George, E. Laurie. "Taking Women Professors Seriously: Female Authority in the Computerized Classroom." *Computers and Composition* 7 Special Issue (April 1990): 45–52.

Gerrard, Lisa. "Computers and Compositionists: A view from the Floating Bottom." *Computers and Composition* 8. 2, (April 1991): 5–15.

Harris, Jeanette. "Student Writers and Word Processing: A Preliminary Evaluation." *College Composition and Communication* 36 (1985):323–330.

Hawisher, Gail E., "Research and Recommendations for Computers and Composition." In *Critical Perspectives on Computers and Composition Instruction,* Eds. Gail E. Hawisher and Cynthia L. Selfe. New York: Teachers College Press, 1989: 44–69.

Hawisher, Gail E., and Cynthia L. Selfe, Eds. *Evolving Perspectives on Computers and Composition Studies: Questions for the 1990s.* Urbana: NCTE, 1991.

————. "The Rhetoric of Technology in Computer Writing." *College Composition and Communication* 42 (1991):55–65.

Herrington, Anne. "Reflections on Empirical Research: Examining the Theories behind our Methods," *Issues in Composition Theory*, Ed. Lee Odell. Carbondale: Southern Illinois UP, forthcoming.

Herrmann, Andrea. "An Ethnographic Study of a High School Writing Class Using Computers: Marginal, Technically Proficient, and Productive Learners." In *Writing at Century's End: Essays on Computer-Assisted Composition,* Ed. Lisa Gerrard. New York: Random House, 1987. (79–91).

Klem, Elizabeth, and Charles Moran. "Teachers in a Strange LANd: Learning to Teach in a Networked Writing Classroom." *Computers and Composition,* forthcoming.

Kremers, Marshall. "Sharing Authority on a Synchronous network: The Case for Riding the Beast." *Computers and Composition* 7 (Special Issue 1990): 33–44.

LeBlanc, Paul. "How to Get the Words Just Right." *Computers and Composition* 5 (1988):29–42.

Moran, Charles. "The Computer Writing Room: Authority and Control." *Computers and Composition* 7 (2): 61–69.

Reid, T. R. "Writing with Microcomputers in a Fourth Grade Classroom: An Ethnographic Study." *Dissertation Abstracts International* 47 (1985): 817–A.

Simon, Roger I., and Donald Dippo. "On Critical Ethnographic Work." *Anthropology and Education Quarterly* 17 (1986): 195–202.

Sirc, Geoffrey. "What Do Basic Writers Talk about When They('re Supposed to Be) Talk(ing) about Writing?" Presented at the *Conference on College Composition and Communication,* 1990.

10

Computers and Composition Studies:
Articulating a Pattern of Discovery

Christine M. Neuwirth
David S. Kaufer
Carnegie Mellon University

This essay is concerned with articulating a "pattern of discovery"—the series of steps a researcher follows in making a contribution to a field (Diesing 1). Thus far, the dominant pattern of discovery in computers and composition studies has involved empirical questions about existing software—asking, for example, "Do word processors improve writing quality or revision performance?"—usually by experimental comparison to some "traditional" technology for writing such as pen and paper (see Hawisher, "Studies in Word Processing," "Research Update," and "Research and Recommendations" for reviews). Such studies primarily grow out of a demand for answers to questions of instructional policy: "What are the costs and benefits of buying into computers for a writing program?". When electronic texts and the tools for their production become, however, a "fact" of our writing lives, we confront a need to re-form our questions.

This essay asks, "What pattern of discovery is appropriate for building knowledge—for representing, validating, and sharing it—when the question we are trying to answer is not 'Should we use computers?' but rather 'What should the computers we use look like?'" In answer to this latter question, the field of computers and composition has been evolving a new pattern of discovery, one that is, we argue, uniquely appropriate to answering it, but its theory and methodology have remained unarticulated. The essay begins articulating such a pattern of discovery and argues its appropriateness for building knowledge in computers and composition studies.

The pattern of discovery we will articulate can be outlined by the following steps:

- Identifying writers (e.g., novices, experts) and a writing task (e.g., co-authoring, synthesis).

- Building a theory- and research-based model of the writing task. Understanding how writers function and hypothesizing the sources of their successes and failures is vital to building tools to support writers. The model draws upon techniques, both cognitive and social, for building models of composing processes, but focuses on *problems* that writers—even experienced ones—have with the task. This model informs the design of technology.

- Designing technology to alleviate these problems. This step involves building a theory of the *prima facie* ways computers can augment writers' performance of the task by drawing upon a theory of the role of external representations and a theory of task activity. The technology represents a hypothesis about a solution, perhaps a partial solution, to some needs or problems identified by the theory- and research-based model.

- Studying the technology in use, with the aim of building knowledge that will help to refine the model of the task and the design of the technology.

Like the subprocesses in composing, these steps are interconnected and often recursive. For example, studying one of our software tools, the Comments program, in actual use led us to refine our model of the task and to design a new software tool, the PREP Editor (Neuwirth, Kaufer, Chandhok, and Morris).[1] Indeed, given that all writing involves technology (e.g., pen and paper), the last step can be thought of as the second step repeated.

It is not necessary for the steps to be carried out by the same group of researchers. A study by a group of empirical researchers observing a software tool in use may be relevant to researchers working at other steps, perhaps on the theory of composing or on the design of software. For example, the work of Haas and Hayes and of Haas identified the problems writers have of getting a "sense" of their texts when using word processors, and added to our theoretical understanding of the process of composing by identifying an additional subprocess, the subprocess of reading one's own writing, and highlighting its importance. This result stimulated further research into the role of reading during writing, both in print and hypertext environments (Goggin), and has been used by other researchers, consisting of an interdisciplinary group from computer science and English, to inform software design (Neuwirth, Kaufer, Chandhok, and Morris).

While it is not necessary, then, for the steps to be carried out by the same group of researchers, it is necessary, or at least desirable, that researchers understand the interconnectedness of the steps in order to increase the likelihood that results they produce at one step will be relevant to other steps. In the remainder of the essay, we elaborate the steps and their interconnections.

Identifying Writers and a Writing Task

"Identifying writers and a writing task" is a step that seems obvious, but it is all too often overlooked. Unless researchers identify "who is writing to whom for what purpose," that is, specific writers and a specific writing task, it hardly makes sense to offer a computer program as a help to writers engaged in the task. Too often, the intended "coverage" of a piece of software is misidentified with its area of effectiveness. This is the case, for example, when word processors, which are intended to "cover" the writing process, with no particular writing task specified, are assumed to augment all aspects of the writing process (e.g., planning, translating, revising) for all writing tasks for all writers.[2] For inquiry to proceed, we need to work with specific writing tasks, where various aspects of the general writing process may exhibit task-specific variants. For example, the process of generating ideas may look quite different for a task in which the writer is drawing upon memory to retrieve what he or she already knows than for a task in which the writer is drawing upon source texts to build new ideas.

What makes one writer or writing task different from another? The answer to this question, of course, depends on the theory of writers and writing that the researcher employs. For example, a cognitive process model of writing such as the one by Flower and Hayes (Flower and Hayes; Hayes and Flower, "Identifying") leads the researcher to see differences in some features (e.g., differences in the process of generating ideas) as defining different tasks and makes it less likely that he or she will see others (e.g., working with a co-author face-to-face or at a distance). What matters, for the purposes of our point here, is not which theory is the "best" but that researchers be self-conscious about their theories and the writers and writing tasks those theories help them to differentiate.

The writing task that we will use as an illustration in this essay is "research writing," that is, the construction and representation of knowledge which the writer intends as a contribution to a field of study. The writers we will be talking about range from relatively inexperienced to experienced.[3]

Building a Model of the Task

Why do researchers interested in asking the question, "What should the computers we use look like?" build models of the task? Don't we already have models of composing processes for various writing tasks? After all, recent empirical research in writing has focused on building models of the writing process, that is, characterizing processes—social (Bazerman and Paradis), affective (McLeod), and cognitive (Flower and Hayes; Witte)—and giving accounts of various writing performances in terms of those characterizations.

Researchers in computers and composition, of course, can draw upon those models in building their own but often need to collect their own data and build their own models because the models built by other researchers were built for writing tasks other than the one they are interested in supporting, or, just as importantly, in order to answer different questions than the ones asked by studies in computers and composition. For example, one question that has focused much of the model building in composition studies is "How do the processes of experienced writers and inexperienced writers differ?" Such a focus directs attention to some aspects of composing and excludes others. Experienced writers are often portrayed as "problem-free," and certainly they are, compared to the novices. But we are interested in the problems that even experienced writers have. And the writing medium (pen and paper, computers) is often viewed as "transparent," that is, as having little role in or influence on the writing process. But we are interested in the role the writing medium plays in the writing process. In short, we are interested in studying and developing ways to enhance the representation of knowledge. These observations are not meant to criticize existing models. As witnessed by the tremendous influence they have had, they are useful for the purposes for which they were built. It is only to say that they are sometimes in need of extension and elaboration when we try to use them for different purposes.

With that said, we outline the following series of steps for building models that are more useful for answering questions in computers and composition studies:

- Collecting empirical observations of writers engaged in the task.

- Constructing a task representation. What goals and sub-goals do writers construct?

- Partitioning the task. Are there ways to partition the task into meaningful and manageable activities that recur throughout the writing process?

- Looking for problems. What problems did writers experience within or across activities?

We will illustrate these steps with our own task—research writing—as the source of our examples.

Collecting Empirical Observations

This step is a familiar one from composition studies. The methods of the empirical researcher are invoked to study the task from a fine grain. In our own work, since the other steps require detailed data from which to build hypotheses of goals/subgoals, recurring activities, and problems, we relied on "think aloud" protocols (Ericsson and Simon; Hayes and Flower, "Uncovering Cognitive Processes") and interviews (Odell, Goswami, and Herrington).

Constructing a Task Representation

As noted above, the theory a researcher develops to analyze the data can depend on purpose. When the purpose is to answer the question, "What should the computers we use look like?" it is useful to analyze the goals and resources of a writer with respect to the demands, constraints, and affordances of the external environment (Woods and Roth). To analyze goals, we constructed a goal tree. A goal tree is a formalism that researchers can use to construct a task representation. A goal tree represents the various goals and subgoals that must be set and worked upon in order to complete the task. A goal tree should not be confused with a process model. Unlike a process model, a goal tree does not specify the sequence in which writers set and act upon goals. It only specifies the goals that are available to be worked upon and their logical relationship to one another. Breaking the general goal of "writing a paper" into the subgoals "think"-"draft"-"revise" represents a very simple (and none too interesting) goal tree. It specifies the three subgoals a writer can be working on at any one time in a writing task. To generate a goal tree from protocol data, one must abstract across the time course of individual protocols and focus on the common goals writers seem to be setting and the logical relationships that hold among them. These common abstractions become harder to make when the task representations across writers vary.

Figure 10-1 illustrates an extremely simplified version of the goal tree we derived from our protocol data depicting the experts' task representation of research writing. There was no strong pattern to how experts,

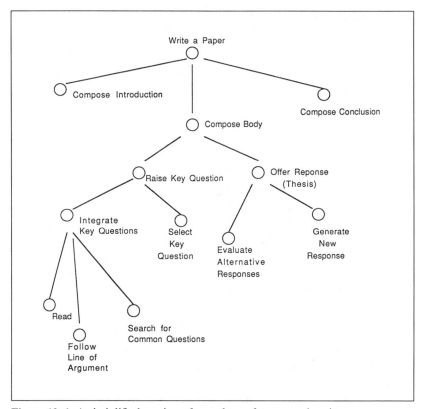

Figure 10–1. A simiplified version of a goal tree for research writng.

as a group, set and worked on the whole span of goals over time. They moved from goal to goal, up the tree, down the tree, from left to right and right to left. What makes the tree an expert task representation is that it contains the goals experts knew they had to account for before claiming to be done with their paper.

The circles represent goals that research writers set and act upon. The downward arcs represent subgoal relationships. The top circle represents the overall goal "write a paper." This goal can be broken down into the goals "compose the intro," "compose the body," and "compose the conclusion." The goal "compose the body" can be further broken down into the goals "raise a key question" and "offer a response (or thesis) to it. The goal "raise a key question" breaks down further into the goals "select a key question" and "integrate possible key questions." These goals further break down into "search for common questions," "follow the line of reasoning," and simply "read." The goal of "offering a response" breaks down into the goals "evaluate" and "generate" responses.

As we mentioned, this goal tree depicts the experts' task representation. Experts knew, for example, that when they were reading source texts, they were following a goal deeply embedded in a hierarchy of goals. They weren't just reading; they were reading in order to follow a line of reasoning that would allow them to explore across multiple lines of reasoning and, eventually, come up with their own. It bears repeating that this goal tree is not a process model.

Partitioning the Goal Tree into Workspaces

Despite the fact that experts showed no uniform traversal strategies of the entire goal tree, they did work on goals in local clusters. For example, all experts worked on the goals of "testing responses" and "generating responses" in proximity. Testing the responses of others apparently allowed experts to arrive at criteria for generating their own. We also noticed that experts tended to cluster goals that operated on multiple sources (e.g., integrating key questions, searching for common questions) as well as goals that operated on single sources (e.g., following the line of argument, reading).

This local clustering of goals is important to researchers because it can give them an idea for software modules or workspaces in the task; it can serve to predict whether a given tool will augment processes (cf. Howes and Young, 1991); and it can serve to deepen an understanding of the component processes involved.

After inspecting our protocol data for the local clustering of goals, we partitioned our goal tree into the workspaces depicted in Figure 10-2. The names of our workspaces are familiar: summarizing, synthesizing, analyzing, contributing, drafting. The names were picked more for suggestive purposes than for their exact correspondence with the ordinary language terms. Our workspace for summarizing refers only to the goals in the goal tree that require a "single-source" view. Our workspace for synthesizing refers only to the goals in the goal tree that require a "multiple-source" view. Our workspace for analyzing refers only to the goals in the goal tree concerned with testing and evaluating possible responses to a key question. We do not by these names mean to invoke *all* the loose associations stimulated by the everyday terms "summary," "synthesis," and "analysis," though certainly some resemblance is intended.

By partitioning a goal tree into workspaces (locally clustered goals), researchers can plan computer tools that are tied to modules. One wouldn't think that software optimized for handling single sources would also be optimal for handling multiple-sources. By defining workspaces, we were able to structure our own design decisions by asking, "What tools do we need to support summarizing, synthesizing, analyzing, and so on?"

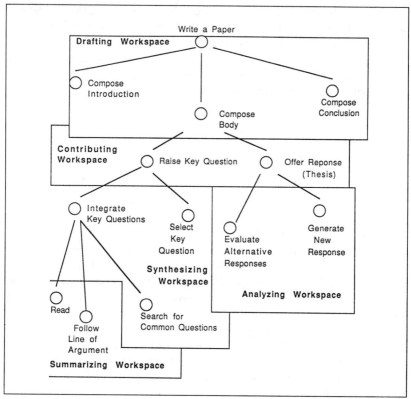

Figure 10-2. A goal tree partitioned into workspaces.

Defining recurring workspaces in the task focuses the researcher's search for software to develop.

Looking for Problems Within and Across Workspaces

Empirically derived workspaces, or task modules, are necessary to search for computer tools to develop. But they are not sufficient. A powerful heuristic for designing writing software is to look for problems that the software can alleviate. The empirical justification for preferring computers as a writing tool lies in showing that they, better than other media, compensate for, if not reduce, the occurrence of problems that naturally arise in complex writing tasks (of course, they can introduce new problems as well). Once researchers have an empirical breakdown of a task, therefore, they need to examine the problems that result when writers work within a workspace or across workspaces. Accordingly, we searched our protocol data for evidence of problems. The following table illustrates some of the more interesting ones we identified and where we identified them.

Summarizing

A writer takes a verbatim note on a source passage. By literally copying the source, the writer feels that she or he is "wasting" time and making no progress interpreting it. Could electronic source texts eliminate what writers perceive as time-wasting transcribing?

A writer interprets a source passage by taking a note on it. Once the note is taken, the writer loses the connection with the original passage. Could a computer tool be built that would keep the connection between the interpretive notes and source texts?

Summarizing to synthesizing

A writer takes systematic notes on individual sources. But this has given him or her no efficient way to view the consequences of these individual summary notes across sources and authors. As a result, the writer needs to take a new set of notes specifically organized across sources. Could a computer tool be built that would help writers move easily from viewing notes on a single source to viewing notes across sources?

A writer prepares "synthesis" notes that show the similarities and differences across individual authors and sources. In preparing these notes, however, the writer breaks the connection between these notes and the original source notes (and source passages). This makes it much harder for the writer to check the accuracy of the synthesis. Could a computer tool be built that helps writers keep connections between their synthesis notes and their notes on individual sources?

Synthesizing to analyzing

A writer has notes on multiple sources. Yet the writer usually has to start a new set of "evaluative" notes to keep track of their strengths and weaknesses. Could a computer tool be built that would help writers move from synthesizing notes to evaluative notes?

A writer organizes source notes for one purpose (for example, to highlight the author's major claims). The writer then decides to reorganize his or her source notes around a different purpose (to highlight flaws in the author's reasoning). Through this reorganization, the writer has broken the connection with the original organization of source notes. Could a computer tool be built that would keep connections across different organizations of source notes?

In research writing, we found that problems often led to what writers perceived as an inefficient duplication of effort. Working on some earlier goal should allow a writer to make as much (implicit) progress as possible on some later goal. Taking notes on a source text, for example, should go far in helping a research writer interpret that text and make cross text comparisons. However, we found numerous problems. Writers took initial notes, but these (verbatim) notes did not help them make as much implicit progress on interpretation as they might have; writers took interpretive notes, but these notes did not help them make as much implicit progress on synthesizing or analyzing as they might have.

For example, writers would take interpretive notes and then ignore them, discard them, or forget to consult them. They lost confidence in their notes, in part, because every note broke the connection with the full text. Still, the urge to take notes did not disappear, resulting in much repetitive effort. In addition, writers used their notes to take many perspectives on the source text, not just one. Yet short of recopying notes, writers had no way to view their notes in multiple organizations. The effect of arranging source notes in a new organization was to break the connection with previous organizations. These broken connections had a particularly costly effect when they spanned different workspaces—say in moving material from summarizing to synthesizing. By the time writers began to synthesize across sources, they were working with material considerably abstracted from source passages. It was not uncommon for our writers to build a synthesis organization in their head and then 1) forget it or 2) fail to be able to confirm it, because of the broken connections between their (abstract) synthesis organization and actual source passages.

Designing Technology to Alleviate Problems

Once the researcher has identified recurring problems, he or she is ready to design technology to remedy them. The researcher attempts to preserve positive aspects of writers' performances and eliminate problems, constrained, of course, by tool building limitations and possibilities. While it is beyond the scope of this paper to discuss software design in detail, we shall just mention two software tools we have designed in light of our analysis of the problems hampering research writers in the summary and synthesis workspaces, respectively.[4] The first of these programs, NOTES, (Neuwirth, Kaufer, Chimera, and Gillespie) is implemented and was extensively used within our institution. The second, PREP, (Neuwirth, Kaufer, Chandhok, and Morris) is currently being used in several pilot sections of a writing course.

Given that writers read and generate too much material to be able to see it all at once (even with traditional technologies), the NOTES program can be thought of as a set of hypotheses about how the material can be represented to help the writer access the right material at the right time (Woods). NOTES is a program designed to restore the broken connections between a writer's summary notes and a source text. It is further designed to eliminate the need for verbatim notes and so with it the problem that forces writers to take verbatim notes as well as interpretive notes. Writers can take notes on electronic source texts by specifying a "take note" option on a region of text. When this option is selected, an automatic link is created between this region and the note. Even when working with tens or hundreds of sources, writers can immediately restore the connection between any note and the original source passage (Figure 10-3). The NOTES program also allows writers to experiment with and save multiple organizations of notes—thus restoring other broken connections that plagued the writers in our protocol study.

The PREP Editor is a program capable of helping alleviate problems that impede the flow of information between summarizing and synthesizing. It is also intended to explore whether a particular external representation of sources, a table, will aid writers in constructing a synthesis. It is a table editor that allows writers to tabularize their source notes easily, through a copy and paste interface. Individual source notes can appear as cells in a table (Figure 10-4).

Figure 10-3. A hypertext link between a source text (Bird) and a note (money-making potential) in the NOTES program.

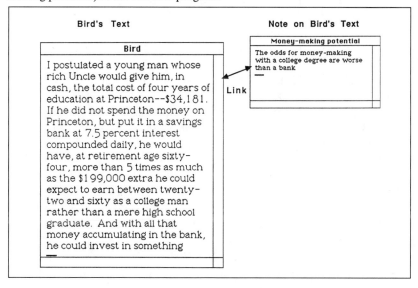

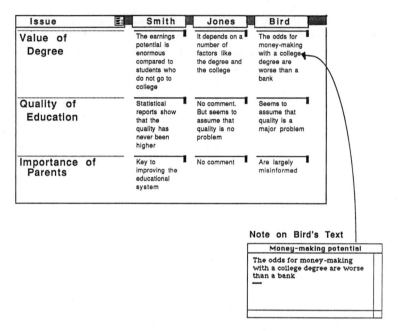

Figure 10-4. The PREP Editor can function as a table editor, allowing writers to move easily from their notes (e.g., the note on Bird) to a synthesis table.

Thus, as in Figure 4, a writer who has taken source notes on three authors (Smith, Jones, Bird) on the higher education issue could easily tabularize these notes with "similar" and "contrasting" notes—where the concepts of "similar" and "contrasting" are user-defined. By tabularizing cross-source notes in columns, writers should be able to induce more general class names to describe the similarities and differences across notes (e.g., the class names "value of degree," "quality of education," and so on). This last statement, of course, is a strong empirical claim in need of testing.

For the sake of exposition, the descriptions here of the problems solved by NOTES and PREP focus on problems of cognition. Proposing solutions to such problems demands a theory of the roles external representations can play in cognitive aspects of writing, such as augmenting processes of encoding, storage, retrieval, monitoring, and so forth (Neuwirth and Kaufer). We are working on developing a theory of the roles external representations can play in augmenting social processes in writing as well (Neuwirth, Kaufer, Chandhok and Morris).

Interface Principles

When computer tools are meant to support writers drawn from different populations (e.g. novice, expert), the researcher needs to think about different interfaces to accommodate them. We believe it is important to single out from among the many interface principles (cf. Gould) two that are especially important for guiding the development of writing tools.

The first principle is *flexibility of task representation*. While the researcher needs a strong model of the task (goal tree, workspaces, problems) to justify a particular software design, the interface should accommodate users who have a variable degree of knowledge or commitment to the implicit task model. Students learning a task for the first time might be well-served working through the goal tree in lockstep fashion. But more experienced writers will want more flexible control over the task representation. They may want to alter the goal tree, elaborate it, or reject it beyond a certain depth of subgoaling. A writer who simply wants a text editor, for example, is interested only in the top goal "write a paper" and will reject every system-sponsored subgoal beneath this ubiquitous writing goal.

Writers should also be able to invent their own goal trees, cluster goals into modules according to their own writing habits, and match modules with the information management tools that are already available in a system. Within this first principle, writers should be able to experiment with their own tasks and try to diagnose and relieve the bottlenecks that hinder them most. Writing systems, under the standards set by this first principle, should be customizable to the needs of different users from their interface alone (Mackay). A simple example of this kind of flexibility are the customized key bindings some word processors currently allow.

The second principle is *flexibility of navigation within a task representation*. Whether a goal tree is system-defined or user-defined, writers using the system should have full control over how they want to move from goal to goal through the goal tree. A dramatic illustration of why this flexibility is essential comes in our experience teaching research writing to students. When our students write research papers, we find that many of them fall into one of two categories. Some students do their serious summary and synthesis writing before they find their own position. They summarize and synthesize other sources as an aid to their own invention. Other students seem to do their more serious summary and synthesis writing after they have worked out their own position. They use other sources less to find their point than to adapt it. Students from both groups can write reasonable research papers. One navigational strategy seems no better than the other. A system that locked writers into a set way of traversing the goal tree would thus do what a computer system should never do—impose a specific process model on writers.

In our own work, we are a long way from satisfying either of these interface principles. Although we have done no work at all on the first, we have made some conceptual progress on the second. A hidden value of defining workspaces in a writing task is that they provide units for navigation. Informally, we have found that finding themselves working as summarizers, synthesizers, analyzers, and contributers can increase the navigational control that even experts (along with students) feel as they make their way through research writing. When textbook writers partition a writing text into chapters, they are often trying to isolate units that can increase a student's navigational control of the writing being taught. The problem is that textbook modules are seldom empirically derived and so make empirically inadequate navigational units. When we design computerized writing systems, we cannot afford to be so casual about defining units.

Studying the Software in Use

Here, we come full circle to the beginning of the paper: empirical studies of computer software. But at this point, we have very specific hypotheses about the effects of the computer on specific aspects of writing processes for a given task rather than general questions about its effect on writing processes. For the NOTES program, for example, we have the question, "Does maintaining a link from a note to the original source text help writers focus on interpreting texts rather than book-keeping?" For the PREP synthesis grid, we have the question "Does the PREP interface enhance writers' processes of searching for similarities/differences across authors?" and "Does the grid representation help writers notice when they have missed encoding an author's position on some part of an issue?" Such specific questions together with observations of writers using the tool can help refine both the models of the task and the software. This is not to say that general questions such as "Do writers using the tool write better?" are not necessary. Indeed, they are important, as mentioned at the outset, in answering questions of policy. But a tool can have a positive effect on one part of the process without resulting in an overall improvement in product quality due to problems the tool does not address. Without finer-grained observations and specific questions, it is impossible to see detailed process effects useful for shaping tools.

Summary and Conclusion

In this chapter, we have articulated a pattern of discovery that, we believe, is appropriate for computers and composition studies. We have focused mainly on what is required to construct a model of a writing task. This profile requires collecting enough data on writers to design a goal tree, to partition the tree into modules or workspaces (goals that cluster), and then to study problems writers experience in and across modules. Software for writing becomes theoretically interesting to the extent that it can be shown to augment processes and eliminate problems. A great deal of theoretical work on interfaces is needed to guarantee that writers can define their own tasks, navigate them as they see fit, diagnose, and correct problems they uncover in their own processes.

Clearly, much general effort lies ahead before the marketplace will make available to us truly powerful writing systems—as opposed to the truly powerful editing systems that now fill the software catalogs. The marketplace is not likely to design these writing systems, moreover, without help from us. To this point in the history of computers and composition studies, research in the use of computers for writing has taken a more retrospective than prospective point of view. Much of our research, that is, comes down to product testing. We use research to test what the market provides rather than to direct where the market should go. To direct the market, we need to work at a finer grain of analysis than product-testing permits—a finer grain more familiar to other research traditions in composition studies.

As with any emerging field, computers and composition studies contains very different perspectives about its patterns of discovery, that is, what its questions are (or ought to be) and the methods most appropriate to answering them. Certainly there are other questions and methods. We have offered one perspective and argued for its significance and appropriateness.

Notes

1. Like most hypertext annotation tools (ForComment, PROSE, Quill), the Comments program prevented users in the social role of commenting from modifying the draft on which they were commenting. In studying the Comments tool in use, we found that, regardless of their social role (either as co-author or commenter), some commenters wanted the ability to rewrite a draft and not simply attach annotations to it. Writers in the role of commenters often copied a region of the draft into a "commenting box" and proceeded to rewrite the copy. Writers who worked in this fashion, however, reported difficulties in revising because their revisions were physically separated from the larger body of the draft. More specifically, they reported needing a "sense of the whole draft" even when commenting on a part. One exasperated commenter went so far as to copy an *entire* draft into a comment box and to revise it from there. Despite its basis in theory and research (cf. Neuwirth, Kaufer, Keim, and Gillespie), the Comments program inadvertently collapsed cognitive needs and social roles. The new design, embodied in the PREP Editor prototype, attempts to solve this problem (as well as others).

2. See Kozma for a study that found an interaction between type of tool (outliner vs. "idea" organizer) and type of writer (beginning novice vs. advanced novice).

3. Five of the subjects were experienced writers. They included three professors of philosophy and two Ph.D. students. Two subjects were novices. Both

were undergraduate students recruited from a writing class. The research team asked subjects to read eight articles on the issue of paternalism and to write an essay that made an original contribution to the issue. The issue of paternalism can be summed-up by the question, "When is it right, if ever, for a society or an individual to limit another person's freedom for that person's own good?" For a detailed analysis of the data, see Geisler ("Toward a Sociocognitive Model," *Nature and Development of Expertise*). Here, the data will be used informally, to illustrate the level of detail about processes of writing that we believe is necessary in order to do the sort of knowledge building we are discussing.

4. It is important to note that we did not judge all problems that we observed as amenable to solutions involving the design of computer technology. For example, in response to some novice problems we observed, we also wrote a textbook (Kaufer, Geisler, Neuwirth).

Works Cited

Bazerman, Charles, and James Paradis, eds. *Textual Dynamics of the Professions.* Madison: University of Wisconsin Press, 1991.

Diesing, Paul. *Patterns of Discovery in the Social Sciences.* Chicago: Aldine Atherton, 1971.

Ericsson, K. Anders, and Herbert A. Simon. *Protocol Analysis: Verbal Reports as Data.* Cambridge, MA: The MIT Press, 1984.

Flower, Linda, and John R. Hayes. "A Cognitive Process of Theory of Writing." *College Composition and Communication* 32 (1981): 365-387.

Geisler, Cheryl. "Toward a Sociocognitive Model of Literacy: Constructing Mental Models in a Philosophical Conversation." *Textual Dynamics of the Professions.* Eds. Charles Bazerman and James Paradis. Madison: University of Wisconsin Press, 1991. 171-190.

———. *The Nature and Development of Expertise in Essayist Literacy.* Hillsdale, NJ: Lawrence Erlbaum Associates, forthcoming.

Goggin, Maureen Daly. *Writing Text for Hypertext: Problems with Conventional Composing Strategies.* Paper presented at the *Conference on College Composition and Communication.* Boston, MA: 1991.

Gould, John D. "How to Design Usable Systems." *Handbook of Human-Computer Interaction.* Ed. Martin Helander. Amsterdam: North-Holland, 1988. 757-789.

Haas, Christina. " "Seeing It on the Screen Isn't Really Seeing It": Computer Writers' Reading Problems." *Critical Perspectives on Computers and Composition.* Eds. Gail E. Hawisher and Cynthia L. Selfe. New York: Teachers College Press, 1989. 16-29.

———. "How the Writing Medium Shapes the Writing Process: Effects of Word Processing on Planning." *Research in the Teaching of English* 23 (1989): 181-207.

Haas, Christina, and John R. Hayes. "What Did I Just Say? Reading Problems in Writing with the Machine." *Research in the Teaching of English* 20 (1986): 22-35.

Hawisher, Gail E. "Studies in Word Processing." *Computers and Composition* 4 (1986): 6–31.

——— . "Research Update: Writing and Word Processing." *Computers and Composition* 5 (1988): 7–23.

——— . "Research and Recommendations for Computers and Composition." *Critical Perspectives on Computers and Composition Instruction.* Eds. Gail E. Hawisher and Cynthia L. Selfe. New York: Teachers College, 1989. 44–69.

Hayes, John R. *The Complete Problem-Solver.* Philadelphia: Franklin Press, 1981.

Hayes, John R., and Linda S. Flower. "Identifying the Organization of Writing Processes." *Cognitive Processes in Writing: An Interdisciplinary Approach.* Eds. Lee Gregg and Erwin Steinberg. Hillsdale: Lawrence Erlbaum, 1980. 3–30.

——— . "Uncovering Cognitive Processes in Writing: An Introduction to Protocol Analysis." *Research on Writing: Principles and Methods.* Eds. Peter Mosenthal, Lynne Tamor and Sean A. Walmsley. New York: Longman, 1983. 207–220.

Howes, Andrew, and Richard M. Young. *Predicting the Learnability of Task-Action Mappings. Computer-Human Interaction (CHI'91) Conference Proceedings.* Eds. Scott P. Robertson, Gary M. Olson, and Judith S. Olson. Baltimore: Association for Computing Machinery, 1991. 113–118.

Kaufer, David S., and Cheryl Geisler. "Novelty in Academic Writing." 6 (1989): 286–311.

Kaufer, David S., Cheryl Geisler, and Christine M. Neuwirth. *Writing from Sources: Exploring Issues through Reading and Writing.* San Diego: Harcourt, Brace, Javanovich, 1989.

Kozma, Robert B. "The Impact of Computer-Based Tools and Embedded Prompts on Writing Processes and Products of Novice and Advanced College Writers." *Cognition and Instruction* 8 (1991): 1–27.

Mackay, Wendy E. *Triggers and Barriers to Customizing Software. Computer Human Interaction (CHI'91) Conference Proceedings.* Eds. Scott P. Robertson, Gary M. Olson, and Judith S. Olson. Baltimore: Association for Computing Machinery, 1991. 153–160.

McLeod, Susan. "Some Thoughts about Feelings: The Affective Domain and the Writing Process." *College Composition and Communication* 38 (1987): 426–435.

Neuwirth, Christine M., and David S. Kaufer. *The Role of External Representation in the Writing Process: Implications for the Design of Hypertext-Based Writing Tools. Hypertext'89 Proceedings.* Baltimore: Association for Computing Machinery, 1989. 319–341.

Neuwirth, Christine M., David S. Kaufer, Ravinder Chandhok, and James H. Morris. *Issues in the Design of Computer Support for Co-authoring and Commenting. Third Conference on Computer Supported Cooperative Work (CSCW'90) Proceedings.* Baltimore: Association for Computing Machinery, 1990. 193–195.

Neuwirth, Christine M., David S. Kaufer, Richard Chimera, and Terilyn Gillespie. *The NOTES Program: A Hypertext Application for Reading and Writing. Hypertext'87 Proceedings.* Chapel Hill: Association for Computing Machinery, 1987. 121–141.

Neuwirth, Christine M., David S. Kaufer, Gary Keim, and Terilyn Gillespie. *The COMMENTS Program: Computer Support for Response to Writing.* Center for Educational Computing in English, English Department, Carnegie Mellon University, 1988.

Odell, Lee, Dixie Goswami, and Anne Herrington. "The Discourse-Based Interview: A Procedure for Exploring the Tacit Knowledge of Writers in Nonacademic Settings." *Research on Writing: Principles and Methods.* Eds. Peter Mosenthal, Lynne Tamor, and Sean A. Walmsley. New York: Longman, 1983. 221–236.

Witte, Stephen P. "Pretext and Composing." *College Composition and Communication* 38 (1987): 397–425.

Woods, David D. "Visual momentum: A Concept to Improve the Cognitive Coupling of Person and Computer." *International Journal of Man-Machine Studies* 21 (1984): 229–244.

Woods, David D., and Emily M. Roth. "Cognitive Systems Engineering." *Handbook of Human-Computer Interaction.* Ed. Martin Helander. Amsterdam: North-Holland, 1988. 3–43.

11

Ringing in the Virtual Age:
Hypermedia Authoring Software and the Revival of Faculty-Based Software Development in Composition

Paul LeBlanc

Springfield College

At a recent meeting of my department I showed my English department colleagues the new IBM hypermedia document on Tennyson's "Ulysses." They watched, rapt, as a user highlighted parts of the poem and with two or three clicks of a mouse called up on-screen a video of professional actors reading those lines. The user could choose to hear the line "This is my son, mine own Telemachus" read first with pride and then with disdain. The user called up definitions of words that included voice commentary and still photo examples. From a list of themes he clicked on "heroes" and an excerpt from Bill Moyers' interview with Joseph Campbell appeared on screen, and he then branched to commentary from various literary critics discussing the theme as it pertained to the poem. In the course of forty minutes the user followed an idiosyncratic path through multiple media and a collection of resources that was both broad and deep.

At the end of the meeting, the most senior member of my department only half jokingly said, "They won't need us anymore." That is, of course, not true. Yet hypermedia dramatically alters the relationship between writers and readers and texts—and between us as teachers of writing and all three. Hypermedia authoring software, now widely available, allows teachers to create hypermedia applications like the one described above and to make the technology their own. These software construction tools, the most well known of which is HyperCard, stand to reinvigorate and fuel faculty-based software development within composition studies. More than any other technology, hypermedia authoring programs invite writing teachers into the virtual age.

Can Writing Teachers Develop Hypermedia?

The history of faculty-based software development in composition hasn't been a particularly happy one in general. When writing teachers have created software their efforts have often gone unrecognized, unrewarded, and unsupported (LeBlanc). While a wide range of commercial software tools for writing have emerged in the last five years, including increasingly sophisticated word-processing, grammar and style-checking, desktop publishing, and electronic-mail programs, the availability of faculty-developed software for composition has been poor. There are indeed some very good faculty-developed programs, the Daedalus Instructional System, PROSE, and SEEN for example, but not many. A complex set of factors has impeded the development of software by composition specialists, but the most costly and time-consuming one for many has been the software programming, writing the thousands of lines of code, that substantiates the program concept and design. For these, and other reasons, most academic software development in the field has moved to either research-based environments like Carnegie Mellon or entrepreneurial settings like the Daedalus Group or XperCom. Thus, one of the richest potential resources for new academic software, the practitioner/ researcher, is being driven from the field. However, the development of low-cost hypermedia authoring systems may change the situation since such systems now allow non-programmers to create software.

While hypermedia's theoretical development has occurred over decades in the work of people like Vannevar Bush, Douglas Engelbart, and Ted Nelson and has been well documented (see Bolter; Beck and Spicer), until fairly recently its practical use was restricted to research settings like Xerox's Palo Alto Research Center (PARC), Brown University's Institution for Research in Information and Scholarship (IRIS), and Peter Brown's research lab at the University of Kent (Beck and Spicer 23). In 1986 Brown's program was commercially released as OWL International's GUIDE. It was followed shortly thereafter in 1987 by Bill Atkinson's HyperCard, packaged with Apple Computer's Macintosh product line and designed to make non-programmers into software developers. There now exist dozens of such authoring programs including

HyperWriter, Hyperties, StorySpace, Folio VIEWS, SuperCard, and Hyper-Word. Most recently, industry giant IBM has weighed in with Asymetrix's ToolBook. The rapid proliferation of hypermedia applications is reflected in the sales of authoring programs, $1.6 million in 1987 and projected at $485 million by 1993 (Fersko-Weiss 242).

The ability for non-programmers to create high-level, complex hypermedia courseware is the defining characteristic of hypermedia authoring software and that which addresses that major obstacle to faculty-based software development in the past, that is, the aforementioned need to program. While there exists in many of the faculty I meet a great deal of interest in creating software, almost all see it as a technical endeavor beyond their abilities. In an authoring program like ToolBook, text, graphics, photos, sound, and video can be combined with no knowledge of programming and little training. Indeed, John Wood, a development expert for Asymetrix Corporation, says, "The initial learning time seems to be quicker for people who have never programmed before" (Johnston 25). An average learning time of 16 hours for HyperCard is reported for novice faculty (Beck and Spicer 24). Authoring programs now enable non-programmers to assemble hypermedia documents, integrate the varied media, create the links between nodes or units of information, and design the interface of the document with stunning ease.

At the same time, the costs of hypermedia development have come down. In fact, the plummeting costs of computer technology are almost as responsible for putting hypermedia in the hands of faculty as is the creation of the authoring programs. Already, one can purchase the hardware necessary for text, graphic, and photograph based hypermedia for about $2,000. While sound and video require additional hardware and expense, there exist thousands of videodisc and CD-ROM titles as a resource for creating hypermedia documents. While most authoring software has a component programming language and familiarity with it may be necessary for some high level effects within a document, animation for example, most of these programming languages are designed for non-programmers. An example of the programs' ease of use is John McDaid's work at New York University, where the students in his freshman composition course create hypermedia essays on topics like Van Gogh and the history of New York's transit system. Using HyperCard, they combine their texts with photographs, graphs, and maps (Apple 36). Robert Beck and Donald Spicer, reporting on the work of the HyperTeam Project at Dartmouth, indicate the liberating effect of these programs. They write, "The development climate was like a return to the 1960s where a faculty member with an idea and a bright undergraduate were an academic software development team" (24).

Should Writing Teachers Develop Hypermedia Software?

Although it has become easy for writing teachers to develop hypermedia software, it may not be immediately clear that they should. Given the inevitable proliferation of commercially developed hypermedia software, one might argue that writing teachers should leave software development in the hands of corporate developers and use the medium as it is developed for us. That argument fails to recognize the professional role we have in the emergence of hypermedia as a pedagogical and communication technology. Writing teachers should develop their own hypermedia software for the following reasons:

- commercially developed software does not often serve well the needs of the classroom;

- hypermedia may enable much current pedagogical theory better than print media;

- our students will have increasing need for hypermedia literacy as they enter the workplace.

As McDaid says, "It seems we are in a 'phase change' between technologies, when the characteristics of the defining medium become momentarily apparent (McLuhan 27). Here is an opportunity and, for composition theorists, a responsibility" ("Toward an Ecology" 217–8). The opportunity we have as teachers is to find new and perhaps more effective ways to teach. Our responsibility as writing teachers, at least in part, is to ensure that our pedagogy reflects the evolving nature of literacy as our students will encounter it in the world—and increasingly, that involves computer-based communications.

Why not commercial software?

Writing continues to be the primary use of microcomputers and commercial software developers are keenly aware of that lucrative market. However, few commercial programs are designed around the needs of the classroom, current composition theory, or the more egalitarian values of the academy. As Richard Ohmann argues, "computers are an evolving technology like any other, shaped within particular social relations, and responsive to the needs of those with the power to direct that evolution" (680). For example, networking software is designed for business use and as such it builds a strict hierarchy of rights for information access and security, while the writing class, in contrast, demands almost the opposite dynamic. "Borrowing" software designed for other fields and applications might, in the short-run, be easier than developing software on one's own.

As a result, however, writing teachers will struggle to make commercially produced programs fit their theory and pedagogy, a reversal of the proper order in which software design should suit theory-based pedagogical goals.

[handwritten margin note: Programs from bus. don't work in classroom]

The need to base commercially developed software on sound theory has led to a greater role for the "content expert" in development efforts. While commercial developers need content experts, the new authoring programs mean that content experts no longer need the commercial developers. With hypermedia authoring programs, expertise, manifested in the information assembled for a program and the links created and/or allowed between that information, becomes the primary determinant in the ability to create software, not technological know-how. As John Thiesmeyer has pointed out, much writing software has been shaped by the programmer's ability to do something technological instead of by pedagogy or theory (75–88). For example, because rule-bound knowledge is most easily programmed, grammar, style, and spell checkers continue to abound, even though they address writing concerns that receive scant attention in current composition theory.

[handwritten margin note: based on tech. not pedagogy or theory]

The implications of our field's reliance on commercial software developers are more serious and subtle than the mere inconvenience of appropriating business software to the classroom or a lack of desirable programs. The danger, as many have articulated it, is that the computer tools we use for writing have the power to alter our conception of writing in fundamental ways (Lanham; Kaplan; Bolter; LeBlanc; McDaid, "Toward"). As Walter Ong argues, "Technologies are not mere exterior aids, but also interior transformations of consciousness, and never more than when they affect the word" (82). Thus we should heed Nancy Kaplan's warning that "in the marketplace for educational materials, many tools deeply rooted in our best understandings of writing and reading . . . may never come into being" (34). That is, of course, unless we take responsibility for developing those tools. As Slatin has argued in an on-line conference, "If we work actively on issues of design, if we work as developers of the technology and not only as consumers dependent upon other people to think about our needs, then we exert influence in profound and subtle ways" (January 1991). With hypermedia authoring programs we can manage the development of those tools, as the experts we are, or we can leave the endeavor to corporate interests who ultimately design software for profit. *[handwritten: profit]*

How does hypermedia support current pedagogical theory?

In higher education, and increasingly within the secondary schools, the number one use of microcomputers has been for writing. Writers of all types and abilities have discovered the power of the computer as a writing

[handwritten note at bottom: #1 use of microcomputers in 2nday schools is for WRITING]

metaphors prove increasingly inadequate, we should begin to more fully tool. In the classroom, writing teachers have similarly discovered profound pedagogical power in computers and attendant technologies such as networking, telecommunications, and software tools. The computer reveals new possibilities for the teaching of writing and makes the traditional writing class seem increasingly constrained. Indeed, computer technology often seems ideally suited to writing and current theories of composition. Discussing networking, for example, Trent Batson has commented, "It was as if some of the current theories about how to write were developed specifically with networks in mind, even though the developers didn't know it" (32). Hypermedia is having a similar impact on those teachers who have discovered it. As Catherine Smith says of those first exposed to it, they "attest to the impact of hypertext on their traditional methods and meanings. They seem minds stunned with possibility" (237). In the few short years that hypermedia authoring systems have been widely available, faculty in a wide variety of disciplines have developed their own courseware for teaching political science, theatre and costume design, physics, foreign languages, nursing, and so on.

Hypermedia, in its least constrained forms, seems by nature to enable many of the pedagogical approaches and practices currently valued in composition studies. As an inclusive medium, hypermedia encourages the linking of multiple texts (Slatin, "Reading" 876). It supports associative thinking, the creation of multiple informational structures, and active knowledge-making on the part of students (Joyce 11). It reflects the recursion we find in the writing process, as well as holistic and integrative thinking (McDaid, "Toward" 215). As George Landow and Paul Delaney point out,

> the implications of hypertext converge with some major points of contemporary and semiological theory, particularly with Derrida's emphasis on decentering, with Barthe's conception of the readerly versus writerly text, with post-modernism's rejection of sequential narratives and unitary perspectives, and with the issue of "intertextuality." In fact, hypertext creates an almost embarrassingly literal embodiment of such concepts. (6)

As the above list of characteristics suggest, hypermedia offers intriguing possibilities for pedagogical applications of cognitive, social constructivist, and other theoretical approaches to composition. As important, and this is a point that many hypermedia theorists make, new theory and pedagogy will undoubtedly emerge from our increasing use of hypermedia and movement away from print literacy and print assumptions (Landow and Delaney; Joyce; McDaid "Toward"; C. Smith; Zimmerman). As Eldred and Fortune point out elsewhere in this volume, we have tended to describe, and thus understand, hypermedia (and other technologies as well) with print-based terms and metaphors. However, as those terms and metaphors prove increasingly inadequate, we should begin to more fully understand in its own epistemological light the theoretical and pedagogical ramifications of hypermedia.

How will we prepare our students for the workplace?

The arrival of hypermedia authoring systems comes at a crucial time in composition studies. While writing in the workplace is being transformed by virtual technologies and hypermedia (Shirk 81), the field of composition, always somewhat resistant to computers, has remained less aware of the transformations in literacy taking place in nonacademic settings. While it may be an uncomfortable fact for many academics in the humanities, what happens in the workplace exerts a powerful influence on the classroom—and perhaps no more so than in the area of literacy. Hypermedia documents are now being used as repair manuals for everything from automobiles to B-1 bombers, for museum exhibits, for information booths at places like Epcot Center, for training medical students, and for delivering engineering reports (Fersko-Weiss 244; Beck and Spicer 23). For our students, its use as an information database and form of communication will be common in almost any field they choose to enter.

Because so much hypermedia in the workplace is still designed as a way of searching a database for specific information (e.g., finding a text in an electronic card catalog or instruction for brake repair), the radically different demands that it places on authors and that "constructive" hypermedia places on readers (Joyce 11-2) are only beginning to be felt. The degree to which our current writing curricula fail to prepare writers and readers for the hypermedia environments they will increasingly use is illustrated in the engineering department of a large aerospace firm where I had an opportunity to observe hypermedia in use. The engineers in this particular division were creating hypermedia engineering reports for their supervisors that combined text, graphics, video, and sound. In one of their reports on a jet engine test, for example, the supervisor could read the text node on the actual firing of the engine, click on the "hotword" compression in a pop-up window and see a graphic representation of the compression data, click on a video button and see a full motion video of the firing in a separate window. The conclusion node of the report was formal and technical text, but a comments button activated the recorded oral comments of the engineering team, each one of which could be called up individually. The supervisor could reconstruct these reports, combine parts of different reports, and build on them in his own reporting to his supervisors.

While the engineers had been trained to use the system to "write" their reports and enjoyed the use of a technical support team who supplied them with the digitized video of the engine test, for example, no one had discussed with them the ways that their hypermedia documents might be effective or ineffective. For example, as one of them pointed out, new users of the system were easily identified because they changed their background templates and color so often, merely because it was easy to do so. Experienced authors had developed some rules of thumb. For example, they tended to use a single background template for the screen. They keyed different kinds of information to different colors. They might have red screen borders for performance data nodes, green borders for engine specifications nodes, and blue borders for analysis. In this way, readers would have color cues to what kinds of nodes they were calling up.

Understanding what makes an effective hypermedia document is the kind of knowledge we will need to impart in the virtual age writing classes where we train students to use hypermedia and other computer writing technologies. In the absence of that training, the engineers were doing with hypermedia documents much the same thing Cynthia Selfe describes her student writers doing in a computer-based writing class, learning on their own screen grammars for improving readability (12). One might even see in the engineers' conclusion sections, where they combined formal technical reporting and informal oral and textual commentary, the creation of a new discourse type that bridges oral and print literacies— that, in the words of Plato's Socrates, "can defend itself, and knows when to speak and when to be silent" (Levinson 3; DiPardo and DiPardo). The experience of the engineers points to our need as teachers for an understanding of the new discourse conventions, grammars, and types which the new medium creates and demands. We might add to that list the need to know what constitutes an effective use of video, graphics, sound, and animation.

As hypermedia becomes pervasive, institutions will feel increasing pressure to prepare students for its use, a phenomenon similar to that which has driven the creation of writing across-the-curriculum-programs across the country. One field related to composition studies, technical and professional writing, is grappling with that pressure now. As illustrated in the case of the engineers, hypermedia is being widely used in technical documentation and manuals, and our colleagues in technical and business writing are struggling to adjust to the paradigm shift in their field (Zimmerman; Shirk; Grice; Alsculer). New textbooks in the area necessarily address the impact of technology on the work of business and technical writers. While Muriel Zimmerman acknowledges the continued importance of print within the field, she asserts:

> it is a mistake to believe that our jobs [technical writing] will continue to
> be the same. We may continue to be called writers; modern truckdrivers
> are called teamsters, and fireman ride diesel trains—but I don't think
> that we will do much . . . of what we presently do. (245)

A similar transformation of communication and information handling will take place in other fields (including academia), yet composition studies has scarcely begun to assess the impact of the new literacy and account for it in our theory, our research, or our teaching.

Will Writing Teachers Develop Hypermedia?

With hypermedia authoring programs, writing teachers can create their own programs and courseware, and, given the transformation of literacy taking place through technology, should do so. Whether or not the profession will enter the virtual age is another question for which there are two formidable challenges to be met:

- the challenge of knowledge-making in an area that is new, dramatically different from what we know, and that seems characterized by rapid and continued change;

- the challenge of overcoming the resistance of our departments and our field to technology and virtual age literacy.

While authoring programs have now given writing teachers the power to explore hypermedia as a pedagogical and communication environment, the potential blossoming of faculty-based software development it presages depends upon increased research and its being valued and rewarded.

Challenge #1: Bridging the knowledge gap.

If we are to know how to use hypermedia and to teach our students how to use it, we need to follow the model of other disciplines like Education and Computer Science which have constructed a much larger research base on hypermedia within their fields than we have in ours. We can give writing teachers authoring tools, but they will find precious little research within their own field for guiding their development efforts. Writing teachers need a strong theoretical base for their pedagogy and that does not now exist for hypermedia. We need more research like Joyce's on exploratory and constructive hypertext, Slatin's on reading hypertext, and Shirk's on metaphor and hypertext if we are to develop effective hypermedia software that takes full advantage of the medium's power. As Shirk points out:

> Communication theorists need to become involved in the evolution of hypertext. . . . If those concerned about communication do not participate in the development of new theories for the new technologies available in the field, others will accomplish the task without them. (198–9)

Colleagues in other fields are exploring questions such as reader disorientation (Conklin), cognitive overload and mode-free operation or rambling (Jones, Gaines and Vickers; Hammond), impact of learning styles (Heller), and design (Kearsley; Eckols and Rossett), questions we need to investigate as we construct effective pedagogy for the virtual writing class.

We can begin to close the knowledge gap by drawing upon other disciplines and research such as that just cited. One of the strengths of composition as a field has been its expansiveness of approach and interaction with fields like cognitive science, literary criticism, reading theory, and philosophy. We might now turn to computer science and art to learn more about interface and instructional design to better understand technology-based pedagogy, to media studies to better integrate video in hypermedia, and information theory to more effectively construct document nodes. That knowledge must not simply be of the "how-to" variety, though that will be helpful as well to fledgling software developers, but must come from sound theory and research. Though the present base of hypermedia programs in composition is very small, as the widespread use of authoring systems occurs, there will exist more and more hypermedia documents to examine and observe in use.

Because the technology is so new and our experience with the medium is so limited, it offers wonderful opportunities for research and for developing new research techniques. As Cynthia Selfe points out elsewhere in this text:

> Indeed, in a virtual age—given the complicating factors of software, hardware, and the lack of training and experience—we might well need more observation and research, and different kinds of research, than we have required in other instructional settings. (Chapter 2)

An increasingly useful tool in that research will be the computer itself, for unlike any other tool for writing, the computer has the capability to record its own use. Many hypermedia programs allow for tracking a user's path through a hypermedia web. That path, termed an "audit trail" by Schwier and Misanchuk, can offer insights into how different kinds of learners construct knowledge within a hypermedia environment (2). As Schwier and Misanchuk point out, the study of such audit trails might reveal the influence of gender, socioeconomic status, age, and religion on the paths learners take through a document (2). John Smith and his associates in the WE project have developed a tracking function in the program that records the use of the system, replays it, and parses the record transcript to create structural representations of the system's use (10-19). Such computer-based research tools are powerful, not only because they have the ability to process a great deal of analytical data quickly, but also because they operate unobtrusively as observational tools, unlike think-aloud protocols, for example (Smith 10). As observational tools in research, computers can supply another source of data for ethnographic research, which Marcia Curtis and Elizabeth Klem persuasively argue is largely missing from computer and writing research and is desperately needed (Chapter 9).

One of the main focal points of research needs to be hypermedia links and nodes, for our ability to create effective hypermedia programs largely depends on our understanding of what constitutes effective nodes and links. The question is complex, as Slatin explains:

> The approach you choose to the problem of identifying links and nodes will depend on several factors: your understanding of the ways in which the material is related; your sense of who your readers are (are they primarily browsers? users? co-authors?). ("Reading" 879)

Research in this area, using such techniques as audit trails and computer tracking and analysis as described above, is vital, for the construction of a hypermedia program is largely a pedagogical endeavor which will require the in-depth understanding of learner behaviors that the aforementioned research techniques may provide. In virtual age research, terms such as linking and constructing will be as common as revising and prewriting are in current print-based composition research.

Challenge #2: Support for software development.

While authoring programs remove the programming hurdle from faculty development efforts, other hurdles which still stand in the way of widespread software development, reside within English departments where software development has historically been unrewarded, unsupported, and often devalued. One of the primary reasons is that software is seen as mere pedagogy, a point echoed in the 1988 report of the FIPSE Technology Study Group:

> The conflict faculty face when forced to choose between the rewards of improving learning in a course and the rewards of publishing research results is deeply rooted in the culture of higher education. We recognize that the traditional and most significant system of faculty reward, tenure, and promotion based on disciplinary research, is not flexible enough at many institutions to encompass work in developing curriculum. (Balestri 46)

English departments, possessing perhaps a deeply held mistrust of technology, have been particularly guilty of discouraging software development, as noted elsewhere (Kaplan; Sommers Chapter 3, this text; LeBlanc).

However, there exists seeds for change in departmental attitudes toward software development, primarily because English faculty are more conscious of computers. At my institution, for example, every member of the department has a computer in his or her office, with modem hookup to our computer writing center and the library. Every section of freshman composition has some scheduled time in the computer writing center. In addition, scholarly interest in the area continues to grow. At the MLA Conference, the NCTE Conference, and the CCCC, computers and composition sessions are well attended. The annual Computers and Writing Conference has been held for almost 10 years now. Slowly, more computer and composition articles are being published in journals like *College English, College Composition and Communication,* and *Research in the Teaching of English. Computers and Composition* has matured from a newsletter to a top-notch journal, and publishers are releasing more computers and composition texts.

Hypermedia authoring software addresses two other areas where departmental support has been poor in the past: release time and funding. In a 1988 EDUCOM survey, sixty percent of the respondents cited a lack of released time as a serious impediment to software development (Keane and Gaither 56). While the time necessary to create quality hypermedia programs should not be underestimated, as mentioned earlier, authoring programs like ToolBook and HyperCard can be learned quickly and require infinitely less development time than do traditional programming languages. As for funding, the faculty developer has no need for hired programmers, cutting a major expense, and the hardware required for development is increasingly affordable.

The slowly increasing legitimacy of computers and composition within English, the growing familiarity of English faculty with technology, and the decrease in development time and cost help make faculty-based composition software a more agreeable venture than it was just a few years ago. That said, faculty software developers still need to educate their colleagues and chairs on the evaluation of software efforts. Joseph Bourque's 1983 *College English* article "Understanding and Evaluating: The Humanist as Computer Specialist" is a still helpful guide in those efforts, though his criteria come close to those one might use to evaluate a textbook. While such criteria would be appropriate for much software, some software—and particularly hypermedia software—might help us redefine our concepts of writing and text, and when accompanied by theory and research, these efforts are substantially different than the production of another textbook and should be evaluated differently.

Conclusion

Composition theorists who have started to explore hypermedia seem to undergo a kind of conversion experience (Joyce 41). I have thus far resisted recounting my own initial experiences with hypermedia, though my tone may reveal the tremendous excitement I feel regarding this technology—as if I were standing with Gutenberg on the brink of a new world. Jay David Bolter asserts in *Writing Spaces:*

> The computer is restructuring our current economy of writing. It is changing the cultural status of writing as well as the method of producing books. It is changing the relationship of the author to the text and of both author and text to the reader. (3)

Until fairly recently, most teachers of writing did not have much possibility for acquiring the technological knowledge or equipment to enter the realm of hypertext or hypermedia. Hypermedia authoring programs have changed all that. However, as T.S. Eliot's Magi reminds us, new ages are attended by uneasiness, uncertainty, and ignorance (67).

Our success in appropriating this technology—and we know how easily computer technology can be misused and its potential never realized— will rely on our increasing understanding of hypermedia as a "writing space," to use Bolter's phrase. To acquire that understanding and promote the creation of effective and innovative hypermedia applications within the field, we must step up our research efforts, integrate new research techniques made possible by computers, and support, within departments and composition studies, research and general software development by writing teachers. Otherwise, as a field, we will become increasingly out of touch with the writing and reading our students will be expected to do as they leave our institutions, out of touch with the new millenium. As Slatin says, "A new medium involves both a new practice and a new rhetoric, a new body of theory" ("Reading" 870). Hypermedia is emerging as the key component within virtual age literacy, and hypermedia authoring systems can give us the power to play our role as teachers and researchers within the new paradigm. Imagine what will happen, then, as hypermedia is placed in the hands of thousands of writing teachers through the availability of authoring programs. Beck and Spicer suggest the power of such programs in their experience at Dartmouth:

> Yet the most enduring influence of this development effort and the emergence of powerful hypermedia authoring tools on the academic computing environment at Dartmouth is its enabling effect on the ability of a faculty member to become involved in software development. (50)

If we are to have a hand in shaping the new literacy, we need to nurture the faculty development and study of hypermedia. What makes the need so urgent is the profound changes in literacy that virtual technologies, but especially hypermedia, engender and the promising potential they hold. It is not that they "won't need us anymore," but that they—and here I mean the culture and certainly our students—need us as they may never have needed us before. They need us as researchers and teachers in the age of virtual literacy.

Works Cited

Alschuler, Liori. "Hand-crafted Hypertext—Lessons from the ACM Experiment." In Hypertext, Hypermedia, and the Social Construction of Information, Ed. Edward Barrett. Cambridge: MIT Press, 1989.

Apple Computers. *Learning How to Write . . . Curriculum Guide.* Cupertino: Apple Computer, Inc., 1990.

Balestri, Diane Pelkus. *Ivory Towers, Silicon Basements: Learner-Centered Computing in Postsecondary Education.* "McKinney: Academic Computing Publications, 1988." A report from the FIPSE Technology Study Group. McKinney: Academic Computing Publications, 1988.

Batson, Trent. "The ENFI Project: A Networked Classroom Approach to Writing Instruction." *Academic Computing* (February 1988): 32–57.

Beck, Robert J., and Donald Spicer. "Hypermedia in Academia." *Academic Computing* (February 1988): 22–50.

Bolter, Jay David. *Writing Space.* Hillsdale: Earlbaum.1991.

Bourque, Joseph. "Understanding and Evaluating: The Humanist as a Computer Specialist." *College English* 45 (1983): 67–73.

Conklin, Jeff. "Hypertext: An Introduction and Survey." *IEEE Computer* 2.9 (1987): 14–41.

Curtis, Marcia, and Elizabeth Klem. "The Virtual Context: Ethnography in the Computer-Equipped Classroom." [In this volume].

DiPardo, Anne, and Mike DiPardo. "Towards the Metapersonal Essay: Exploring the Potential of Hypertext in the Composition Classroom." *Computers and Composition* 7.3 (August 1990): 7–22.

Eckols, Steven L., and Allison Rossett. "HyperCard for the Design, Development, and Delivery of Instruction." *Performance Improvement Quarterly* 2.4 (1989): 2–21.

Eliot, T.S. "Journey of the Magi." *The Wasteland and Other Poems.* New York: Harvest: 1962.

Fersko-Weiss, Henry. "3-D Reading with the Hypertext Edge." *PC Magazine* 10 (May 1991): 241–269.

Gaines, Brian R., and Joan N. Vickers. "Design Considerations for Hypermedia Systems." *Microcomputers for Information Management* 5.1 (March 1988): 1–27.

Grice, Richard. "Information Development is Part of Product Development—Not an Afterthought." *Text, Context, and Hypertext.* Ed. Edward Barrett. Cambridge: MIT, 1988.

Hammond, N. "Hypermedia and Learning: Who Guides Whom?" In *Lecture Notes in Computer Science: Computer-Assisted Learning,* eds. G. Goos and J. Hartmanis. Berlin: Springer Verlag: 1989.

Heller, Rachelle S. "The Role of Hypermedia in Education: A Look at the Research Issues." *Journal of Research on Computing in Education* (Summer 1990): 431–441.

Johnston, Stuart J. "Software Reusability Depends on Teamwork and Cooperation." *InfoWorld* 11.25 (June 1989): 19.

Jones, W. "How Do We Distinguish the Hyper From the Hype in Non-Linear Text?" *Human-Computer Interaction.* Eds. H. Bullinger and B. Shackel. New York: North-Holland: 1987.

Joyce, Michael. "Siren Shapes: Exploratory and Constructive Hypertexts." *Academic Computing.* (November 1988): 10–42.

Kaplan, Nancy. "Ideology, Technology, and the Future of Writing Instruction." In *Evolving Perspectives on Computers and Composition Studies: Questions for the 1990s.* Eds. Gail E. Hawisher and Cynthia L. Selfe. Urbana: *Computers and Composition* and NCTE, 1991.

Keane, Dorothy, and Greg Gaither. "The Effects of Academic Software on Learning and Motivation." In *Facilitating Academic Software Development,* ed. Jerry W. Sprecher. McKinney: Academic Computing Publications, 1988.

Kearsley, Greg. "Authoring Considerations for Hypertext." Educational Technology (November 1988): 21–24.

Landow, George, and Paul Delany. "Hypertext, Hypermedia and Literary Studies: The State of the Art." In *Hypermedia and Literary Studies,* eds. Paul Delany and George Landow. Cambridge, MA: MIT, 1991.

Lanham, Richard. "The Electronic Word: Literary Study and the Digital Revolution." *New Literary History: A Journal of Theory and Interpretation* 20 (1988–9): 265–290.

LeBlanc, Paul. *Software Development and Composition Studies.* Urbana: NCTE, forthcoming.

Levinson, Paul. "Intelligent Writing: The Electronic Liberation of Text." Paper presented at Annual Meeting of the American Association for the Advancement of Science. San Francisco, 1989.

McDaid, John. "Toward an Ecology of Hypermedia." *In Evolving Perspectives on Computers and Composition Studies: Questions for the 1990s,* eds. Gail E. Hawisher and Cynthia L. Selfe. Urbana: Computers and Composition and NCTE, 1991.

———. "Breaking Frames: Toward an Ecology of Hypermedia." Paper presented at the Computers and Writing Conference. Minneapolis, 1989.

McLuhan, Marshall. *Understanding Media.* New York: McGraw-Hill, 1964.

Ohmann, Richard. "Literacy, Technology, and Monopoly Capital." *College English* 47.7 (November 1985): 675–689.

Ong, Walter. *Orality and Literacy: The Technologizing of the World.* New York: Methuen, 1982.

Schwier, Richard, and Earl Misanchuk. "Analytic Tools and Research Issues for Interactive Media." Paper presented at Meeting of Association for Media and Technology in Education in Canada. St. John's, NFLD, 1990.

Selfe, Cynthia. "Redefining Literacy: The Multilayered Grammars of Computers." In *Critical Perspectives on Computers and Composition Instruction,* eds. Gail E. Hawisher and Cynthia L. Selfe. New York: Teachers College Press, 1989 (3–15).

Shirk, Henrietta Nickels. "Hypertext and Composition Studies." In *Evolving Perspectives on Computers and Composition Studies: Questions for the 1990s,* eds. Gail E. Hawisher and Cynthia L. Selfe. Urbana: Computers and Composition and NCTE, 1991.

Slatin, John. "Reading Hypertext: Order and Coherence in a New Medium." *College English* 52.8 (December 1990): 870–883.

——— . Comments on Megabyte University Electronic Conference. January 11, 1991.

Smith, Catherine. "Reconceiving Hypertext." In *Evolving Perspectives on Computers and Composition Studies: Questions for the 1990s,* eds. Gail E. Hawisher and Cynthia L. Selfe. Urbana: *Computers and Composition* and NCTE, 1991.

Smith, John, and Mark Rooks and Gordon Ferguson. "A Cognitive Grammar for Writing: Version 1.0." *Text Lab Report TR89–011.* University of North Carolina-Chapel Hill. April 1989.

Sommers, Elizabeth. "Political Imediments to Virtual Reality." [In this volume.]

Theismeyer, John. "Should We Do What We Can?" In *Critical Perspectives on Computers and Composition Instruction,* eds. Gail E. Hawisher and Cynthia L. Selfe. New York: Teachers College Press, 1989 (3–15).

Zimmerman, Muriel. "Reconstruction of a Profession: New Roles for Writers in the Computer Industry." In *Hypertext, Hypermedia, and the Social Construction of Information,* ed. by Edward Barrett. Cambridge, MA: MIT Press, 1989.

12

What Are They Talking About?
Computer Terms That English Teachers May Need to Know

Richard J. Selfe

Michigan Technological University

Although the editors of this book and the authors of the various chapters have tried to keep specialized terminology to a minimum, there are certain terms—that appear here or that will come up in later discussions you might have with colleagues—that may need further definition. The short glossary that follows should provide definitions for and information about many of these terms. For explanations of additional terms or for further detail on specific terms, I suggest obtaining a copy of Brian Pfaffenberger's *Que's Computer User's Dictionary* (1990). Many of the technical definitions in this chapter are derived from information presented in that volume. For those readers who would like a basic and more discursive definition of key terms connected with word processing written specifically for writing teachers, I would suggest "A Writing Teacher's Guide to Computerese," by James L. Collins (Collins and Sommers).

GENERAL

ASCII An acronym that stands for the "American Standard Code For Information Interchange," this term is generally used to refer to "plain vanilla" text (or other data) that can be easily transferred from one computer to another because it is stripped of all the control characters that are particular to a specific software or hardware environment. Most word-processing packages now have the ability to *import and export* files in ASCII format so that users can send them to other users who work on different hardware and software systems.

Consultants In a virtual classroom or computer-supported writing facilities, consultants are often, but not always, students who have some special training or expertise. Technical consultants, for example, generally have some hardware or software expertise, or both, on one or more systems (e.g., Macintosh, DOS, UNIX). Other consultants may have expertise in particular applications (e.g., word-processing software packages, drawing programs, page-layout programs) or in providing support for communicators. Some facilities pay their consultants for their work, others use volunteer consultants (who work in exchange for access to the computers, for experience in teaching, or for the fun of it), others provide course credit for such work, still others use a combination of such methods to entice these talented people into their lab/classrooms. One can never have too many consultants.

Distance Learning Using computers hooked to WANs (see "Network" below) and equipped with telecommunications software, learners can attend "classes" offered at sites distant from their own. Sometimes, distance learning involves an exchange of video or television images.

DOS An acronym that stands for "Disk Operating System," this is the most common operating system for IBM compatible systems. This software essentially runs the computer, telling it what to do with the commands that you and your software send to the computer.

High Density This is a strategy for packing more information onto a computer disk by using very small magnetic particles. On a high density disk, one can store up to a megabyte of information. As you might guess, such disks cost more than regular disks.

Icon A picture that represents a location (e.g., a trash can or a disk), an application (e.g., Microsoft Word or HyperCard), or a tool (e.g., a paintbrush or an eraser).

Mass-Storage or Optical-Storage Devices A device connected to a computer on which users can store documents, graphics, or other projects. Mass-storage devices are particularly handy for teachers dealing with video, complex graphics, large databases and other information that requires an extensive amount of memory. This term can refer to several kinds of devices: for example, 5.25" and 3.5" floppy drives (even though the 3.5" drives don't "flop" because of their hard cases) that store from .36 to 1.4 megabytes (or "megs") of data, internal or external hard drives that store from 6.0 to 660 megs and more, removable-platter harddrives that provide the capability of storing information on platters (containing

40 megs or more of memory) and can be removed and stored on a shelf, and tape backup systems that store information on specialized cassette tapes. Currently, the computer industry is developing optical-storage drives (an audio CD is one example of this type of technology) that store much larger amounts of data. Currently most affordable optical-storage devices are "read only," which means that they permanently store one set of data (graphics, audio, video, text, etc.). Users cannot store new information on these read-only devices. However, the computer industry is moving toward "read/write" optical storage systems that will allow users to read *and* write on such devices.

Megabyte A term that refers to an amount of stored data equal to one million characters (letters, numbers, symbols) of text. It's equivalent to 1000 kilobytes, commonly refered to as 1000 "KB" or 1000 "K." The word megabyte is often abbrievated as "meg."

Menu Driven Refers to systems that allow users to choose from a menu of items (programs, applications, drives), rather than typing in commands consisting of *alphanumeric characters*—letters or numbers. *Pull-down menus*, like those on the Apple Macintosh system, pull down from the top of the screen like window shades to reveal choices to users.

Navigate The process of moving about purposefully within a virtual environment. For example, readers of a hypertext or hypermedia document navigate from node to node via links. Each reader chooses his/her own path of navigation, depending on interests, curiosity, associations, directions, etc. The term navigation suggests the wide-open spaces involved in virtual environments and the need to find one's way with the help of *navigational devices* (nodes, links, web maps, files, menus) that are particular to electronic environments.

Platform Describes a unique and complete computer system. Each platform—such as the IBM, UNIX, or Macintosh—approaches computer-use problems from different perspectives. Each computer configuration generally has both advantages and disadvantages. For instance, an IBM platform has a very open system that is easily manipulated by sophisticated DOS system programers, while their applications are somewhat more difficult to learn. The Macintosh system is less available to most users but allows them to focus on easy-to-use, sophisticated applications such as word processing, graphics, desktop publishing, and desktop video.

Video Capture Refers to the process of freezing a video image and storing it digitally so that it can be displayed on a computer screen or printed as a still image in a document. Video capture requires special hardware and software as well as large amounts of memory.

Virtual Refers to things that are stored in the digital domain of a computer; they are not physical entities. Hence, classes held via computer, which never meet in a traditional classroom, are termed "virtual classrooms" (Hiltz). Text which exists only in the computer's memory is called "virtual" text.

DESKTOP PUBLISHING

DTP An acronym that stands for "DeskTop Publishing," the use of personal computers and the appropriate software to produce publications that approach typeset quality (1200 DPI). Generally, desktop publishing systems use word-processing software, graphics software, and a WYSIWYG (see below) page-layout program—to combine text and graphics on the same page—as well as a laser printer for high quality output (300–600 DPI). Some high-end desktop publishing systems are linked to computerized typesetting systems like CompuGraphics.

DPI An acronym that stands for "Dots Per Inch," DPI is a measurement of the *resolution*, clarity or sharpness, of text and graphics. DPI refers to the number of dots a printer can produce within the space of a linear inch.

Fonts Fonts are complete sets of characters (capital letters, lowercase letters, end punctuation marks, internal punctuation marks, etc.) in a particular family (e.g., Helvetica, Bodini, Times) and style (e.g., Helvetica Narrow, Bodini Bold, and Times Roman). On a desktop publishing system, two kinds of fonts are generally used: *bit-mapped fonts* and *outline fonts*. The letters of bitmapped fonts are composed of individual patterns of dots, and the computer must store, in its memory, every pattern for every letter used. Users who want different sizes of bitmapped fonts (e.g., Helvetica Narrow 24 or Avant Garde 48) must store a complete character set for each size of this font in their computer's memory: bitmapped fonts cannot be enlarged or shrunk (scaled up or down) without distortion. Outline fonts, in contrast, are formed mathematically and can be enlarged or shrunk without being greatly distorted. These fonts, however, require special processing capabilities within a computer. Storing fonts, as you might guess from this description, can be a problem. There are two main ways to store fonts. *Built-in* or *resident fonts* are stored permanently in the computer's or printer's ROM (See ROM), but they also take up valuable memory space. *Downloadable* or *soft fonts* are sent transferred from the computer's hard drive to the printer's RAM (See RAM) when requested by the user—this approach takes time and many users consider it an inconvenience. Such a strategy does, however, eliminates the problem of devoting large chunks of ROM memory to font storage.

Multitasking Allows users to work with several programs at once without exiting any one program. The different programs are shown in different windows on the computer screen, and a user can work in different windows as needed. For example, in one window, a user can be working in a word-processing program on a document; while in another window she uses a graphics program to draw a diagram; and, in a third window, she refers to data from a spreadsheet program.

WYSIWYG An acronym that stands for "What You See Is What You Get," this term is used to refer to programs that show users, on the computer screen, exactly what a page will look like when it is printed out. Related acronyms such as WYSIAWYG ("What You See Is Almost What You Get") and WYSIMOLWYG ("What You See Is More Or Less What You Get") are used to accentuate the slight differences that characterize some programs' screen representations and page copy.

HARDWARE

C-D ROM Compact Disks (CDs) are used as mass storage devices that allow users to store large quantities of information (i.e., 100 megabytes to 1000 megabytes currently) on one surface. These disks are read by a light beam, and the information is fed into a computer. Currently, unlike floppy disks, most affordable CDs can only be read by a user: users cannot write, erase, or change information on them. Hence, teachers may come across the term CD-ROM, referring to compact disks that provide only *"read only"* memory. Soon, however, the profession may have access to CDs that can be both written and read by teachers, much like large floppy disks. Some companies supply multiplatter machines that allow users to access (usually relatively slowly) more than one CD. For instance, a user could employ such a device to access an encyclopedia, a graphics database, and a listing of government documents during one work session!

CPU This acronym stands for "Central Processing Unit," the brains of the computer. The storage units, processing circuits, and the control units that make up the CPU, are components that control and make sense of the directions users and programs give to the computer.

LCD An acronym that stands for "Liquid Crystal Display," this term refers to the screen displays used for some laptop computers. These screens are flat—and, thus, take up little room—but they also can irritate some users, cause headaches and eyestrain, because the image they produce is not as bright or sharp as many individuals would desire.

MHz Stands for "megahertz," a unit of measurement "equal to one million electrical vibrations per second" (*Computer User's Dictionary*, 288). Megahertz is the unit of measure which describes the rate at which computers process instructions. It is used to compare the speeds of VERY similar computers but is not a very good measure of computer speeds between platforms. Today, personal computers commonly work at 25 and 33, and into the 40 + MGz range.

MIPS Stands for millions of instructions per second. It is used in combination with MHz and is a better measure of the relative speed among DIFFERENT makes of computers.

Mouse A peripheral device that fits into a user's hand and is hooked to a computer by a small wire (hence, the mouse and its tail). With a mouse, the user gives the computer commands. By rolling the mouse on a pad alongside the computer and clicking one or more of its buttons, a user can move a pointer or cursor on the computer screen and select items, make menu choices, or give commands. The term *point-and-click* refers to the ease with which even novice users can, by manipulating the mouse, move a pointer on the computer screen, click one or more of the mouse's buttons, and select their choice of commands and actions.

Monitors The primary video output device for a computer. A monitor may be monochrome which means it is capable of displaying shades of only one color. Monitors have a variety of attributes including size, resolution, number of colors displayed, and video format. You might hear people talk about various kinds of monitors, among them the following: RGB (red, green, blue), CGA (color graphics array), VGA (video graphics array), or MCGA (multicolor graphics array). Another category of monitor includes full-page and double-page monitors. These larger displays can provide either color or grey-scale (black and white) images and measure either 8 1/2" by 11" inches (for the one-page variety) and 11" by 17" (for the double-page displays).

Pixel Stands for "picture element." This is the smallest definable element of a monitor's display. Pixels are defined by their attributes: location and color.

ROM An acronym that stands for "Read Only Memory," memory that contains information the user cannot change. Generally this memory, in the form of computer chips, is filled with instructions for the computer's CPU.

RAM An acronym for "random access memory," the "primary working memory" (*Computer Users Dictionary* 378) of the computer's CPU. It makes data and commands immediately available to the CPU so that it can compare and initiate commands quickly. Depending on the type of program a user is employing (e.g., word processing, programming languages, or graphics) the CPU needs different information readily available. Because of this demand, what is stored in RAM changes depending on the demands of software.

Scanner A peripheral device that digitizes images (e.g., line art or photographs) and text and stores these in a file so that users can work with them or change them. Using a scanner, students can take a drawing that they have produced, digitize it, store it on a disk, and import it into papers they are writing. Similarly, with scanners that allow for *Optical Character Recognition (OCR)*, a teacher can, among other things, digitize the best and the worst examples of a set of essays and store them in computer files so that students can refer to them.

286, 386 and 486 These numbers refer to the different microprocessing chips found in DOS (IBM compatible) personal computers. In this series of microprocessing chips, all manufactured by Intel Corp., the 286 chip is the older, less powerful chip, and the 486 chip is the most powerful and most recent chip.

Videodisk These are optically scanned disks that can store large quantities of video and graphic data (both images and sounds) and retrieve them for playing back on a monitor. They are currently read only, meaning that you can read from them but not store any new information on them.

SOFTWARE

AppleShare is a program that allows a Macintosh computer to be a file server so that it can control an AppleTalk network.

GUI An acronym that stands for "Graphical User Interface" and is pronounced "gooey." A GUI allows users to work with graphical icons of files and tools by using a mouse to point to and select various items on a computer screen.

PostScript A standardized page-description language developed by Adobe Systems, Inc. that describes how to print or to display the elements on a page or screen. Postscript commands allow users, among other things, to identify typical formatting commands (e.g., right or left justification), the shape and location of objects such as text or graphics, and how to portray fonts. Laser printers used on desk top publishing systems generally require Postscript commands for high-quality output.

SCSI An acronym that stands for "Small Computer System Interface," and is pronounced "scuzzy." SCSI interfaces allow personal computers to communicate with peripheral devices such as printers, scanners, and mass storage devices.

Systems 6.0 and 7.0 Macintosh numbers its systems software on an ongoing basis so that they can keep track of the various versions. System 7.0 for the Macintosh, for example, is the latest upgrade. System 7, according to Macintosh (Applegram), for example, features improved multitasking and filesharing in comparison to System 6.

NETWORKS

Asynchronous Communication Networks Networks that allow the exchange of information or written messages, but in a slightly delayed fashion. Messages are exchanged among computers on a network much like letters are exchanged within a postal system, only faster.

Bulletin Boards Bulletin Boards (BBs) are virtual "spaces," located within some computer's memory, that are used to post and receive messages of interest to various groups of people—hence, the analogy to traditional bulletin boards. The messages on bulletin boards are generally directed at people with something in common (a hobby, a profession, a chronological age, a problem) and are transmitted and received within minutes for relatively little expense. Users generally get access to these BBs through personal computers equipped with modems and connected to telephones—users pay the phone costs. Frequently, BBs can also be accessed through educational, governmental or some business computer systems. BBs are popular because they provide virtual spaces for users to talk about topics of general interest (e.g., problems with specific computer platforms and/or software packages), a variety of academic and scholarly projects (e.g., cold fusion research, the use of computers in composition instruction), areas of personal commitment (e.g., abortion, environmental news), or personal concerns (e.g., computer dating, vampires, alternative sexual practices).

E-Mail Refers to "electronic mail," mail sent via computer from one person to another or from one person to many people. E-mail can only be sent from one computer on a network to another computer on the *same* network or from one computer on a network to another computer on a *linked* network. E-mail works much like the postal system (only much faster!) in that messages are forwarded to individuals or groups who have *addresses*—the name of the computer at which one receives or sends mail (e.g., MTUS5 is the address for the IBM System 5 computer at Michigan Technological University)—and an *id*—the name which identifies the particular person at that address (e.g., my id is RSELFE, which stands for Richard Selfe). To use e-mail, a user also needs a *communications software package* that allows one computer to speak to other computers. Typical communications packages are Kermit, Xmodem, or PC-Talk. These programs also allow users to set the *communication protocols* (the settings and the parameters) for their machines to match the protocols for the machine they are sending information to.

ENFI An acronym standing for "Electronic Networks For Interaction" and used most often to refer to networks that allow for real-time written interaction, or synchronous exchanges. The first ENFI system was originated in 1985 by Trent Batson at Gallaudet University.

File Server A file server is a computer—hooked to a hardware network and using network software—that stores files centrally so that they can be shared by many users (e.g., a Mac IIci with AppleShare software, an IBM PS 2 Model 70 with Novell software, or a SUN Sparc workstation with NFS software). File servers are the machines that run networks and determine many of their operating characteristics. Back up file servers frequently!

Filesharing Exchanging files among computers on a networked system.

Network Collections of computers that are linked electronically so that they can exchange information and share peripheral devices such as printers and scanners. *Local-area networks (LANs)* link computers in a single location (a classroom, a building, or a campus, for example) by some kind of cabling system. Typically, LANs are used when computers are located within one to two miles of each other. *Wide-area networks (WANs)* link computers in different and more far-flung locations via high speed, long distance communications networks or satellites. BITNET, ARPANET, and Internet are WANs that connect people in various locations for various purposes: the Internet, for instance, is a system of linked networks that connects several million users around the world. ARPANET, a WAN under the aegis of the U.S. Defense Advanced Research Projects Agency (DARPA) is "intended to support defense research." (*Computer Users Dictionary* 31) There are *gateways* that allow people on ARPANET, for instance, to send messages to people on the Internet.

Network Operating Systems (NOS) The controlling software associated with a network is called a *network operating system*. The topology of these systems varies with their particular characteristics. *AppleTalk*, for example, is the LAN software that Apple developed for Macintosh computers. AppleTalk, because it uses a computer's serial port, is relatively slow for a network (320 bits per second), but it allows the linking of IBM PCs to Apple Macintoshes by a simple and inexpensive cabling and system (twisted pair or telephone, cables). In contrast, EtherNet, LAN software developed by Xerox Corporation, is a high speed networking system (2 to 3 megabits per second), which requires the installation of *interface cards*—electronic circuit boards—and is, thus, more expensive to install. These boards allow the rapid transmission of information via the computer's *internal bus system*, the circuitry pathways that carry information from one location to another within the computer.

Server In LANs, the server manages the traffic on the network, orchestrating demands on peripheral devices and central files so that multiple users' requests get responses in a timely and efficient manner.

Synchronous Communication Networks Networks that allow users to exchange written information at very high speeds so that written conversations take place in "real time," much like regular conversations, rather than in a delayed, or asynchronous, fashion.

HYPERTEXT AND HYPERMEDIA

Authoring Systems (or Language) This term refers to computer languages (like HyperCard, SuperCard, ToolBook, or Inkway) that use "real" language (in a limited sense) to represent programming commands. The intent of such systems is to make it easier for users to program their computers without having to learn the more obscure terms and syntax of most programming languages such as FORTRAN, Pascal, and C.

Digitizer (Audio) These devices—with accompanying software—allow users to digitize sounds and place them into various computer-based projects. The "beeps" and "boings" and "clanks" that you hear on Mac computers, for example, are digitized sounds.

Digitizer (see scanner) Used by itself, this term refers to a device that can take visual information (graphics or text) and—employing some of the same technology as photocopy machines—translate that information into a digital format. This digitized information can then be edited on a computer. Scanners can range from hand-held devices, costing a few hundred dollars, that provide relatively poor resolution to large color scanners, which cost over $20,000, that provide excellent resolution. Most DTP systems, especially in academic settings, operate on the low to medium end of this spectrum with hand-held and flat-bed scanners.

Digitizer (Video) Video "cards" (internal hardware for computers) are used to "capture" still video images, digitize them, and place them into multimedia or DTP projects. Some of the more expensive hardware/ software systems allow the capture of video clips as well as still images. Some systems also give users the option of transferring digitized computer-generated graphics onto video tape. These cards and their software cost anywhere from $500 to $5,000 dollars.

Digitizing Pad A peripheral device that allows users to draw freehand images with a stylus (electronic pencil), digitize these images, store them in a computer file, and manipulate or change them at will using appropriate graphic software.

HyperCard An authoring language developed by Bill Atkinson at Apple Computer in 1984, HyperCard allows authors to create hypertext stacks, or files, that contain text and graphic components. Using HyperCard, authors can create hypertext stacks without knowing traditional programming languages. SuperCard is another version of an authoring language that allows for enhanced hypermedia applications.

Hypermedia A hyper-document that mixes all or any one of the following—text, still photography, video, sound, and synthesized voice—in a hypertext environment. Various nodes in a hypermedia document about Virginia Woolf's life, for instance, may contain a video clip about education in Victorian England, a speech from the suffrage movement during the time that Woolf was writing, photographs of a number of Woolf's original diary pages, and several published chapters from *A Room of One's Own,* among many other potential items.

Hypertext A term coined by T. H. Nelson in the 1960s (Landow and Delany 45), hypertext refers to the non-sequential arrangement of text-based information. Hypertexts are broken down into *nodes*, small units of text (screens of text of text and graphics, or scrolling screens of text and graphics, for instance), which are *linked*, or connected, to other nodes in *webs*, or connected sets of information (a web of nodes may be a set of critical essays on existentialism, a set of poems by Emily Dickinson, or a set of definitions of terms from a single page). In most hypertexts, each node will contain several "hot" words. If the reader chooses these words or icons, they jump to a node containing related information. In a *pure* hypertext, every node is connected to every other node, so each reader must choose which nodes to view and the order in which to view these nodes. Typically, hypertexts present readers with alternative paths through a document; as a result, each reader creates his/her own path through a hypertext.

Stack, Stacks, or Stax A hypertext or hypermedia file is often called a "stack" and contains several *cards*, or nodes, linked to each other which readers can view in the order they choose. The analogy is to a stack of cards that can be shuffled and reshuffled at will. (Hypertext *cards*, which are meant to represent pieces or chunks of information, should not be confused with hardware *cards*, which are internal circuit boards placed within a computer for a specialized function.)

Works Cited

"Apple Introduces System 7." AppleGram 7.4, (May 1991): 1–2.

Collins, James. L., and Elizabeth A. Sommers. *Writing On-Line: Using Computers in the Teaching of Writing.* Portsmouth, NH: Boynton/Cook, 1985.

Hiltz, Starr Roxanne. "The 'Virtual Classroom': Using Computer-mediated Communication for University Teaching." *Journal of Communication,* 36.2 (1986): 95–104.

Landow, George P., and Delany, P. "Hypertext, Hypermedia and Literary Stud-
    ies: The State of the Art." In *Hypermedia and Literary Studies*, Eds. Paul
    Delany and George Landow. Cambridge, MA: MIT Press. (1991): 3–49.

Pfaffenberger, Bryan. *Que's Computer User's Dictionary.* Carmel, IN: Que Corpo-
    ration, 1990.

Contributors

Hugh Burns is Chairman and Vice President of The Daedalus Group, Inc. Hugh also holds adjunct appointments in both Liberal Arts and in Education at the University of Texas in Austin. For over twenty-five years, his leadership in the education and computer training community has impacted, not only how computers are being used in education, especially the language arts, but also in technical training where artificial intelligence approaches are being successfully designed, developed, and demonstrated. With James Parlett and Carol Redfield, Hugh recently edited *Intelligent Tutoring Systems: Evolutions in Design* [Lawrence Erlbaum, 1991]. Among Hugh's recognitions are scientific and management achievement awards from the United States Air Force and appointments to several prestigious editorial and advisory boards.

Marcia Curtis is an assistant director of the University of Massachusetts/Amherst Writing Program, and director of its basic writing component. Her writings on computer-based teaching, basic writing, and multi-cultural education have appeared in *The Journal of Basic Writing, College Composition and Communication,* and *The Harvard Educational Review.*

Janet Eldred received her Ph.D. in English from the University of Illinois and is currently an assistant professor of English at the University of Kentucky and Berea College. Her research interests include the work of M. M. Bakhtin, the relationships between law, language, and literacy, and the role of computers, particularly computer networks, in composition studies. Her articles have appeared in *The Journal of Narrative Technique, College English,* and *Computers and Composition.*

Ron Fortune, who received his Ph.D. from Purdue University, is an associate professor in the English Department at Illinois State University. His research and teaching focus on composition, rhetoric, and the connections between the study of writing and the study of literature. He has directed several funded projects examining students' writing processes and the teaching of writing. Most recently, he has been involved with a National Endowment for the Humanities project concerned with connecting the teaching of writing and literature through the use of literary manuscripts, a project enhanced by his innovative integration of hypertext applications. His published research includes articles on writing and problem solving, learning theory, and English studies, and connections between instruction in writing and literature. In 1986, the Modern Language Association published *School-College Collaborative Programs in English,* a book he edited and contributed to.

Gail E. Hawisher is an associate professor of English at the University of Illinois, Urbana-Champaign where she also directs the Center for Writing Studies. With Cynthia Selfe, she edits the *CCCC Bibliography on Composition and Rhetoric, Computers and Composition,* a journal for writing teachers, and the book series *Advances in Computers and Composition Studies.* Currently she is serving as Chair of the NCTE Instructional Technology Committee and is a member of the CCCCs Committee on Computers. Among the collections she has co-edited are

Critical Perspectives on Computers and Composition Instruction, On Literacy and Its Teaching, and *Evolving Perspectives on Computers and Composition Studies.* Her articles have appeared in *Research in the Teaching of English, Collegiate Microcomputer, English Journal,* and *College Composition and Communication.*

David S. Kaufer is an associate professor and associate head in the Department of English at Carnegie Mellon University. He received his Ph.D. in Communication Arts from University of Wisconsin—Madison. He has published extensively in many journals, among them *Philosophy and Rhetoric, Research in the Teaching of English, Rhetoric Society Quarterly,* and *Written Communication.* He is currently working on a book examining the impact of technology on the social interactions of authors and readers.

Elizabeth Klem is a doctoral candidate in the University of Massachusetts/ Amherst English Department. Her work on computer-based teaching has appeared in various publications; her most recent ethnographic study of a networked classroom, conducted with Charles Moran, appears in *Computers and Composition.*

Paul LeBlanc is an associate professor and chair of the English Department at Springfield College. He received his doctorate from the University of Massachusetts—Amherst, where he also won a Walker Gibson Prize for Research in Composition. He was the first finalist for the 1990 Hugh Burns Dissertation Award. He is a member of the NCTE Committee on Instructional Technology, Software Editor for *Computers and Composition,* and pursues a special research interest in software design and development. He has published in *Thalia, Computers and Composition,* and co-authored with Charles Moran a chapter for *Computers in English and the Language Arts. Forthcoming are a chapter on the politics of literacy and technology in secondary schools in an MLA volume on literacy and computers and a book entitled Software Development and Composition Studies* to be published by NCTE. With Gail Hawisher, he is co-editor of the technology section in the forthcoming *Encyclopedia of English Studies and Language Arts.*

Charles Moran is a professor of English at the University of Massachusetts— Amherst. He serves on the NCTE College Editorial Board and on the editorial boards of the *Journal of Basic Writing,* the *Massachusetts Review,* and *Computers and Composition.* He has written on the teaching of literature, the teaching of writing, writing across the curriculum, and the effects of computer technology on the teaching of English. He served from 1982–1990 as Director of his university's Writing Program; from 1978–87 he directed the UMass/Amherst Writing Project. He has received his university's Distinguished Teacher Award and, from the Massachusetts Council of Teachers of English, the Andre Favat Award for service to English. With Paul LeBlanc, Marcia Curtis, and Elizabeth Klem, he has designed and configured two computer-equipped writing rooms at his home institution. With these same co-conspirators he has attempted to discover how the new technology can be used and how, in actual writing classrooms, it is being used.

Christine M. Neuwirth, who received her Ph.D. in Rhetoric from Carnegie Mellon University, is an associate professor in the Department of English there and director of one of the freshman writing courses. She has published numerous papers on computers and writing and developed several software tools. She is currently working on a study that analyzes the cognitive effects of social interaction during the writing process.

Cynthia L. Selfe is a professor of Composition and Communication in the Humanities Department of Michigan Technological University. Currently a co-editor of the *CCCC Bibliography on Composition and Rhetoric* (with Gail Hawisher), Selfe has chaired both the NCTE Assembly on Computers in English and the NCTE Instructional Technology Committee. She has served, as well, as a member of the NCTE College Section Steering Committee, the CCCC Executive Committee, the CCCC Resolutions Committee, the CCCC Committee on Computers, and the MLA Committee on Emerging Technologies.

In addition to her journal articles and book chapters on computer use in composition classrooms, Selfe is the author of *Computer-Assisted Instruction in Composition: Create Your Own* (NCTE) and *Creating a Computer-Supported Writing Facility* (*Computers and Composition* Press). Selfe has also co-edited several collections of essays on computers, including *Evolving Perspectives on Computers in Composition Studies: Questions for the 1990s* (with Gail Hawisher, National Council of Teachers of English and Computers and Composition Press), *Computers in English and Language Arts: The Challenge of Teacher Education* (with Dawn Rodrigues and William Oates, National Council of Teachers of English), *Critical Perspectives on Computers and Composition Instruction* (with Gail Hawisher, Teachers College Press), and *Computers and Writing: Theory, Research, and Practice* (with Deborah Holdstein, Modern Language Association).

In 1983, Selfe founded the journal *Computers and Composition* with Kate Kiefer; she continues to edit that journal with Gail Hawisher.

Richard J. Selfe is a Technical Communication Specialist and an Instructor in the Scientific and Technical Communication Program at Michigan Technological University (MTU). He is currently managing a communication-oriented computer facility, a video production lab, and a print production lab. He teaches courses in first-year English, publications management, video production, and print production and is currently working on his Ph.D. in Rhetoric and Technical Communication at MTU.

His interest is in composition pedagogy and the social, political, and cultural influences of electronic media on that pedagogy. Papers delivered at conferences include Interaction as a Function of Play: Computers and Collaboration (CCCC, 1988) A Computer-Supported Communication Facility as a Site for Collaborative Student Activities: A Naturalistic Study (CCCC, 1990); and a co-authored piece with Johndan Johnson-Eilola called Theory and Practice in Computer-Supported Communication Facilities (*Computers and Writing*, 1991).

Elizabeth Sommers is an assistant professor in the English Department at San Francisco State University, an institution renowned for political activism, where she teaches theory and practice courses in a graduate program for writing teachers. She continues to teach various undergraduate writing courses as well. Her long interest in computers in writing classrooms originated at SUNY/Buffalo, where she completed her Ph.D. thesis in 1986 on computers and writing instruction. After all of this time she still remains intrigued and worried by computers in composition instruction. Her curiosity usually overcomes her apprehension, and she continues to develop writing classroom curricula, write articles, construct computer-supported writing facilities, teach graduate courses, and direct workshops on computer-supported literacy.

Paul Taylor received his Ph.D. in Rhetoric from the University of Texas in 1991 and joined the English Department at Texas A & M University the same year. Since 1985 he has developed several computer programs for research and teaching in the field of rhetoric and composition.

William Wright, Jr. has degrees from Sewanee and Middlebury Colleges (English), as well as the Harvard Graduate School of Education (Administration, Planning, and Social Policy). He has worked as a middle school teacher and, after graduate work, as a project director at American Institutes for Research (AIR) in Washington, DC. With AIR he directed development projects for IBM and other large computer companies, projects that involved applying research to make manuals and screens easier to use. In 1983, he proposed the idea of a teacher network for the Bread Loaf School of English, a summer graduate program of Middlebury College in Vermont. The idea was funded by Apple. Since then, with support from Middlebury and a private foundation, he has been able to experiment with ways to set up effective projects using this technology. Some of the groups he has helped with networking projects include: Foxfire Outreach, the Cleveland Education Fund, the National Council of Teachers of English (NCTE), the Texas Education Agency, CHART (a large consortium supported by the Rockefeller Foundation), AT&T, and Apple. He has written several articles—and chapters in three books—about educational telecomputing.